COMMUNICATION GOLDMINE

For a complete list of Management Books 2000 titles,
visit our web-site on http://www.mb2000.com

COMMUNICATION GOLDMINE

Russell-Oliver Brooklands

2000

To John McWhirter - with thanks

Acknowledgements

There are loads of people who've helped me make this book a reality. In particular, thanks to Yvonne Ash and Ron Stone, for going through numerous early versions - and still being prepared to come back for more. Thanks also to Jo Livesey and Jennifer McAleer, for reassuring me it would work for agencies, to Sian Everson for an alternative author's view, to Andrew Fox for helping me with the calculations, to Jerry Grayburn, David Sims and James Hill for having enough faith in me to give me time to 'think about it' in the first place. And finally, to my numerous clients who, over the years, have probably taught me as much as I've taught them.

First published in 2006 by Management Books 2000 Ltd
Forge House, Limes Road
Kemble, Cirencester
Gloucestershire, GL7 6AD, UK
Tel: 0044 (0) 1285 771441
Fax: 0044 (0) 1285 771055
E-mail: info@mb2000.com
Web: www.mb2000.com

Printed and bound in Great Britain by 4edge Ltd of Hockley, Essex

British Library Cataloguing in Publication Data is available

ISBN 1-85252-518-5

Contents

How to Get the Most from the Goldmine

Welcome to a treasure hunt, of a very different kind. We'll be following a trail that will unravel mysteries stretching far back to the very dawn of business communication, and recover untold riches that have lain hidden for all time. For ten years, I've been piecing together the clues and mapping out a route that can lead you to rewards you might never have dreamt possible: rewards you'll be able to tap into throughout the rest of your career. For although the mysteries are ancient, they are still very much alive today...

When something goes wrong in business or government, likely as not it will be attributed – at least in part – to 'a communication breakdown'. This seems always to have been the case, so is it just a convenient way of fudging the issue and absolving everyone from blame? It would be naive to suggest that this never happens, but no more so than to pretend that communication breakdowns don't occur – even when, on the surface, everything seems to be going well. And that's where the real mysteries lie.

- Why does business communication break down? (**Many reasons**)
- How often is it happening? (**More often than most people realise**)
- Whose fault is it? (**Rarely any one person's**)
- How big are the commercial consequences? (**Usually spectacular**)
- What can you, as a business communicator, do about it? (**Loads, potentially**)

In each chapter of this book we'll uncover a logical succession of clues as to why, where and how the breakdowns are going on, and develop insights which will enable you to solve the puzzles – and even help others to do so as well. In the process, you will unlock the secrets of the communication goldmine: unearthing your own amazing commercial potential and that of the organisation or clients who pay you. But before going any further, there are one or two things we need to get straight.

This book tackles challenges facing people in four different types of communication role:

- **Communication owners**, who 'own' various messages that need communicating to internal or external audiences

- **Communication professionals**, who write, or manage the production of, these communications
- **Communication approvers**, whose job is to vet, edit and approve communications
- **Communication planners** who engage in long-term communication planning

Sometimes these roles are carried out by different people. At other times, some or all of them can belong to just one person wearing different hats. And here's a single book trying to talk to everyone about the challenges facing all four roles. It could get a bit messy unless we can establish a few ground rules up front.

1. Whether or not it's your main job, chances are you'll have to fulfil the communication professional's role at least some of the time. This book therefore looks at business communication challenges from that point of view. Even if communicating is not your full time occupation, I believe you'll find it useful to look at the problems we tackle through the eyes of someone for whom it is. For example, you'll probably recognise some of the difficulties they face when trying to get communication owners to be clear about what they want – even if you're playing both roles yourself.

2. If you are a full time communication professional, you may be working as a freelance, for an agency, or maybe as part of an in-house comms team. I therefore had to use a form of shorthand for 'the people for whom you do your work'. After much deliberation, I've settled for *'the business'*. If you're an in-house employee in a commercial concern, this should present no problems. If you work for a non-profit making organisation, I hope you will be able to think of it as 'the business' for the duration of this book. If you're a freelance, please take 'the business' to mean that of any one of your clients. And if you work in an agency, you'll have to decide for yourself whether to take it to mean your employer's business, or that of your clients. In the main, of course, I do mean your clients, but if the agency itself is big enough, who knows – maybe some of what I talk about could apply equally to your employer too. I appreciate that this shorthand is not ideal, but I hope you'll understand the need for it.

    Similarly, when talking about the writing, editing and approving of text, I have had to use more shorthand, talking about 'your text'. If you have a different role in communication approvals, please take this term to mean 'the text being approved'.

3. The ideas in this book will work for marketing, recruitment, customer, shareholder, press and internal/employee communications. For reasons that should become apparent as the book unfolds, I will be focusing mainly (but not exclusively) on the internal communication arena, as this is by far the stickiest. This is partly because it's often subject to much more business politics. More significantly, though, many of the challenges involved in communicating with internal audiences are more complex than those presented by any other group. Not least, internal communications can pose linguistic problems that simply can't arise in other arenas.

On top of that, if you have to do communications for any other audiences, chances are you will be doing some internal communicating too (even if only face-to-face and email). And if you can solve the puzzles of internal communications, you can be sure these solutions will work for any other business audience.

My research has shown that if there's one thing business people want more than anything else when it comes to communicating, it's confidence: confidence that they're 'getting it right'; confidence that they are adding value. Therefore, given the emotive nature of the subject matter, and the entrenched positions that some people can take, I believe you need to understand not just how to solve the communication puzzles we'll be discussing, but why these solutions make sense. I've therefore recounted a number of experiences from my careers as a corporate writer, a brand manager and an independent consultant and trainer, to illustrate how these ideas have solved particular problems.

But I would never claim that what I'm presenting here is the final solution. In a dynamic business environment, any such claim would be naive, for the journey never ends. In fact, I hope you will see this book as just a beginning, stimulating you to develop and refine these ideas still further for yourself – once you really understand how the principles work. I offer that caveat because it takes time to appreciate the linguistic precision in some of these principles. As clients have told me time and again, with some of this material you have to 'do it' for a while before you really 'get it' (i.e. understand instinctively how and why it works). And without that appreciation, some people might be tempted to start modifying the questioning techniques I've developed, before having really understood how they work. And then they would wonder why they weren't getting the results they wanted. The desire to run before we can walk is a common one. But as the whole purpose of this book is to make your working life easier and more rewarding, it makes little sense to read it, and then set out to make your life more difficult and frustrating. So please take your time.

4. This book has a clear bias towards the linguistic aspects of planning, briefing, writing, editing and approving business communications. Naturally there's more to communicating than simply working out what to say and how to say it; the visual impact of most communications is also vital. Although this book focuses mainly on language, rather than on graphic design issues, many designers have found the ideas contained in these pages to be of immense value when it comes to helping clients to articulate clearly what they want.

To make it as easy as possible for you to find your way around the Goldmine, I have organised it into four parts.

As a starter, I will put the 'goldmine' approach into context, establishing why your communications are potentially so valuable, how high you could now raise the bar, and why it's worth going for. It will reveal why the very *raison d'etre* of business communication is often misunderstood. You'll understand how those misunderstandings impact on your work, and on the astonishing value that the goldmine could hold both for you and for those who pay you.

The next part delves into the numerous ways in which the briefing process can go awry. You'll discover a host of new navigation tools for identifying what needs communicating to whom, when and how – on a communication-by-communication basis. You'll travel inside your own language, meet up with phantoms, have your first brush with the seven triggers that can spell death for any business communication, and learn to disarm the first of them.

Part three will throw light on the unanswered conundrums of communication strategy: why strategies are often unsustainable over the long term, and how to make them work indefinitely. You'll be introduced to a new, more powerful strategy, without which all others are almost certainly doomed.

The final section answers some of the greatest puzzles of all: how and why things can easily come unstuck during the writing, editing and approving of communications. You will finally come face to face with the remaining six deadly triggers, and learn how to disarm them all. You'll discover how to navigate the treacherous linguistic minefield, and to track down and tame the mischievous and elusive linguistic chameleon.

By the end of this journey you will know how business communication breakdowns happen – and how to stop them. For good. You'll have a wealth of knowledge that will make you invaluable to business leaders everywhere – for the rest of your career.

So without further ado, let's go.

Chapter 1
Being Taken Seriously ... Enough

'You don't have to be ill to get better.'

Jim Cronin

In this chapter we will uncover:

➤ some of the signs that will tell you you're sitting on a potential goldmine

➤ a critical communication owners' blind-spot

➤ the threat of a bottomless pit that no one speaks of

➤ a vicious circle that can stop you from fulfilling your potential

➤ a poisoned chalice that few dare touch.

If someone were to tell you that you're worth a fortune, you might be forgiven for thinking they're away with the fairies – or at least ill-informed. But would they necessarily be wrong? If you have a job that involves the production or management of business communications, I think anyone would be on pretty solid ground if they were to tell you that you're worth a fortune – to the people who pay you. At least potentially. Perhaps you've had at least an inkling of this yourself. You may not have sat down and worked out any specific sums, but most business communication professionals, it seems, instinctively feel that their work has much more commercial potential than they or their employers or clients ever get around to exploiting. And this failure to exploit the commercial potential of your role means that everyone's losing out: you, the people you work for, their audiences; everyone. So why does this situation persist?

The unspoken threat of the bottomless pit

If you ask the directors, partners or senior managers of any commercial or non-commercial organisation, they'll almost always tell you they take communication seriously. Then again, who wouldn't? Can you really imagine a company director saying:

'We don't give a monkey's about communicating.'

That's just not going to happen. But ask them if they take it seriously enough, and suddenly they hesitate. And they often respond with something like:

'When you say seriously enough, what do you mean, exactly?'

Such responses suggest they may not have fully thought through their claims about taking communication seriously. But so what?

The business is probably doing at least reasonably well. And when it comes to communicating, it's often difficult to know just how high is high. How much more seriously *could* they take communication? What would doing so involve? And what results would it produce? Would it really be worth the time and effort? Let's face it, they've got loads of other things on their plates, and isn't it possible that 'taking communication more seriously' could simply be a bottomless pit? I think such concerns are perfectly valid. Yet it's also fair to say that whatever the attitudes of the people you work for, the potential almost certainly exists for you to be making a much bigger commercial impact for them than you currently do, and having an easier life into the bargain – should you so wish.

Too much stress, not enough recognition

Even if your job is already great, and whether or not you want to put a turbo-charger into your career, don't you sometimes feel that, if things were different, you could save a lot of time some weeks, and have more influence with the people for whom you're working? Does your job not sometimes cause you more frustration or stress than it really needs to? And would it not be possible at times for you to add more value, receive more recognition, have more confidence, job fulfilment and, long-term, more career potential? I believe you would have to be in an exceptional position not to be able to answer 'Yes' to at least some of these. This book will help you to understand many of the reasons why this is so – at least to some degree – and how you can bring about some radical changes to make your personal working life easier and more rewarding. Better still it will demonstrate how such changes can spawn huge commercial and logistic benefits for your business.

From my years of working as an in-house communication professional and an independent consultant and trainer, I've discovered that most senior people don't take business communication nearly as seriously as they may think they do. I've also established some solid commercial reasons for them to start doing so, and some methods you can use to help them do just that. Many communication professionals don't think it can be done; perhaps because their bosses are too intransigent, and the difficulties they're experiencing are something they feel they just have to live with. If you've ever been tempted to think that way, I've got news for you (in fact, I've got news for you even if you've never thought anything of the kind). Not only can you change the way you work with your bosses or clients, those changes could be much easier to introduce than you might currently believe – provided you can break the vicious circle that almost always seems to come with the territory in which you work.

Breaking the vicious circle

I don't think it's any great secret that, on the whole, a lot of business communications are less effective than they could be, and that this is rarely any one individual's fault. I believe it's also true that at least some of this ineffectiveness may come from a vicious circle in which most communication professionals find themselves – at least to some extent. Naturally I don't know the situation you're in yourself, but working with numerous clients over the years has shown me that the vicious circle can often work a little like this. Maybe the individuals for whom you're working don't appreciate what you'd be truly capable of, given the chance. And this could mean that perhaps they don't give you as much time or influence to do the job as you really could do it, if only you had that time and influence. This could easily result in you frequently having to work in the dark, or without enough political clout, or up against time pressure, any one of which will stop you from demonstrating what you'd be truly capable of, and from adding the value you could. And perhaps this means the people who are paying you never get to see how much better you could do the job if only they'd let you, so they never raise their expectations of what you could do for them and the business. And so it goes on.

Worse still, that very lack of time may also be denying you the luxury of sitting down and working out how you could break this vicious circle. But I got lucky. A few years ago, I was given time to 'think about it'. The specific 'it' I was initially charged with thinking about was the way in which my employer's business was doing its writing.

As a corporate brand manager within a large financial services company, I was given responsibility for developing a set of writing standards for the business. In short, my job was to 'work out the right way for us to write stuff'. At first I was really chuffed about getting this role, but I soon discovered that I'd been handed a poisoned chalice. Writing is, after all, a very personal activity. And as I was soon to discover, saying to someone, *'Er, do you think you could write this a bit differently?'* will elicit about as warm a reception as you'd get from asking them, *'Excuse me, but have you ever heard of deodorant?'*

But why are many people so touchy and closed-minded? While I was a corporate writer myself, I used to think that I was the only one in the world who wasn't entirely confident of his ability. But once I started working with communication professionals in other businesses, I found that they too were, if not hungry to know they were 'getting it right', then certainly fairly peckish. And if you think about it, this is perfectly understandable.

Where's your comfort zone?

On the whole, business communications tend to be made up mostly of words, with maybe some pictures and diagrams, and sometimes a few numbers as well. The people who take care of the numbers in any business – the accountants – can know they've got their job right. A balance sheet either balances or it doesn't. No ifs, no buts, no doubts. The people who take care of the visuals: the graphic designers, tend to be on reasonably safe ground too. They may not be able to work with the same numerical precision as the accountants, but that's okay. I used to work with a group of designers, and I know how often other business people say to them, *'Oh I'll leave it up to you; you're the expert; I can't draw for toffee'*. Designers, then, can know their skills are 'special'. But it's much rarer to hear someone say, *'I can't write for toffee'*.

It seems that many people in business, especially senior people, believe they can write well, so professional business writers are much less able than designers to consider their skills 'special'. And unlike the accountants, there's no security to be found in any empirically 'right way' of writing. Perhaps it's no real surprise that anyone whose job it is to write or manage the production of business communications might spend their career living with an undercurrent of uneasiness, lest some senior bod suddenly pops up and whispers, 'The Subjunctive Mood' in their ear. People who've been trained as journalists tend to suffer from this uneasiness less than those who haven't. But even an in-house journalist can often come up against people who can't articulate clearly what they want to communicate, or who insist on having it written their way.

It was this uneasiness and frustration that drove me to look for a way of introducing more certainty into the whole process. Of course, I never set out to achieve the same degree of security as the accountants: language being incapable of the precision of mathematics. But could there be a way of at least reducing some of the doubt, some of the woolliness in the discussions about what a person wanted to communicate, or how it should be written? Would it be possible to unearth some immutable truths about writing business communications, which could not only bolster the confidence of communication professionals, but make their jobs easier and demonstrably add massive value to any business? If it were possible to do this, might such truths not change the whole dynamic of planning and producing business communications? Might they not, in short, force the issue: getting people, even at the very top, to take communication professionals more seriously; dare one almost say 'seriously enough'? Given adequate time to 'think about it', I discovered that all this would indeed be possible.

An antidote for the poisoned chalice

Shortly after I got the brand management job, I was introduced to behavioural linguistics (which, among other merits, helps to explain numerous ways in which language affects people's behaviour). It's a discipline which started being developed in the early 1970s, initially under the cumbersome title of Neuro Linguistic Programming (NLP), principally for use in psychotherapy. By the 1990s, it had spawned various more sophisticated hybrids, and made its way into the business arena, but even there it was only being used to help people with their face-to-face communications. No one seemed to have applied it to the discipline of producing communications that people would receive through written media. I quickly realised that I'd stumbled across something that could help me to solve the very problems I was facing. Firstly, it would help me to work out various 'right ways' for us to write things in different situations (or at least 'wrong ways' to avoid). More importantly, it would enable me to develop a radical new approach for identifying what needed to be communicated in the first place – with the very rigour and precision I craved. As it turned out, I also ended up understanding numerous other little quirks of business communication (including what causes people to want to argue about 'the right way to write stuff' in the first place – and I bet it's not what you might currently think it is). What followed was a lot of study and development, during which time two things became apparent:

1. Although I've had numerous people tell me that these ideas are 'blindingly obvious when you think about it', I would say that many of them only become so when you 'think about it' in a particular way. And that particular way is not always so obvious.

2. It would have been a great deal quicker and easier if someone else had already done the thinking for me.

That said, even though many of these ideas remained frustratingly elusive for ages, along the way I experienced many 'Eureka' moments – which often had me wanting to shout my solutions from the highest mountain. But I recognised that doing so would hardly have been an effective communication, given that I can't speak a word of Nepalese. So instead, I'm delivering these ideas in book form.

And I hope this book will enable you to understand not only that you're worth a fortune: that you're sitting on a potential goldmine. I also intend to show you how you to exploit it – for your own benefit, that of the people you're working for, and all the stakeholders as well. It's the result of hundreds of training days, client briefings and consultancy sessions, all of which have produced a reliable system for delivering amazingly valuable communication results with ease and confidence. In time you may feel you want to build on this approach. But for now all you have to do is sit back, relax, and gently acquire the benefits of ten years' hard thinking – in a matter of a few hours. No sweat – the question of deodorant doesn't even arise.

Chapter 2
Beginning at the Beginning

*'Three minutes' thought should suffice to work this out. But thought is
irksome; and three minutes is a long time.'*

A E Houseman

In this chapter we will uncover:

➤ the two commercially justifiable purposes for business
communication

➤ the problems of defining communications as 'need to know' or
'nice to know', and a new more useful categorisation

➤ why taking communication seriously enough will not be a
bottomless pit

➤ why journalism training doesn't teach people how to identify or
generate business communication results.

At a certain point during children's development, something rather magical
happens: they discover the question 'Why?' – and then spend the following
weeks and months driving people nuts with it. Eventually, though, many
children appear to lose their all-consuming fascination with this question –
never, it seems, to regain it. But some kids (like me) don't; and we grow up
to be thorns in the sides of managers who want to focus only on 'what' they
want done, or 'how' they want it organised. To them, it's irritating to have
someone wanting to know 'why' they're doing it at all, because having to
think about 'why' distracts them from driving all the activity, and it might
momentarily slow down the output. That the activity may be unnecessary
and the output useless seems less of a concern to them than it is to the
confirmed Why-er.

As I discovered, being fascinated with the question 'why?' can be a
double-edged sword. Often, it can enable you to add extraordinary value.
But equally, if you repeatedly ask 'why', it can annoy the hell out of some
people; and, perhaps less obviously, if you then hold your tongue it can also

quietly gnaw away at your self-confidence. Take something like 'the purpose of business communication', for example.

As soon as I got the brand management job, I stepped up my reading of books and articles on business communication. I also began to review training courses for the company, and to attend conferences and seminars on the subject. But I never got very far with any of it because, each time I tried, I'd have a nagging feeling that I'd arrived in the middle of the story and that, if only I'd turned up earlier, I wouldn't have missed the bit where they'd explained the purpose of it all. (And because it was seemingly my own fault for being tardy, they certainly weren't going to go back over it all again just for my benefit.) But the truth was that I hadn't turned up late; I'd been there from the beginning. So what was going on?

Had they explained, in an earlier book perhaps, the purpose of all the communication processes and activities they were now discussing, or covered it in some pre-course reading that, for whatever reason, I hadn't received? Possibly the purpose of business communication was a secret, known only to members of a Masonic-style society to which I didn't belong. Maybe one of its members would divulge this secret to me, if only I would roll up my trouser leg and vow to put a horse's head in the bed of the next person who got up their nose. Was that it? Or did everyone consider the purpose of business communication to be so blindingly obvious that they all took it for granted, and no one even bothered to talk about it any more? Had it now become something that was simply passed on through the genetic code, and did I have a defective chromosome that meant I was the only person in the world who didn't know it? Was my continued ignorance final proof that I really was, after all, just a bit of a thicky? Certainly it seemed that every time I read a communication book, sat in on a strategy meeting or attended a conference, I would feel like I was about four years old again, standing there in my short trousers, ankle socks and sandals, desperately wanting to scream out: 'But why?' Surely there's something missing. And maybe that missing something is hiding in the very broadness of the term 'communication'.

The need for a clear purpose

When I became an independent consultant, I started asking people – experienced, intelligent, dedicated communication professionals – to give me their definition of the purpose of business communication. My request was almost always met with blank faces. And an awful lot of staring at the carpet. But let's be honest here. Can we really have a sensible discussion about how to improve 'what' we're doing, or 'how' we're doing it, without first taking care of 'why' we're bothering to do it at all? Can we seriously expect to improve our ability to fulfil the purpose of business communication if we don't first establish what it is? Call me a loony, but I'd say not. So what is the purpose of business communication? Can it be defined? Are there not different purposes, depending on the communication in question? Or could there be a single umbrella purpose for all business communication – regardless of its content, circumstances, 'owner' or audience? Instinctively, I felt there just had to be. And because, seemingly, no one else was going to tell me what it was, I would just have to work it out for myself.

Different types of communication

I often found myself getting irritated when a business person said something like: *'Of course I'm a good communicator; I've been communicating all my life'*. To me it always sounded somewhat fatuous, rather like: *'Of course I'm good with children; I used to be one.'* If either of those statements were true, everyone would be good with children and everyone would be good at communicating. Clearly there's a logical fallacy here, and I believe we need to make two key distinctions to sort it out.

Firstly, let's recognise that, although everyone has been communicating all their lives, the sort of communicating they've been doing has been social. Starting out when we were born as nothing more than the ability to cry and gurgle, social communicating develops into a very sophisticated system for interacting with others, so we can function in the world. From the age of five or six, we also begin to learn academic communicating – particularly writing – which uses many of the rules and tools of social communicating. But its purpose is different from that of social communicating. Generally, it is for us to demonstrate our knowledge of particular subject in order to gain some kind of personal reward and recognition (be it a gold star or a university degree). And crucially, to fulfil that purpose successfully, we also need to learn some new disciplines (spelling, punctuation, and some additional rules of grammar and syntax). So although it's still 'communicating', it's got a different purpose, and there are extra rules to follow if we want to do it successfully.

Until people go out to work, then, these are the only forms of communicating they've done. And while being skilled in both disciplines can be immensely useful, it would be naive to think they'll guarantee someone's ability to communicate effectively with large business audiences – whether internal or external. Just as academic communicating has a different purpose from social communicating, and more stringent disciplines that need to be adopted to fulfil that purpose successfully, so too does commercial communicating have its own purpose – *and* its own disciplines. But maybe when some people enter the workplace they still think their purpose in communicating is simply to demonstrate knowledge of their subject in order to win gold stars. Even if that's not the case, it's still easy for people who've been successful social and academic communicators to believe that they must therefore be good at commercial communication – and therein lies the root of the logical fallacy.

Often when asked, people say that the purpose of commercial communications is to inform, motivate or educate. These may seem reasonable answers, but do they go far enough? Some people get right to the heart of the matter and say that, as with any business activity, its ultimate purpose is profit. If you work in a commercial operation, this can be at least partially true (certainly its purpose won't be to compromise profit). But, again, does it tell us all we need to know (especially if the business is non-profit-making by design)?

Commercial communication

When thinking about commercial communications, many people distinguish between 'need to know' and 'nice to know'.

Need to know	Nice to know

But when I looked at it, I discovered that this categorisation was not the most useful. For one thing, it could be taken to suggest that the two types of communication are mutually exclusive. The very making of such a distinction could imply that nice to know communications are unnecessary in business (because the information they contain isn't needed) and, similarly, that people shouldn't enjoy reading things they need to know (because such communications aren't meant to be nice).

Unfortunately, these distinctions have become self-fulfilling in many businesses. Many so-called 'nice to know' communications are largely pointless, and fail to motivate anyone (except perhaps the people being talked about). Similarly 'need to know' communications are often quite un-nice: so drab and uninspiring that many people can't be bothered to read them – even though they contain information that the audience 'needs to know'. Furthermore, when people discuss the idea of nice to know communications, it becomes all too clear that even within this term there's room for confusion. Just what makes a communication 'nice to know'? Take a look at the following list of subjects:

1. notification of a company party
2. one of the sales teams winning a major new contract
3. a member of staff graduating with a degree from the Open University
4. one of the company's new office buildings winning an architectural award
5. a pay rise.

All of these might be considered 'nice to know'. But are they really all the same type of communication? It's at least questionable, wouldn't you say? So perhaps we need to come up with a more useful way of distinguishing between different types of commercial communication. And fortunately it's staring us right in the face.

How commercial communications pay their way

We can also cut the cake a different way: distinguishing between 'business communications' and 'recreational communications'.

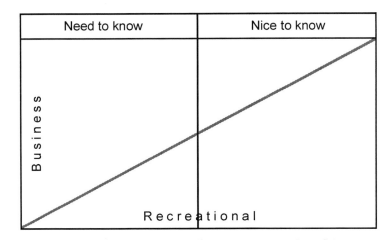

☐ **Business communications** may take the form of reports, meetings, promotional literature, advertising, annual sales conferences, in-house bulletins etc.

☐ **Recreational communications** include theatre plays, TV and radio shows, newspapers, magazines, books, computer games and so on.*

It costs money to produce both types of communication and get them in front of an audience. Clearly they both need to justify themselves commercially. But there's a crucial difference in how they do so.

If you want to see, say, *Les Miserables*, or read *Time Magazine*, whose money do you have to spend? Probably your own. And with a TV programme (*Fawlty Towers*, for example) you'll usually have to pay for a television licence or cable subscription. (*Fawlty Towers* and *Time Magazine* may, of course, also receive sponsorship from advertisers. But the amount of money they get from this will be determined, at least in part, by the size and type of audiences they are able to command.) Furthermore, whose time are you spending while receiving these communications? Your own. With a recreational communication, then, the audience will spend their own time and money to receive it. This means that a recreational communication can cover its costs and generate a profit if the communicator simply gets enough people to receive it – to engage in the *process of being communicated with*. Nothing beyond that is necessary. (Naturally, it helps if the audience goes off and tells other people how good it is. But this is only to get more people involved in the process of being communicated with.)

However, what happens if we apply the same questions to a business communication? Whose money is being spent on the communication? The business's. And whose time is the audience spending while receiving it? If it's an external communication, it's their own, but if it's an internal communication it's usually the business's. So when it comes to a business communication, the audience doesn't pay a penny for the communication process. Instead, it's the communicator who carries all the costs of both production and distribution, and (with employee communications) the considerable additional cost of the audience's time as well. Therefore, unlike a recreational communication, simply getting people to engage in 'the process of being communicated with' will do nothing to cover its costs.

---

* Some people question the existence of 'need to know' recreational communications. For someone learning the piano, their books of piano pieces are 'needed' for that recreational activity. And if you think about the commercial dynamics, this very book you're reading could be considered a need to know recreational communication.

And with a commercial operation it will reduce rather than increase profit. Such communications can only recover their costs (and generate profit) when they prompt and/or enable their audiences to take or avoid actions of some kind, once those people have finished being communicated with.

In summary, then, the recreational communication process has already been paid for by its audience and/or advertisers, before it takes place. But the business communication process is paid for by the actions of the audience only after it has been completed.

(This doesn't mean that a recreational communication can't also prompt people to take or avoid actions; it's simply not necessary. A BBC television news report once prompted Bob Geldof to set up Live Aid, but BBC news would still have carried on anyway, whether Bob had done so or not. Furthermore, it's clear that recreational communicators often need to engage in business communications too – whether internally among their own staff, or externally, to get the public to want to receive their recreational products.)

Business communication's pivotal role

Whether profit-making or not, each business has its own *raison d'etre* – whether it's encapsulated in a long-term vision or mission statement, in a business plan, or simply in the daydreams of its owner or CEO. And communication has a pivotal role to play in the fulfilment of that raison d'etre.

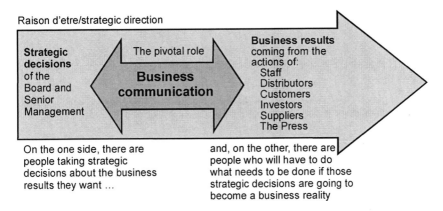

Sitting in between these two groups, communication plays a pivotal role in helping to turn strategic decisions into business results, by directing the thoughts, feelings and ultimate behaviours of those who make the results happen.

The functional purpose and the ultimate purpose

This being the case, we can indeed identify an umbrella purpose for all business communications (whether need to know or nice to know) as follows:

**Directly and/or indirectly
to prompt and/or enable people
to take and/or avoid actions
immediately and/or eventually.**

Despite the inescapable logic behind this purpose, some people don't like it. They say it smacks too much of a 'Command & Control' mentality. Surely, they say, there needs to be a more consultative approach in today's business environment? Interestingly, this purpose, far from being in conflict with a consultative approach is actually crucial to making it work. What, after all, do the business's senior managers want to be able to do, or avoid doing, as a result of having consulted with their employees/customers/shareholders and so on? If they don't know, how can they possibly find the right questions to ask? This is something we'll be looking at later on.

When I first identified this purpose, I was well satisfied. It seemed to cover all the bases, but it also left something nagging in the back of my mind. Although this purpose seemed not to leave any gaps, it somehow felt incomplete. Eventually, I realised that it was the very word 'purpose' that was niggling me. There was no doubt in my mind that all business communications must fulfil the above in order to justify their existence. But you could still ask, 'What is the purpose of them doing so?' I decided that what I'd identified was what I call the **functional purpose**, over and above which there is also an ultimate purpose:

**to help enable the business to fulfil its *raison d'etre*
as effectively as possible, and to develop its ability
to do so increasingly.**

A bottomless pit no more

As we shall see, these purposes have huge potential implications when it comes to identifying what needs communicating, and how to write and design it. For one thing, they make it all too clear that *there can never be any such thing as a valuable 'for information only' business communication.* Furthermore, these purposes have massive implications for 'being taken seriously enough'. One of the key reasons why senior management can be reluctant to take communication more seriously is their fear of that bottomless pit. These purposes remove that fear. To fulfil any business goal, plan or mission, there will always be a finite number of actions to be prompted and/or enabled among the business's audiences, and therefore a finite amount of communicating to be done. And the better the communications, the more efficiently they can prompt and enable those actions, and the lower that finite volume. I believe this is a crucial insight for you to get across to the senior management, because it means that taking you seriously enough will no longer mean pouring resources into a bottomless pit. The dimensions of the pit are at last quantifiable and, with investment in the right areas, even reducible.

A developmental note for journalists

Many journalists end up working in the business communication environment. But journalism training is designed to enable people to produce communications for newspapers, magazines, radio and television – all of which have their roots in the recreational arena. Journalism training teaches how to identify, write and edit content that engages readers, and how to write snappy headlines to grab people's attention, pull out quotes, and so on. All of this can be necessary for many business communications too. But business communications require more. Journalism training is not intended to teach anyone how to identify the content necessary to prompt and/or enable people to take or avoid actions, nor (as we shall discover shortly) how to identify audiences with the precision necessary to ensure those actions happen. Indeed, as we shall also be discussing later on, even a business communication's phraseology has to be much more disciplined than that of its recreational cousins, if it's going to succeed.

But before we concern ourselves with how to put business communications together successfully, we may need to make the commercial case for change a little more tangible for those at the top.

Chapter 3
Dormant Riches

'Make visible what, without you, might perhaps never have been seen'
Robert Bresson

In this chapter we will uncover:

➤ the potential wealth that can lie dormant in any business

➤ how to tell whether that potential wealth currently exists in yours

➤ why your communications can bring that potential wealth to the surface

➤ how to start building your personal influence, by proving your commercial potential to the people at the top - in cold, hard cash terms.

It's all very well to be sitting on a potential goldmine. But that doesn't mean others are going to let you start exploiting its potential – not unless they recognise it too. So before getting into any discussion about how to exploit the dormant riches, it seems sensible to take an honest look, as objectively as we can, at what those riches could amount to.

Any business is kept alive by money and communication; money and communication rely upon each other for their existence. Communicating in business costs money: whether it's the price of a telephone call, or the cost of printing brochures, producing CD ROMs or running a website, or the bill for hiring a conference venue. This is true whether your organisation is a commercial one or not. If it is a commercial enterprise, a failure to communicate will mean it isn't going to make any money. And even if it's a non-commercial operation (a trade association or government department, perhaps) it won't be able to fulfil its purpose without communicating. In short, any business that fails to communicate fails – full stop. Including yours.

Communicating is *not* an option.

But even though your business doesn't have a choice about whether or not to communicate, it does have a choice when it comes to how badly or how well it does so. And I'm not talking just about people's ability to write or design well. Of at least equal importance is the ability to identify what needs to be written or talked about in the first place.

Your communications play a vital and incredibly valuable role. And if you're going to fulfil your potential, you may need to shake a few people out of a complacency of which, by definition, they're probably not aware. Before we look at how you could improve the way your business communicates, then, maybe it would help to have a compelling commercial argument which can get the senior management right behind you.

Of course there's more to business than just making money: there's adding value to the lives of stakeholders, helping people to grow, contributing to the community and so on. The point is that all of these can only be enhanced by better communicating. And it's equally true that many senior managers will only countenance the investment of time, effort and money necessary to make these improvements if they can see that such an investment will add to the bottom line. The good news is that it can do so in spades.

Business fitness

Many people think of money as the life-blood of their business – and with good reason. This being the case, maybe it can be useful to think of communication as the respiratory system.

I grew up in Wimbledon, when Bjorn Borg was at the height of his powers. And every time the tennis was on, my biology teachers would make a point of mentioning that his resting heart rate was about half that of average people. This was because he was extremely aerobically fit. In other words, when a human body is breathing efficiently, its cardio-vascular system doesn't have to work so hard to get oxygen to the cells. With an unfit person though, the heart has to pump more blood through the system to get the same results. And I think this is a useful metaphor to use when thinking about business communication. After all, the more effectively a business communicates, the less money it will have to pump through the system to get the results it's after.

It's obvious enough, but also gives rise to the question of why many businesses could still be communicating so much better than they do. Why so flabby? One reason could be the manner in which many people end up 'owning' communications as part of their job remit. Often, they've joined a company from, say, university. And if they've got on well they've been promoted through the business's hierarchy. They may have changed businesses en route, but their upward climb has eventually got them to a point where they have responsibility for getting key messages communicated to either internal or external audiences. Sometimes (particularly if they have a marketing role) they may have had some business communication training. Often though, they won't have. But this hasn't stopped them getting the job. And it also doesn't stop many of them believing that they know how to do it. Why is this? Why do people who may have displayed no natural aptitude for communication ownership, and who have had no relevant experience or training, believe that they know how to do it? Why *should* they know?

Communication ownership skills shortfall

I'm in no way suggesting that any communication owners are careless, foolish or lazy. In fact, I believe part of the problem stems from the very broadness of the term 'communication skills'. If you were to ask these people 'do you have good communication skills' many of them would probably say yes. And they'd mean it too. After all (as some are often keen to point out) they've been communicating all their lives. But what would their answers mean? Some might say 'yes' because they believe themselves to have good interpersonal skills, or because they've had an education which now enables them to identify a split infinitive at 100 paces. Some might feel they're good communicators because they're skilled at winning arguments in meetings, or because they enjoy giving presentations and are highly charismatic on stage.

These are indeed all examples of good communication skills. Yet none of these skills mean that such people can accurately identify a business communication outcome, or audience. Their skills also don't indicate that they know how to identify the content necessary for an effective business communication, or the most appropriate medium or media to use. The rules of grammar are, after all, of only the most peripheral relevance when putting together a communication plan. And personal magnetism just doesn't translate onto a brochure or web page.

The necessary skills

The question, then, is not 'do your communication owners have good communication skills?' but 'do they have the necessary business communication ownership skills?' Do they have the skills to:

1. identify what needs communicating in the first place?
2. articulate that clearly to you or your colleagues?
3. objectively appraise the work you produce for them?

4. provide only constructive feedback which is consistent with their original brief?

In many instances the honest answer is 'No'. And to be fair, since 'communication ownership' is not a widely recognised concept (to be honest, I'd never heard the term used by anyone else; I made it up a few years ago) hardly any of them have ever been taught how to fulfil this role, so there's little reason to expect that they should have such skills.

Tell-tale signs of a potential goldmine

Perhaps it's not surprising, then, that many business communications produce less effective results than they could, and that you can be left facing a whole raft of unnecessary challenges – any one of which is a clear sign that your business is not communicating effectively, and that there's a potential goldmine sitting there just waiting to be exploited:

- having to produce communications for people who don't know what they want (but they'll know it's what they want when they see it)
- having to do numerous re-drafts
- not having enough time to do the job properly
- having people re-write the text (often quite badly) or just asking you to produce communications 'wot they've writed themselves'
- having to spend ages getting communications approved, because so many people want to stick their oars in, and often correct each other's corrections
- investing loads of time and effort into a project only to have it pulled at the last minute.

In addition to this, people around the business may be complaining that they aren't being kept informed and (paradoxically enough) that they're suffering from communication overload. And to top it all off, senior management often complain that their people are engaging in 'silo-thinking': concentrating only on their own parochial interests rather than the wider needs of the business as a whole.

Little wonder, then, that the communication owners may be wasting a lot of time and effort (theirs, yours and the audience's) and that the quality of the finished communications may sometimes be poorer than necessary, given your skills and those of your colleagues. And if we return to our earlier metaphor, and think of communicating as the respiratory system, this situation suggests that your business is not nearly as fit as it could be.

But so what? Why should anyone care? Apart from the frustration, stress and knocks to your confidence, what does it matter if your business's communication processes leave the whole operation wheezing a bit, and stopping every few yards holding its sides? Many people look at the above list of problems, shrug their shoulders and say, *'Well that's life. That's just the way it is, and you have to make the best of it.'* Often they'll say, *'You just have to work around problems like that.'* But maybe it doesn't have to be that way any more – not if you can work *through* those problems. And from a commercial perspective, perhaps there are good reasons for doing so.

Counting the cost

Business communication is much more expensive than most people think. It can have up to ten costs associated with it, and many businesses recognise only part of one of these. And when you start to appreciate not only the number of hidden communication costs that your business could be incurring, but their magnitude as well, you may begin to appreciate the staggering potential that exists for both cutting costs and, if appropriate, increasing income. In other words: mining the dormant riches that are lying there, right now, within your business's communication goldmine.

These costs fall into three categories. The first category is made up of three necessary costs (albeit some of them may be unnecessarily high). The other seven costs are unnecessary: three are the result of wasteful production and distribution decisions, and the other four arise from the finished communications failing to do their jobs properly. Not surprisingly, then, some of these ten costs overlap, so it might look like I'm double counting. In fact, my intention is simply to separate them out so we can see more clearly what's going on.

Necessary costs

Cost 1 – the hard costs of producing and distributing communications

This is the cost that everyone recognises (or at least thinks they do). It's the cost for which there is often a specific budget set aside, to cover expenses such as printing and telephone bills, postage, agency fees, the cost of hiring conference venues, running websites and so on. While this cost may be recognised for a central communication team, there are often communications being produced on an ad-hoc basis by other departments (finance, HR etc) which aren't being counted. And even if they are, they represent the only communication costs that most businesses pay attention to – which is a bit of a shame really, because they're often among the smallest. However, some businesses do recognise at least part of the second cost.

Cost 2 – the cost of people's time spent producing communications

While the cost of employing agencies or freelances is a hard cost, in-house communication professionals often get accounted for differently. Such an overhead may be baked into the business's overall communication budgets, or it may not. But even if it is recognised as a communication cost in its own right, the cost of other people's time invariably gets overlooked. Many communication owners are senior people, whose time is expensive. And those senior people have to spend time commissioning you or your colleagues to produce the communications they want.

Once these communications have been drafted, they then often do the rounds of a whole group of people (including the owner of course) who need to vet and approve what's being said. I used to be involved in many such reader groups, one of which had no fewer than nine members. We were approving five standard customer service letters, and the elapsed time between the beginning and end of the process was more than six months. How many iterations we got through I've no idea, but the combined number of working hours involved must have been up in the hundreds.

I once took the Internal Communications team of a British water company through these costs. They estimated that their Managing Director alone spent an average of four hours a day doing nothing but vetting and approving internal communications (at an estimated cost to the business of some £300,000 a year).

Cost 3 – audience time

This is where it starts getting serious. Of course, when it comes to paying for the audience's time, we're talking principally about internal communications. But it's worth bearing in mind that many people in business need to keep up to date with what's being said to customers, prospects or distributors etc. So it's not only internal communications that can incur this cost.

Although it's obvious, many people forget that communicating with 60 staff for one minute doesn't cost your business one minute, it costs one hour. So it costs 2,100 minutes (or 35 working hours – one average working week) to communicate with 210 employees for just 10 minutes.

A few years ago, a major British high street retailer, with 14,500 staff, set itself an internal communication budget of £1.2 million. When I asked them how much time they felt an average employee would spend each week going through internal communications, they estimated that it would be about three hours (and this was in the days before they got e-mail). Until it was pointed out to them, they hadn't realised that, in fact, this amounted to nearly 26 working years a week. So this business, which thought it was spending £1.2 million on its internal communications, was incurring well over £60million on this third cost alone. What's important here is not so much the cash figures (although they certainly caused a few jaws to drop at the business in question) but the ratio. In this instance a 50:1 ratio between the cost of the audience's time and the communication budget. Not every business has a ratio as high as this; in some, it can be estimated as low as 3:1. But the growth in electronic communication has meant that centrally produced communications account for a diminishing percentage of this cost – and the real ratio may be considerably higher than many people estimate.

Of course, no one is saying that this money is necessarily being wasted. Your business needs to incur all of these first three costs just to get the communications out there. But it's fair to say that these costs may be higher or lower than necessary. If people around the business are complaining that they aren't being kept informed of what's going on, it's possible that this may be because not enough money is being put into getting the communications out there. Then again, one could just as readily argue that if people are complaining they've got too much to read, there may be too much being spent on these three costs. In many businesses, of course, staff are making both complaints, suggesting that:

- they're not being told everything they want
- they're being told, but they can't find what they want because it's buried under a mass of useless stuff they don't want and can't use
- they're getting to the stuff they want, but something about the way it's written is switching them off. (This is a mammoth problem in itself, and one we'll be looking at later.)

I believe that it's too early to start making decisions about this. One thing we can start identifying, though, is whether this money – however much it may be at present – is all being spent efficiently. To do this, we have to look at the first three unnecessary costs.

Wasteful production and distribution costs
These wasteful costs come from spending more than you need to, just getting the audience to have received the communications. In short, the unnecessary part of the necessary costs.

Cost 4 – ill-defined or moving goalposts
Once you've put together an initial draft or design visuals, communication owners can often change their minds about what they want (or remain just

as uncertain as they were first time around) – asking you to go away and try again. Or drafts can get caught up in an approval process in which different people want to make changes (seemingly 'because they can'), correct each other's corrections, or argue about 'the right way to write this'. These inefficiencies not only increase Cost 2 unnecessarily, they can also push deadlines to such an extent that any printing that's required can also be more expensive (Cost 1).

Cost 5 – ditching communications

In some circumstances, a communication project gets started, and a load of work can be done, when suddenly the whole thing gets ditched before the communications ever see the light of day (or shortly after they've gone out). And it means that all that time (Cost 2) and possibly some hard costs (Cost 1) will have been incurred in vain.

Cost 6 – back covering and ladder climbing

This is one that's exploded exponentially with the growth of e-mail. Many finished communications get sent to people who don't need and can't use them, either to cover the communicator's back, or to get themselves noticed by more senior people. These communications are increasing Cost 3 unnecessarily and, with printed communications, Cost 1 likewise.

Communication failure costs

So far we've looked at costs associated with the process of just getting the communications out there. But that's only half the story. There's no point in getting business communications in front of audiences just for the sake of doing it. These communications have a job to do, and if they don't do it they can rack up a whole bunch of other costs.

Cost 7 – the cost of re-doing the communication

This cost could be said to have a foot in two camps. Like the three inefficiency costs we've just looked at, this one also eats unnecessarily into the communication budget, soft production costs and audience time. However, this is because the communication process has been ineffective, rather than inefficient: the end product hasn't done its job. Interestingly, the way in which it wastes this money can depend on whether the communication is dealing with a long-term issue or a short-term one.

In the case of longer-term issues, a communication can be redone if it didn't work first time. And this will mean incurring Costs 1-3 all over again. Sometimes the communication is dealing with a short-term issue. And if the communication doesn't work, it may often be too late to do anything about it. In such instances, two scenarios become possible:

a) the first three costs already incurred in producing it were unnecessary, because it clearly wasn't needed
b) the communication's failure will incur one or more of the following three cost (these next costs can also kick in with long-term issues until the communication eventually gets redone).

Cost 8 – the cost of correcting mistakes and misunderstandings

If a communication fails to produce the results you want, chances are it's going to produce results you don't want. One British financial services company estimated that some 30%+ of its customer service staff time was being spent correcting mistakes and misunderstandings. These were found to come from two sources. The first was ineffective internal communications, which meant that staff weren't following procedures properly. The second was ineffective customer communications, which had customers on the phone, asking to have their most recent letter explained to them. The annual cost to this business was some £7.5 million, about 7% of its profit.

Cost 9 – the lost opportunity cost

Again this can really be two different types of cost, depending on whether the issue was a short- or long-term one. With a short-term issue, a communication's failure will probably mean that the business's opportunity to capitalise upon it (by either saving money or generating income) has been missed. Longer-term issues, though, incur a different sort of opportunity cost. Most people are employed to contribute to business profitability (or stakeholder value) either directly or indirectly. So all the time they spend on the receiving end of useless communications, or correcting the resultant mistakes, is not only incurring the cost of employing them. The business is also losing out on the additional profit/stakeholder value that those employees could have generated during that time.

Cost 10 – the cost of lost or lower audience good will

The impact of losing this good will depends on the audience. With staff, it could mean lower productivity, and more people leaving (with the inevitable higher recruitment and training costs, not to mention the interim inefficiency caused by the loss of experienced people). With customers, it can mean fewer sales, re-sales or referrals. With recruitment communications, it could mean fewer and lower quality applicants. And with shareholders, lower confidence and a dropping share price. (With public service communications from, say, a government department, it could mean more disgruntled voters.) In strictly numerical terms, these costs may be virtually incalculable. But common sense suggests that every time a communication fails to hit the mark, its cumulative knock-on effect on behaviour can be massive – and may easily put all of the other nine costs in the shade.

For example, official statistics released at the end of 2002 showed that the number of days' sick leave taken in Britain during the year had risen from 18 million in 1995 to 33 million in 2002. And that huge increase (85% in just seven years) was attributed almost entirely to stress. It's certainly true that stress can have a number of contributory factors, but it's undoubtedly the case that ineffective communication can be one of the main ones. People complaining of communication overload is now an almost universal phenomenon in business. And communication overload can lead to them stressing themselves out in several ways:

1. They diligently go through all the communications they've been sent, knowing all the while that they're not getting on with the work they have to do, and which is still lurking there, awaiting their attention. And many of the communications they read, or listen to, are useless to them, so they know they've just had their time wasted: time in which they could have got on with their work.

2. They know that a lot of the stuff they get sent is useless to them, so they only bother reading communications from certain individuals. Even then, some of the communications they read may still be irrelevant. And on top of that there can always be the nagging doubt, gnawing away at them, that they may be working without all the information they need.

3. As a result of either of the first two scenarios, deadlines get missed and/or work gets rushed and mistakes made which means that a lot of it may have to be done again.

And it's not only communication overload that can lead to stress. Often, an absence of effective communicating results in many people becoming disconnected from the purpose of what they're doing, or the employer for whom they're doing it, giving rise to frustration, apathy or both. This can add to the stress, or result in many people choosing to 'throw a sicky' when there's nothing wrong with them.

Looking at these ten costs, several things become clear.

- Communicating is an expensive business
- Get it wrong and it can become monumentally expensive
- If you can make your communication owners aware of these costs

(and better still, get the finance division to start doing the sums) they may be much more interested in taking communication more seriously.

The upside benefits

Ideally, your business would want to eliminate costs 4-10, and turn 1-3 from costs into investments: ones which, directly or indirectly, would generate valuable returns:

- ✓ increasing customer loyalty
- ✓ better quality recruits
- ✓ a happier workforce and working environment
- ✓ greater staff productivity
- ✓ greater staff creativity
- ✓ less sick leave
- ✓ lower staff turnover (meaning greater skills retention)
- ✓ a more nimble business
- ✓ increased competitive edge
- ✓ increasing income
- ✓ more confident investors and a growing share price

… and so on.

But how? Do the communication owners know? It would seem not. After all, whenever money gets tight, the knee-jerk reaction of many businesses is to try saving it by cutting the amount they're spending on Cost 1: the communication budget. Such a policy suggests that those responsible for setting communication budgets have been doing so without being clear about what returns they have expected to get from that investment. And simply cutting these budgets is both short-sighted and pretty much certain to fail, as it's almost bound to increase the communication failure costs, which will always be exponentially greater than the budgets. (We'll be looking at why this is so in a later chapter.)

Valuing the goldmine

It's likely that they may pursue such a course because they don't recognise the other costs. Appendix F will help you to start working out some of these costs, so you can bring them to the attention of your business's key decision makers. This will be a crucial first step towards exploiting your communication goldmine. But let's not get ahead of ourselves. Recognising and quantifying these costs is not enough. After all, just suppose that the Financial Director were to recover from the subsequent apoplexy, and the will to change existed at boardroom level, chances are they would still carry on as they were – unless they could find a better way of thinking about business communication.

Developing just such a 'better way' (one that could enable your Finance Director to breathe more easily) is exactly where we're headed.

Chapter 4

The Briefing Sequence

'So tell me what you want. What you really, really want.'

The Spice Girls

In this chapter we will uncover:

➤ the five potential subject areas for any communication brief

➤ the most effective sequence in which to delve into those subject areas

➤ what communication owners really want.

I've always believed that a robust, precise brief is the necessary foundation of an effective communication. Get it right, and the writing, editing and approval should follow easily. Muddling through with an inadequate brief, though, can often be like trying to put together a flat-pack wardrobe. Without the instructions. Or a screwdriver. In the dark.

Effective communication briefing is a skill that seems not to be taught in business – certainly not to communication owners – and is perhaps one of the main reasons why people can often end up saying, *'I don't know what I want, but I'll know it's what I want when I see it.'* As a result, if business communications were to receive report cards, they would often read, 'could do better.' Over the next few chapters, I'd like to share with you a robust briefing process for business communications. Because the purpose of business communication is different from that of its recreational counterparts, the briefing process also has to be quite different too. And because, with internal communications, you often can't afford to have people selecting themselves out of the audience, this process also has to go beyond that of marketing communications.

This process has been tried and tested successfully in many commercial and government organisations. Perhaps more important still, its efficacy is pretty much self-evident, and you can prove it for yourself as you go along. It's quite possible that you may already be doing some of this already.

However, I've discovered a whole bunch of subtle linguistic nuances that can often arise, and which can store up problems for later if we don't address them here. And I've no way of knowing which of these subtleties might be waiting to ensnare you. Even if much of this is already familiar to you, therefore, I'm confident there will be a number of new ideas in this process, any one of which could be worth a fortune to your business and your career.

The key ingredients

As I see it, to be able to do this briefing thing effectively, you have to know three things:

1. what information you need to be looking for from the communication owner
2. what questions to ask to get that information (including what to do when you get a 'don't know' answer)
3. the most useful sequence in which to ask those questions.

We'll be cycling round these three factors several times, but we'll begin by looking at the sequence.

When putting together a brief for any communication, there will usually be five different subjects you can consider. They're listed here in alphabetical order, and it might be interesting to think about which of these you would habitually try to identify first.

- **Audience**
  - **Content**
    - **Logistics** (e.g. deadlines, budgets etc)
      - **Medium**
        - **Outcome**

Most people (and these are experienced, dedicated communication professionals) tell me they go for the audience first, and then often the medium or the content. So let's think about this for a moment. Just imagine that someone has come up to you and asked for your advice. They're intending to go on holiday, and they want you to suggest the best way for them to get there. What's the first thing you're going to need to know before you can help them? Surely it's going to be the destination isn't it? Without knowing that, you're stymied. How can you possibly help someone to get to the place they want to go if you don't know where that place is? Travelling is, if you like, a process: a sequence of activities. So is communicating. Yet it's rare for anyone to say that, when they're taking a brief, they identify the outcome first. Admittedly, sometimes the audience may be predetermined (or at least may seem to be). But even if this appears to be the case, it may still be negotiable. Indeed, we will be discussing later why it may have to be. For any brief to be effective, the outcome has to be the first item you identify, followed by the audience, the content and then the medium (often returning briefly to review the content again at the end).

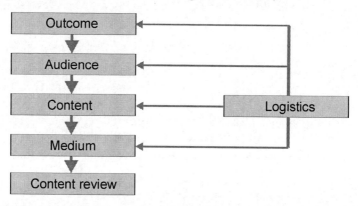

The 'outcome-focused briefing' sequence

The logistics can float around and come into play at any point after the Outcome (or even as the Outcome is being identified). Some people, of course, start with a deadline, or a budget. Sometimes these may be fixed by external forces, but they're often negotiable. And if people don't know what outcome they're going for, they can't possibly identify the cost of not getting it, and therefore how much they ought to invest in order to get it. They are therefore ill-placed to take decisions about anything else until they're clear about the outcome. If the logistics haven't already cropped up by the time you're discussing the medium, they will have to do so then.

Soon after I began my research, I concluded that 'the right way to write stuff' would be the way that produced the outcomes we were after. Put simply, if a given communication produced the outcome we wanted, it must have been written in the right way (both in terms of its content and its phraseology). If it didn't, it hadn't been. A simple enough idea, but one which raised two challenges. Firstly, it seemed to require a trial and error approach, as one could never know until after the event whether it had been written correctly. Secondly, it made me realise that I didn't know what a communication outcome was.

This was a somewhat disconcerting realisation for someone whose very mortgage payments relied on his ability to deliver communication results.

But I took consolation from the fact that no one else seemed to know either. Indeed, the conversations I found myself having with various communication owners around the business proved this to be the case. These conversations used to go something like this.

'Yes, it's very good, but it's not quite what I want.'

'So what do you want?'

'Well, I don't really know ... oh, but I'll know it's what I want when I see it.'

And I'd think to myself, *'Oh thanks, that really helps!'* as I returned to my desk none the wiser, but with a deadline looming larger than ever.

This sort of conversation always left me with a whole bundle of questions, clambering over each other to be heard. Questions like: How were we able to have that conversation? After all, if someone doesn't know what they want, how can they possibly tell that what they've been presented with isn't it? And if they are capable of knowing what it is when they see it, they must be able to know what it is that they want. So why can't they identify it up front? And, if they do identify it up front, why do the goalposts so often move?

I believe there are two main reasons why many people can't say what it is they want, either up front, or when they're critiquing a first or even second draft, or why it is that they're just plain uncomfortable with what's been presented to them. The first of these has to do with identifying outcomes; the second, with the way the communication is written. I'll be spending the latter part of this book looking at how and why people respond differently to the same piece of writing – and how to get the response you want.

What people really, really want

But what any communication owner wants – what they really, really want – is an outcome. Often, though, they think they simply want to say stuff. So before we can go any further, we need to establish a clear definition of a communication outcome – something that everyone can agree upon, and which can apply to any type of business communication. Only then will it be possible to identify – in advance perhaps – 'the right way to write things' to produce such outcomes. With this in mind, here's a set of questions for you to ponder. What is a business communication outcome? What does it look like? What does it sound like? And how do you go about identifying it?

Chapter 5
The Language of Outcomes

'If a picture paints a thousand words, it's every bit as true that a word can paint a thousand pictures too.'

Reginald Milton

In this chapter we will uncover:

➤ where you need to focus a communication owner's attention

➤ some limitations of the question 'Why?'

➤ why it's a surprisingly ineffective idea to set communication objectives

➤ the three key criteria of an effective communication outcome.

Within my first year as a brand manager, I arrived at a conclusion which I still hold to be true – even if it appears at first sight to be somewhat odd: one of the biggest reasons why business communication problems exist is that we all speak the same language. And the reason it's a problem is that it tends to make people believe that they understand each other. Or to be more precise, that they understand each other identically: that Person A not only understands what Person B means, but that Person A's understanding is identical to Person B's understanding. But the reality can frequently be somewhat different.

When I mention this to clients, some immediately appreciate what I'm on about (and had already arrived at pretty much the same conclusion themselves) while others blink at me a little, as if I'd just produced a small curtain rail from my ear and begun to fricassee it in their office. As I've no idea into which category, if either, you might place yourself at present, I think it would be useful to explain the problem in a little more depth; and not for the sake of having an academic discussion. If you want to start mining the riches that lie hidden in your communication goldmine, you need to know what obstacles and pitfalls you're likely to encounter, what tools you need to use to overcome them, and how to use those tools to best effect.

What follows therefore has practical implications for how you start sorting out many of those niggling challenges that can crop up in your work, and for making inroads into those unnecessary communication costs we spoke of earlier. (If you're already familiar with neuro-linguistics, the next section is going to be stuff you already know, but I've put it in for anyone whose knowledge of neuro-linguistics is limited or non-existent.)

How language works

Understanding how language works is something that most people have never been taught, nor ever felt the need to learn, any more than many drivers have felt the need to learn about the workings of the internal combustion engine. Even the most skilled drivers don't really need to understand how that works in order to be able to get safely and efficiently from A to B. Similarly, most people blithely use their language to get along, without knowing how it works.

Language (in our case English) not only makes up a large chunk of what we're thinking; it's also integral to how we're thinking. As human beings, we experience the world by taking in information through our five senses, and doing various things with that information through electrical and chemical discharges in our bodies – principally in our brains. All that activity gives us the raw data of our reality: what we see, hear, feel and so on. But it's principally through language that we create the meaning of that raw data – that we 'make sense' of what our senses are giving us. Language therefore not only describes our experience, it prescribes how we are understanding that experience. Knowing how language really works, then, has nothing to do with protracted debates about whether or not to split an infinitive, or end a sentence with a preposition. We're talking about something much more powerful: your ability not only to understand what someone else means, but to recognise, through the very words they're using, how and why your 'meaning' may be different from theirs – and how to close the gap. Might such skills not be useful to acquire if you want to put together robust, precise briefs in the shortest possible time? Might they not also be useful if you want to know that the words you're writing stand the best possible chance of producing the outcomes the communication owner wants? My experience has shown these skills to be invaluable. Numerous clients have told me that when they've 'got' this, it's as if they've been able to start thinking in 3D. When they're taking a brief, certain types of word or phrase leap out at them, clamouring for attention. And when editing draft text, they also find similar words and phrases drawing attention to themselves. And they talk with enthusiasm about how such abilities are increasing their confidence, saving them time, enabling them to add massive value and making their working lives easier.

Throughout this book, I'll be introducing numerous such words and phrases (many of which may be new even to aficionados of neuro-linguistics) so you'll know what to look for in the future, and what to do once you've spotted them. In short, it's my intention to give you a 'linguistic toolkit'. To keep it practical, we'll look at these tools in action, so you can understand not just how they work, but when and how to apply or avoid them. And as we're starting our exploration at the beginning of the briefing process, I believe the first linguistic tool that we need to understand is the word 'why'. When it comes to starting a communication brief, many people believe that 'why' is the ultimate navigation tool – but is it as reliable as they'd like to believe?

Where are you looking for the answer?

When I ask clients how they identify outcomes, they often say that they ask: 'Why do you want this communication produced?' The question 'Why?' is, after all, a useful one for identifying reasons behind any activity. But will it necessarily enable you to identify the outcome? Perhaps surprisingly, it hardly ever does so. This seems to be because, when considering the reason for engaging in any activity, people can put their attention on any of these different subjects:

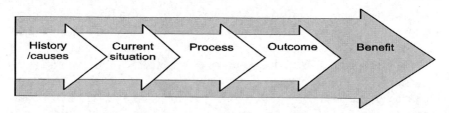

If you ask someone *why* they want to get something done, they can focus on the current situation they'd like to address, or they might describe to you the history that has led up to that current situation. They might also put their attention on the process they'd like to engage in to address the current situation, or the benefits they perceive will arise from doing so. Or they might focus on the outcome they want the communication to produce.

Crucially, though, you can't make any process effective if you don't first know what outcome it has to produce, and the outcome is only one of at least five different places that a person might go to when asked 'Why?', which makes this question hopelessly imprecise. It doesn't direct the communication owner's attention to one specific place or another; their minds free to wander wherever they choose. (This doesn't mean that 'Why' is a bad question in itself – it just doesn't work that well when looking for communication outcomes.) And there are other questions you can use which would be better at focusing people's attention on one particular place or another – most particularly on the outcome. But even knowing what these questions are isn't enough. Chances are you may well have had the experience, in either your work or personal life, of asking someone a question and having them give you an answer which didn't tell you what you'd asked for. This can certainly happen in communication briefing. Knowing what questions to ask, then, is only half the skill; you also need to understand what the answers look and sound like – otherwise you may still come unstuck.

Focusing people's attention where you need it

To illustrate this, I'd like to relate a story about a former colleague of mine. To spare his blushes, let's call him Brian.

Shortly after he joined the company, Brian had taken a shine to one of the Directors' secretaries, whom I'll call Cathy. He was on his way to get himself a cup of coffee one morning when a Director came out of his office with a box of chocolates and started handing them around. Cathy said she didn't want one. But because she was the Director's own secretary, he was a bit more insistent than he had been with the others:

'Go on, have a chocolate.'

'No, really. I'm on a diet.'

When Brian heard this, two very 'bloke-ish' thoughts started jostling with each other in his mind. He was both dismayed at the thought of her trying to ruin what he saw as a perfect figure, and also delighted to have an excuse for chatting to her. As he was passing her desk, he stopped and said: 'You're not seriously on a diet are you?' (Not the greatest chat-up line perhaps, but then Brian had never heard of interpersonal skills.) Cathy said that yes she was, to which Brian (trying to pay her a compliment and missing by several miles) said in a rather plaintive voice, 'But *why?*'

At this, Cathy – aware that all her workmates were now listening in – dropped her pen on her desk in a rather marked manner, looked at him levelly and said, 'Because I'm fat. Okay?'

Having been asked 'why' she was engaging in the activity of dieting, Cathy's focus of attention is not on the outcome, but on the **Current Situation** (as *she* perceives it).

45

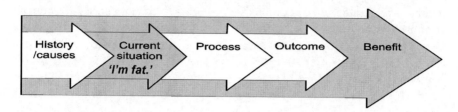

This can often be the case when you ask people why they want a communication produced. Let's say, for example, that the communication has to do with the introduction of new security procedures. If you ask the communication owner why the communication is needed, he might say 'because we've got a security problem we need to sort out.' Or he might even focus on the history of the current situation and say something like 'because we've had several computers pinched over the past few weeks.' The question 'why' can, after all, allow people to focus anywhere they like. And if you use it when trying to identify a communication outcome, it may leave you (as it did Brian) feeling that perhaps a different question might yield a more productive answer.

While getting his coffee (during which time he told himself that maybe he hadn't got his wooing off to the brightest of starts) he thought he'd come at it from different angle. He stopped at Cathy's desk on his way back and asked her:

'What's the objective of your diet then?'

To which she replied, 'To lose a stone.'

Where's her focus of attention now?

With this answer almost everyone says that she's now focusing on the outcome. But maybe she's shifted her attention onto the process. Losing weight is, after all, a process. (At this point in my workshops, some people say that if she were focusing on the process, surely she'd be talking about things like exercising and cutting out certain foods. I would suggest that these are indeed parts of the process: they're simply at a lower logical level than Cathy's currently attending to. She's focused on the process's top line.)

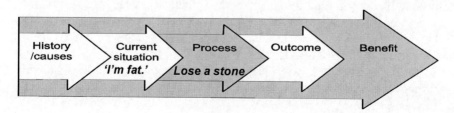

46

That she's focusing on the process is something which, for many people, becomes apparent only when they hear her answer to Brian's third question (which she provided just before she stood up and chinned him):

'So what outcome do you want to achieve as a result of having dieted'?

'I'll be a size 10.'

In this story, being a size 10 is the outcome Cathy wants, and losing a stone is the process through which she has decided she has to go in order to get that outcome.

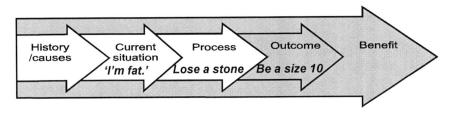

What makes this story interesting from a business communication perspective, is that most people just as readily confuse the process and the outcome – particularly when dealing with internal communications. They think they're talking about the outcome when, in fact, they're focusing on the communication process. This is not just a fairly common occurrence – it's an almost universal one. And it's often a hugely expensive error. After all, as I was observing earlier, how can you expect any process to generate the outcome you want if you don't first know what that outcome is?

What people see

That said, it took me ages to be able to distinguish clearly between a process answer and an outcome answer. And once I got clear about the differences, I realised there were three key distinctions. My clients have told me that these distinctions alone have had a massive impact on their confidence, influence and productivity. To help me explain the first of the distinctions, I'd like you to do a little visualising. Just imagine, for a moment, that you are at an archery range. Give yourself a moment to do this, now.

Once you've got this set up in your mind's eye, I want you to imagine that you've got a bow and arrow, and that you're stepping up to the place from which you're going to take your shot. The target is, say, 25 metres away in the distance. And as you stand there, I want you to picture your objective in your mind's eye. Before going any further, give yourself a few seconds to picture your objective, now.

Many people talk about identifying communication objectives. But this is rarely the most effective expression to use. To understand why, let's return to the archery range in your mind's eye, and notice what happens if we make a tiny linguistic shift. The set up is exactly as before. You've got your bow and arrow and the target is 25 metres away. And this time I want you to picture the *outcome* you're going for. Again, give yourself a few seconds to picture the outcome in your mind's eye.

Was there any difference between what you saw in your mind's eye when picturing your *objective* and what you saw when looking at the *outcome*? For about 20% of people there's no difference, but with 80% there is. When picturing the outcome, almost everyone sees the arrow in the centre of the target, but when picturing the objective – even though they're looking at the target – four out of five people have the arrow still in the bow waiting to be fired, or flying through the air but not yet in the target. (For the 20% of people who see the same thing both times, the arrow is usually in the target when they picture their objective. There are other possibilities too, but these are the most common.)

Many people fall into the trap of thinking that they can interchange the terms objective and outcome with impunity, but this simply isn't true. For only a minority of people do these two words prompt the same mental image. For most people, it is only the word 'outcome' that gets them seeing the – well, the outcome; the word objective merely gets them looking in the general direction in which the outcome is to be achieved. And, importantly, the process (whether it be firing the arrow, or communicating) is still to be engaged in. If you ask someone for a communication objective, what they will spontaneously picture in their mind's eye – and therefore describe to you – is much more likely to be the process than the outcome. Talking about communication outcomes is therefore more useful than communication objectives.

Outcome v process

So what is a communication outcome? And how can you tell, just from someone's conversation, whether they're telling you about the outcome or the communication process? This requires us to understand another subtle linguistic distinction. Forgive me if this gets just a bit technical, because it concerns the way we use verbs – particularly the *Continuous Tenses* (those that end with 'ing', e.g. I am walking). And, rather than getting into a technical discussion, I think it would be more useful to illustrate how this linguistic tool works. So, I'd like you to answer the following question:

Do you like learning?

Most people say that they do; in workshops I always get a 100% yes to this question the first time I ask it. But let's consider the idea of learning for a moment. Learning, when you think about it, can often be quite a disagreeable experience. After all, it means having to accept that there are things you don't know how to do, and makes you acknowledge that, in some respects, you're not as capable as other people. It can also mean having to go outside your comfort zone, in danger of becoming confused perhaps, or concerned that others are learning more quickly than you, or it can leave you feeling in danger of looking foolish, or possibly becoming frustrated if you don't seem to be 'getting it'.

When one looks at it coldly, then, learning is not necessarily always a bundle of laughs is it? And yet 100% of the people I work with say that they like it. Are they just saying it, because they're in a learning environment and daren't admit otherwise, or do they really mean it? In which case, are they all masochists? Or do they only think they mean it because they're answering a different question entirely? In fact, this last scenario has proved to be the case for almost everyone. Most people, it would appear, do not usually enjoy the learning experience all that much. But what they do enjoy – what they *love*, what they're prepared to put up with all the discomfort of learning for – is so they can get to the point of *having learned*. That's what almost everyone really likes.

This distinction between expressing an idea in the present continuous tense (learn*ing*) and the future perfect continuous (hav*ing learned*) is one which pretty much everyone seems to miss until it's pointed out to them. And although it may seem like nit-picking, the impact of confusing these two can be immense, because within this distinction is the difference between the language of process and the language of outcomes: between communicat*ing* and having communicat*ed*.

Who's doing the doing?

Apart from the difference in tenses, there's the question of who's doing the doing. An 'outcome' answer will focus on what the audience is doing once they've been communicated with. But a 'process' answer will be focusing on the activity of the communicator in communicating. And if we put all this together: the purpose of business communication, the verb tenses and the question of who's doing the doing, we arrive at the conclusion that a communication outcome will always tell you what the audience are:

- **doing** and/or
- **not doing** and/or
- **able to do** and/or
- **able to avoid doing**...

...as a result of *having read,* or *having watched,* or *having listened to* the communication.

This phraseology (the *'having read...')* means that the process of communicating is over, so we must be focusing on the outcome. Therefore, the first question we need to ask any communication owner is:

'What do you want people to be doing (not doing/able to do) as a result of having read (watched/listened to) this communication?'

(Naturally I've had to give you a generic version here; in real life the words in brackets would be alternatives to use as the occasion demanded.)

If we return to the security bulletin example, the difference is easy to see. An answer that's focusing on the process would say something like:

'We need to make sure that people know about the new security procedures.'

(Here, the 'making sure' is being done by the communicator.)

An answer that's focusing on the outcome would be saying something along the lines of:

'Staff are locking away their valuables and challenging strangers in the building.'

And what a difference it makes, wouldn't you say? Being clear about the outcome (and enabling the communication owner to be clear about it too) can often mean the difference between being able to quickly produce a communication that generates that outcome, or taking ages to produce one that doesn't. This is because (apart from the whole issue of 'the right way to write stuff') if you don't have the outcome clear in your mind, it's often impossible to identify either the audience or content effectively. This single distinction can do much to stop them saying, *'I don't know what I want but I'll know it's what I want when I see it'* – because it gets them to nail down what they really want up front. **What they really really want is the outcome.**

Two way outcomes

This is all very well for outbound communication. But to be truly effective, of course, business communication needs to be a two-way process. So how about communications, such as questionnaires and surveys, that are designed to bring information back in? In fact, exactly the same principles apply. Many people start out by scratching their heads and thinking, *'Now what questions should we include?'* This is again a process-focused question (as is 'what do we want to know?'). An outcome-focused question would ask:

'What do we want to be able to do as a result of having received their feedback?'

Whether you're working on outbound or inbound communications, if you use these questions up front every time, there will be a fat chance of anyone asking you to produce a worthless communication in your business ever again...

...or will there?

Chapter 6

Lighting Up the Darkness

'The limits of my language mean the limits of my world.'

Friedrich Nietzsche

In this chapter we will uncover:

➤ the need for linguistic orienteering: why it's useful, and how to do it

➤ why a certain type of English can make it impossible for you to see what someone else means - and what you can do about it

➤ how to get people's thinking moving if they're stuck.

You could say this is where the detective work really begins. It's just about impossible to overstate the importance of these next two chapters. Without them, everything we've discussed so far, and most of what comes afterwards, will be rendered redundant.

We've established what a business communication outcome looks and sounds like. And many people might think we could let the matter rest there. But we can't. This goldmine isn't going to give up its riches that easily. After all, it's common when people are having a discussion for Person A to ask a question of Person B, and for Person B's answer to leave Person A thinking:

'Huh? You haven't answered the question. Well, yes, I suppose you have answered it, but ... Huh?'

When it comes to identifying communication outcomes, the 'Huh?' factor can kick in all too often, so we need to spend a little time understanding what's going on, and what to do about it. First of all, we need to recognise that, in these circumstances, the 'Huh?' factor can have two sources:

1. The communication owner is talking about an outcome – albeit obliquely – but the way they're doing so makes it difficult to understand them clearly.

2. They're not talking about an outcome at all, but they think they are because they're discussing a 'phantom outcome'.

We'll look at phantom outcomes in the next chapter. Before we do so, though, we need to delve once more into our linguistic toolkit, so we can understand how to clarify a communication owner's thinking – whatever they happen to be talking about. We'll look at four ways in which your language can affect not just what someone thinks about, but how their very thinking processes are operating. You may or may not already be familiar with some of what follows, but even if you have come across some of it before, it may be useful to review it, now, with an eye on identifying and fulfilling business communication outcomes. Indeed, what follows here can be useful in many aspects of your work, and even in your personal life too.

Audience motivation

Your communications need to get audiences to respond, so we need to bear in mind what it takes to get them to do so. At our most primal level, all human beings are instinctively motivated to move away from discomfort, and towards comfort (it's a survival thing). Apart from physical pain itself, we generally experience discomfort as various types of fear or angst, or both. And at the other end of the spectrum, we tend to experience emotional grooviness as a sense of safety, or fulfilment or both. And when people are deciding to do or not do things, as a result of having been communicated with, they can focus on any or all of the following:

- the discomfort they want to move themselves away from
- the discomfort they want to move other people away from
- the comfort they want to move themselves towards
- the comfort they want to move other people towards.

The fact that people motivate themselves in these ways has some important implications when you're taking a brief and/or writing copy.

Firstly, it helps explain why so many communication owners don't have a clear outcome in mind when they ask you to produce something for them. What they're aware of is a 'current situation' that they want to *move away from*. This is enough for them to know that they need a communication produced. And it means that when taking a brief from them, you may sometimes find them telling you what they want the audience to be moving away from: what those people are not doing as a result of having read the communication. In other words, the communication owner is answering your 'outcome' question by telling you about the current situation. For example, a simple communication for a staff kitchen might be intended to stop people leaving dirty coffee cups lying around in the sink. This is useful as far as it goes, but it's even more useful if you can also find out what the communication owner wants the audience to be doing instead. After all, it's almost inevitable that the audience will do something instead; it just may not be what the owner needs. (They might, for example, just put dirty cups back in the cupboards.)

This example may seem almost facile, but it really can happen – and when the outcome has bigger business implications, the consequences can be much more serious. When I finally worked out what I needed to be looking for when it came to communication outcomes, I found that people were often asking me to produce communications only to move away from a current situation, without having any idea of the outcome they wanted the audience to move towards.

That's why I believe it's vital that you can recognise how people are orientating their thinking, and change that orientation if necessary – from focusing on what they don't want to happen, to what they do want to happen instead. This will enable you to identify what the audience's actions need to be.

To illustrate why this is important for you, let's return to the archery range that you visualised in the last chapter. Just imagine that someone has seen your marksmanship and, being mightily impressed, has asked you if you could possibly hit a target for him. And (if you'll indulge me a little here) can we also imagine that, flushed with glory, you've agreed to do so. This person takes you with your bow and arrows through a door and into a large room. There are no windows in this room, no lights on and with the door closed, it's pitch black inside. And in the darkness he asks you to hit the target for him. Naturally, you can't see where it is. *'Never mind,'* he says, *'I've got a torch.'* And with that he throws a large circle of light on the far wall – where the target isn't.

'So, where's this target, then?' you ask.

'Well it isn't there,' he says.

Of course it isn't. You can see that it isn't, but where is it? How are you supposed to hit this target for him if all he's prepared to let you know is one of the many places where it isn't?

Such a scenario may seem absurd, but it does illustrate a problem which is common to many human interactions – both inside and outside business. Often, if you ask people what they want, they don't tell you. Instead, they tell you what they don't want. You hear this a lot with some parents (or other adults) who give many instructions to young children about what they shouldn't do. For example:

'Mind you don't spill that.'

And how often is such an instruction followed, less than 30 seconds later, by the dismayed cry of:

'I thought I told you not to spill it?'

But the child's behaviour is hardly surprising, when you recognise that they've just had their attention drawn to the idea of spilling it, and not given any alternative to move towards instead. And before you say that only a child would respond like that, try following this instruction:

Don't think about a black cat.

That instruction is impossible to follow. Even if you're now thinking about something else, you had to think about a black cat just to make sense of what the instruction was telling you. The very act of understanding what you weren't supposed to think about caused you to think about it. You had no choice.

This same dynamic can operate in business communications. Indeed, without a specific desired behaviour to move towards, an audience may stop one undesired behaviour, and then simply go off and do something else you don't want instead. So if you find yourself discussing what the audience is not doing as a result of having been communicated with, it's always worth using the following question:

'If you don't want them to do that, what do you want them to do instead?'

Concrete and abstract language

Some communication professionals bemoan the fact that they can sit down with someone to identify what that person wants to communicate, and come away after an hour or 90 minutes still feeling none the wiser. There can be several reasons for this. One of them is that the communication owner has been using a lot of abstract language.

There are many ways of dissecting the English language; one of them is to distinguish between *concrete language* and *abstract language*. Concrete language describes direct sensory experience: that which you can see, hear, taste, touch or smell. Sun, table, grass, tap, loud, soft, bitter and warm are all concrete words. And because concrete language describes information which is in the world outside us, there is a common pool of information out there in the world, which different people can draw upon to build their understandings. Abstract language, on the other hand, describes intellectual concepts. Community, education, professional, deliberate, unnecessary and poignant are all abstract words. These concepts exist only in people's minds, which means there is no common starting point from which different people derive their understandings. That people *think* they have a common understanding is almost always an illusion.

For example, if someone were to stand up in a team meeting and say, *'We must be professional,'* it's quite possible that everyone in the team will agree. *'Yes,'* they may chant, *'we must be professional.'* It's highly unlikely, after all, that anyone's going to sit there and say, *'Nah. I reckon we ought to behave like a bunch of rank amateurs.'* So there is an illusion of consensus. But what is each person really agreeing with? Numerous studies into people's understandings of abstract language have shown that, within a group of just four people, there will be widely differing, even contradictory meanings attached to the same abstract word.

You can try this for yourself if you want. Get a group of four people together – including yourself – and do a quick word association exercise together, with each person writing down the first ten words that they associate with the word 'professional'. (Word association is not intended to give you a definition of the word, but it will give you an idea of the meaning that people spontaneously attach to it.) Give the team a maximum of 90 seconds to do this (otherwise some people will agonise over it for ages). Then get one person to read through his or her list, and note how many words all four of you have in common. Although a couple of people may occasionally have the same word on their lists, it's unlikely that there will be even a single word that all four of you agree on exactly.

Most people are quite shocked by this, but the following exercise should make it clear as to why this happens. Try visualising the following sentence:

The President is sipping the hot coffee, quickly.

Give yourself a moment to picture that idea in your mind's eye. And notice how clearly you can do so – how clearly you can see what it means. Do it now, before continuing.

Now try visualising the following sentence:

It's important to rationalise communications satisfactorily.

How clearly could you picture that, when compared with the first sentence? It's rare to come across anyone who is able to create a clear mental image of the second sentence. And even then, they usually have to add in lots of stuff that isn't in the sentence itself. The reason? It's entirely abstract, whereas the first sentence was full of concrete words.

The greater the number of abstract words you string together, the tougher it becomes for people to see clearly what you mean, and the more difficult it can be for people to trust what you're saying as well. By creating a sort of mental fog, or blackout in the mind's eye, abstract language can be highly effective at either obscuring the intended meaning or, as often as not, obscuring the fact that there is no such meaning. That's why politicians use it so much – as do corporate bosses when they feel that they have to say something, even though they don't want to. Abstract language is great for people who want to communicate nothing. Of course, it's impossible to avoid abstract language altogether; business is full of abstract words (this sentence alone contains over half a dozen). But you can play the percentages, by making your communications more concrete.

If you need to get a clearer picture in your mind's eye of what a communication owner wants you to communicate, and be sure that the audience have a clear idea of what you mean, the following questions can help you to clarify abstract ideas. There are two approaches you can take to this. Sometimes, a person will throw a particular abstract word into a sentence which you want to make clearer. And sometimes it may be an entire abstract sentence that needs clarifying.

When it comes to dealing with individual words, the questions that will serve you best will depend on the type of word you're trying to clarify. In the example sentence I gave you, I used the following abstract words:

Adjective:	important
Verb:	rationalise
Noun:	communication
Adverb:	satisfactorily

The questions with which you can challenge them are based on Kipling's, *'I keep six honest serving-men (They taught me all I knew); Their names are What and **Why** and When And How and Where and Who.'* (and although Kipling didn't include the word 'Which', it can often serve us well too).

When faced with an **abstract adjective**, the most useful questions to use are frequently: When?, Where?, or For whom? ('Why?' will tend to give you more abstract answers, while 'How?' or 'In what way?' often just lead to blank faces.) So, in our example: 'It's important to rationalise communications satisfactorily,' you could ask, 'When is it important?' or 'Where is it important?' or 'For whom is it important?'

For an **abstract verb**, the most useful questions are How?, When?, Where? and For whom? Again, the question 'Why?' will usually lead to more intellectualising. So the question here would be 'Rationalise how?' (That's not to say that you shouldn't be interested in understanding why, but simply that the answer to such a question will often be an abstract one. The purpose of these questions is to make it easier for you to see in your own mind's eye what the communication owner means.)

For **abstract nouns**, the questions What? and Which? are often most useful. And if the abstract noun is the word 'people', then asking Who, specifically? will tend to get you a more concrete answer. Here, you could ask 'Which communications, specifically?' Indeed, for any of these questions, tagging on the word 'specifically' is great for pinning people down.

Abstract adverbs are rarely worth bothering with on their own. They're usually best dealt with by addressing the sentence as a whole. For this, a couple of 'catch-all' questions often do the business. The first of these is:

'Can you give me an example of that?'

Often, people use abstract language to make generalisations. And when they do so, they've frequently got an example in mind upon which they're basing their statement. This question gets you to the example. And it may not only help you to get more concrete detail, it may also enable you to challenge the generalisation itself. So, with our example, you could ask: *'Can you give me an example of rationalising communications satisfactorily?'*

The second 'catch-all' question is:

'How will you know?'

The first catch-all question tends to focus someone on the current or historical evidence upon which they're making their generalised statement. This second question focuses on the future evidence. People often use abstract language to describe their own expectations, without ever making it clear precisely what those expectations are. This question can draw out that information. For example: *'How will you know that communications have been rationalised satisfactorily?'*

The answers you get may still contain a bit of abstract language, but the idea is not necessarily to make it completely concrete, simply more so. What you're trying to do is get to a point where you can see something as clearly as possible in your mind's eye. And some abstract words are easier to see clearly than others, because some concepts are more abstract than others. For example, 'party' is an abstract concept. But it might still allow you to see a room with people in it, drinking, talking or dancing perhaps. So even though it's an abstract word, it's not as abstract the word 'professional', which tends to leave most people enveloped in a mental fog. Furthermore, making abstract language more concrete is only one way to tackle it. Another is to make it dynamic.

Static and dynamic language

To explain this linguistic distinction, I'd like you to do a little more visualising. Think of a relationship you have with someone. It could be a work relationship, a family relationship or a social relationship. Just pick one, and then, in your mind's eye, make a picture of that relationship. Give yourself a few seconds to get a clear picture in your mind's eye, now.

There are numerous differences that we can bring into play when we're creating pictures in our mind's eyes. For instance, we can make pictures in colour or in black and white. We can make them clear or fuzzy, sharp or grainy, small or large, bright or dark, and so on. And these differences can influence how the images we're making affect us emotionally, which, in turn, can impact on how we respond behaviourally. Bearing this in mind, let's return to that relationship you pictured a few moments ago, and do the exercise again, but making another of those tiny linguistic shifts. This time, rather than picturing the relationship, I want you to picture yourself *relating with* that person. And when you're picturing yourself relating with that person, it may be interesting to notice if there are any differences not so much in what you're picturing (although there may be differences here too) but in how you're picturing it, and the emotional response you get to that. Give yourself maybe fifteen seconds or so to picture yourself relating with that person, now.

When I've got my clients to do this exercise, I've found that about 75% of them will notice a particular difference in how they're doing their picturing. You may or may not be in that 75%, but even if you're not, this difference is worth being aware of. Most people, when asked to make a picture of a 'relationship', create a still picture. And when it's 'relating', their mind's eye manufactures a movie. (Interestingly, the other 25% invariably make a movie both times.) And, in seeing a movie, most people comment that they get more concrete detail, and a bigger emotional hit from what they're picturing.

Grammatically, the difference is simple: an abstract noun 'relationship' has been changed into a dynamic verb 'relating'. This is once again making use of the Continuous Tenses we spoke of in Chapter 4 (in that it ends with 'ing'). The evidence suggests that this spontaneously gets the mind's eye to create dynamic images and, in doing so, helps to get the audience's thinking and emotions moving. If you're taking a brief from someone whose thinking appears to be stuck, they may well be expressing their ideas with a number of abstract nouns. Changing just one of these into a dynamic verb can work wonders in getting their thinking moving. For example:

'We've got a <u>communication</u> problem.'
'So what will it take for us to be <u>communicating</u> effectively?'

Of course, some people love abstract nouns, and it may take you several attempts to finally get their thinking moving. But there's a second reason for persisting, which is that dynamic verbs tend to give people a sense of ownership that they wouldn't otherwise get. For example, it's not uncommon to hear people (in the pub perhaps) saying things like:

'I feel really trapped in this relationship.'

And, given the way they're thinking about it, it's hardly surprising that they have that feeling. After all, they're using an abstract noun, which is almost certainly getting them to make a stuck, static picture in their mind's eye. But just as significantly, abstract nouns are also impersonal. The implication is that the relationship is something beyond the individual, almost like a box that they can be 'trapped' in. And you could respond to this with a question such as:

'So how would you like to be relating differently?'

Doing so turns that abstract 'thing' into a dynamic activity. And, most importantly, it's an activity which that individual is doing. Suddenly, they've got control back again. It's no longer a 'thing' that's beyond them, but an activity that they're doing, and that they can choose to do their way.

But not all abstract nouns will turn into verbs. If, for example, someone were to tell you they want more confidence, you wouldn't get far by asking them how they want to be 'confidencing'. But there's usually an adverb you can use instead: *'What do you want to be doing confidently?'* So dynamic verbs and adverbs engender moving images in the mind's eye, which tend also to have more detail, feel more personal and evoke a bigger emotional 'hit' than static abstract nouns. Naturally, then, if communication owners' thinking is stuck, dynamic verbs and adverbs can help to get it moving. And, of course, it will have a similar effect on the people who read your communications too, making it much more likely they'll engage with what they're being told. Another way of shifting people's thinking is to change its 'range'.

Directive and permissive language

Just spend a moment thinking about the following question:

'What will you do for the homeless this month?'

Give yourself a few seconds to think about it. And now try this question:

'What could you do for the homeless this month?'

Again, give yourself a few seconds to think about it. Did you find that you had more ideas come to you with the second question than you did with the first? The simple and obvious difference here is that the word 'will' was replaced with the word 'could'. And what these two words do is encourage you to organise your thinking in different ways. The word 'will' encourages you to narrow your focus of attention, whereas 'could' is much more permissive, encouraging you to expand your attention to encompass more possibilities.

Each of these is useful in different circumstances. For example, if someone is stuck for ideas when trying to identify, say, the benefits to an audience of taking a particular course of action, simply asking them, *'How could they benefit from doing this?'* will enable them to see a greater number of possibilities. Conversely, if someone is feeling bewildered by too many choices, or is struggling to distinguish between what's possible to say and what's useful to say, asking them *'What will make them respond as you want?'* will usually enable them to make a decision and move on.

Chapter 7
Phantom outcomes

'Everything should be made as simple as possible. But no simpler.'
Albert Einstein

> ### In this chapter we will uncover:
>
> ➤ why some communication owners get stuck in 'process' thinking, and how to move them out of it
>
> ➤ how to spot seven 'phantom outcomes', and what to do with them
>
> ➤ the importance of noticing the 'logical level' at which someone is thinking
>
> ➤ what to do with communication owners who simply don't know what outcome they want, or say 'It's for information only'
>
> ➤ other uses for outcome-focused thinking.

When I first worked out how to identify a business communication outcome, I thought it would be dead easy to get people to tell me what they wanted their audience to do, avoid doing, or be able to do as a result of having read the communication. I simply needed ask them for that information. What could possibly go wrong? Plenty.

Apart from the linguistic stuff we looked at in the last chapter, there seemed to be loads of ways in which communication owners could come up with answers that weren't outcomes. How could this be? Were they being deliberately obtuse? Were they just winding me up? It certainly felt like it. But over time I started to notice a series of patterns emerging. And I realised that, together, the communication owner and I were chasing shadows – phantom outcomes – some of which even had the ability to lurk behind each other. I've identified seven in all, and to save you from getting frustrated, as I was, it's time to 'out' them.

1. A process answer
I spotted this one fairly early on, when taking a brief from a Facilities Manager for a communication about the introduction of some new security procedures:

'What do you want people to be doing as a result of having read this communication?'

'Well we need to tell* them about the new security procedures we're introducing from the beginning of next month.'

*Sometimes, the word 'tell' is phrased differently, e.g. 'make sure people know'.

Clearly, this response just isn't answering the question at all. So how could someone come up with it? It seems that people can sometimes start briefing sessions having already identified what they want to say, but not having identified the outcome they want to get from having said it. But because they know (or think they know) what their message is, they almost can't think of anything else until they've got it off their chest. The initial question therefore doesn't really register, so it simply needs repeating. Or you could slightly tweak the question in response to what they've just said:

'And what do you want them to be doing as a result of having been told that?'

This should get you either the outcome or, sometimes, another phantom.

2. A benefit answer

This example comes from a training session I ran with a manufacturer of kitchens and bathrooms. The marketing manager was working on a press ad, and this is what he came up with:

'What do you want people to do as a result of having read this ad?'

'I want them to be buying our kitchens!'

You could argue that this is an action, of sorts, but it's not an outcome. One clue is that 'buying kitchens' is somewhat abstract. What's happened here is that this manager has made the all too common error of leaping to what we could call a higher logical level.

Logical levels

One of the common mistakes that people often make when giving briefs is that they confuse communication outcomes and communication benefits. Hardly any business communication works in isolation. It's almost always going to be part of a chain, with some communications happening before it, and others following on afterwards. And this chain of communications exists to address a particular business project, such as a product launch, or office relocation, or a longer term business issue, such as product sales, staff recruitment, or health and safety.

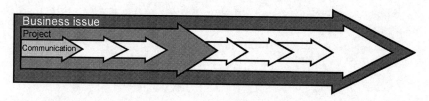

For our purposes, we could say that an outcome is something that you get from an individual communication, while the benefit is something you get from completing a whole project, or dealing with a business issue. And, at the risk of getting technical again, people confuse outcomes and benefits because they're muddling ideas that belong at different 'logical levels'. A logical level is simply a way of categorising information. For example, apples and pears are ideas that belong to the same logical level, but at a lower logical level than fruit, which, itself, is at a lower logical level than vegetation. And, similarly, apples are at a higher logical level than Cox's or Granny Smiths.

Vegetation					
Fruit			Vegetables etc		
Apples		Pears			
Cox's	Granny Smiths				

Communication benefits belong to a higher logical level than outcomes, and some people can confuse the two – with potentially damaging consequences. When the marketing manager identified his outcome as 'people are buying our kitchens' he had jumped up a logical level, from the outcome of this individual communication, to the outcome he wanted from the business issue. Our conversation continued along the following lines:

'Will this ad have an order form built into it?'

'No.'

'So, how am I supposed to buy the kitchen?'

'Well, you visit one of our showrooms.'

'Right, and that's where I actually do the buying?'

'Well, yes, obviously. That's where you can view the products, and that's where our sales people are.'

'So although this ad is going to make me want to buy the product, the specific action you would want me to take as a result of having read it is to visit the showroom, where I might find another of your products that I want

to buy even more.'

'Yeah, true enough.'

The mistake he had made was a common one: expecting a single communication to deliver a bigger outcome – one that will take a number of communications working in tandem to achieve.

Business issue: product sales

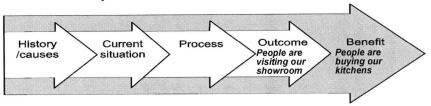

(At the risk of getting technical, the benefits of some short-term projects are sometimes the same as they are for long-term business issues – as in this example. But sometimes they can be different – at a logical level between the business issue benefit, and an individual communication outcome. For example, with the security procedures issue, the project was intended to ensure that the company's IT equipment was secure, but this was part of a broader business issue of ensuring that people were able to work in a safe environment.)

This distinction between outcomes and benefits is subtle and it's one that, even when I'd realised the distinction was there, took me a while to spot efficiently in live situations. It's something that I believe comes with practice. For now, I think it's enough to be aware that the distinction is there, and you may well find yourself able to spot it quite readily if you put the other ideas into practice. The same could also be said of the next distinction as well.

3. Subsequent outcomes

I'm not going to try pretending here. This one can be a real pig to spot, because it is an outcome; it's just not the outcome that the owner needs from this communication.

I discovered this phantom during another training session, where a divisional manager was working on a communication to let his people know about a team building day he was organising for them.

'What do you want people to be doing as a result of having read this communication?'

'I want them to be turning up on the day, ready to rumble.'

There's no getting away from it: this is an outcome. The problem here was that the team building day was voluntary, and this manager had over forty people in his team. So what sort of venue was he going to need? How many people were going to turn up? Surely some would be on holiday, or have made other commitments they either couldn't, or didn't want to, get out of. Maybe some would think that team building days were just a waste of time. As a result, he might book a venue for forty people, and have only five turn up. The more pressing outcome he needed, then, was to get responses from people to let him know if they were going to be there.

What he had first identified, then, was what we could call a Subsequent Outcome. It's not up at the logical level of a benefit (which would come from this and other team building activities) but, timewise, it is beyond the most immediate outcome he needs. In fact, he needs both outcomes, although a future communication could tell those attending how to get to the venue and so on. The important point here is that, even though he does need the subsequent outcome, he can't afford to overlook the more immediate outcome he needs first:

Business issue: team building

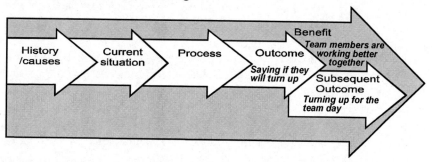

One way of checking whether or not you're dealing with a subsequent outcome is simply to ask:

'Is this the most immediate thing you need them to be doing?'

4. No known outcome at all

This is one you may encounter a lot, especially when working with communication owners who haven't been used to thinking about outcomes. In response to the question:

'What do you want people to be doing as a result of having read this communication?'

People often say either, *'I don't know,'* or *'I don't want them to do anything. This is for information only.'*

(In fact, there is a third answer they often give in these situations: *'You know, that's a very good question,'* in which case it's easy enough to ask them for a very good answer.)

Any of these answers suggests that the owner may have identified only the current situation they want to move away from, and probably needs help to identify the outcome. (It's often the result of someone thinking about business communication as if it's recreational communication.) Importantly, there are two problems with a business communication being 'for information only'. As we shall discover in the next couple of chapters, without a clear outcome it will be impossible for you to identify either the audience or the content effectively. After all, how can you possibly know what information people need to be given if you don't know what you want them to do, or be able to do, as a result of having been given it? And similarly, how will you ever be able to work out who needs that information? It doesn't take a genius to see that 'for information only' communications are the main reason why so many staff complain of communication overload.

But there are two main reasons why people may still think they're valid:

1. The proposed information is intended to enable actions, more than prompt them, and those actions may be some way off in the distance, in which case, it's usually a good idea to ask, *'What do you want them to be able to do'*. This may give you your answer, or it may highlight the second challenge:
2. A communication owner has identified a current situation that she needs to move away from, and has settled on some content to move the audience away from where they are now. And she can become so attached to the content she wants to communicate, that her thinking can get stuck there; stuck in 'the process of communicating'. Or the current situation concerns her so much that she almost doesn't care what outcome she produces. It's a case of 'anywhere but here'.

To guide them effectively, therefore, we can use some simple questions to get them to talk themselves round to one of two conclusions:

1. There is a valid outcome for their communication after all, or
2. The communication doesn't need to exist.

To do this, we can use either a 'towards' or an 'away from' motivation question. Toward motivation sounds like this:

67

'If you don't want people to do anything as a result of having read this, what's the benefit of telling them?'

The away from question, which is often the more potent, sounds like this:

'If you don't want people to do anything as a result of having read this, what would happen if we just didn't tell them?'

In response to either of these questions, communication owners may immediately identify the actions they want the audience to take or avoid. Often, though, they identify the following phantom: the most common of the lot:

5. Intellectual or emotional responses

It may sound bonkers, but I've found that I need to make a big song and dance about what constitutes an action. Unless I make this clear to the people I work with, they often think they've identified an outcome when they say that the audience 'knows' or 'understands' or 'believes' something. But knowing something is not an action. And neither is believing. Nor is any other intellectual or emotional response, whether it's 'Feeling X' or 'Being aware of Y' or 'Being bought into Z'. The key question here is:

'What do you want them to do (not do/be able to do) as a result of knowing (or understanding/feeling etc) this?'

Only when it turns into a behaviour have you identified the outcome.

If people come out with an emotional or intellectual response, there are two ways of pointing them towards their outcome. You may find it useful to use these two in tandem with each other until you finally get the owner to give you an outcome (or to realise they don't need the communication at all)

1. *'What do you want them to be able to do as a result of knowing (feeling/understanding/etc) this?'*
2a. *'What's the benefit of them knowing (believing/being aware of/etc) this?'*
2b. *'What would happen if they didn't know (buy into/appreciate/etc) this?'*

Often, when people respond with answers about intellectual or emotional responses, I've found that the question, 'So what?' is a rather handy one to tag onto the beginning of my follow-up question. It's great for shaking people out of their process-focused thinking. To show you how this kind of questioning sequence can work in practice, here's an example from a real briefing I did as a demonstration during one of my workshops:

'We want a communication to tell other staff about the major sale which our team made last week.'

'And what do you want people to be doing as a result of having read about it?'

'We don't want them to do anything.'

'So what would happen if you didn't tell them?'

'Well nothing would happen.'

'Okay, so what could happen?'

'Well, for one thing, they wouldn't know about the sale.'

'So what? What would happen if they didn't know about it?'

'Well, we only got this sale because of the collaboration of our finance team and the product technicians. And this new collaboration means we can now sell into markets we haven't worked in before.'

'Right, so?'

'So, as a result of having read about this new sale, people can know that we can work in this way, and there are opportunities in these new markets.'

'And what's the benefit of them knowing that?'

'Well, apart from feeling good about this sale, the benefit is that they can look for more of these opportunities themselves, and maybe see what other collaborations might also be possible within the business to create further selling opportunities.'

'And is that what you'd like them to be doing as a result of having read about this sale?'

'Absolutely, yes.'

This method of questioning can ensure that every communication has a clear and valuable outcome in mind, which serves the audience and the business as a whole – rather than just the communicator or the people being talked about. It doesn't even matter if the actions may be a long way off in the future. The communication still has a valid commercial reason for its existence.

6. Deciding

This one often crops up with reports and such like, especially if several people are going to discuss the communication before any action is taken. One person I was working with had done a piece of work on tightening up the business's accounting procedures, and was making recommendations to the board. Initially, she articulated her outcome as follows:

'I want them to take a decision about the new accounting procedures.'

There are two pieces to the 'decision' phantom. Firstly, it's worth recognising that the word 'decision' is an abstract noun, which can always be turned into the dynamic verb 'deciding'. Secondly, when the audience is deciding upon an action, they'll be considering any or all of the following three types of decision:

1. to take action themselves
2. to prompt and/or enable other people to act
3. to enable the communication owner to do something.

I've found it's quickest to simply present these three options to the communication owner, and get him or her to tell you which of the three it is, before identifying what the specific actions are.

'What are they going to be doing themselves, or getting other people to do, or allowing you to do, as a result of having agreed/decided?'

7. Telling

This phantom is probably the sneakiest of the lot. I first got wise to it when working with some planning people in a high street retail company.

'What do you want people to be doing as a result of having read this communication?'

'I want them to tell their staff about the changes to store layouts.'

Is that an action? It would be hard to argue that it isn't. The audience is not just thinking about telling people; they don't just 'know' what to tell their staff; they're actually doing it. The question here is who is really the audience? Is it the people to whom the communication is being sent, or the people to whom those recipients are going to be passing on the message? The word 'telling' is a dead give-away. Clearly, the intended recipients of the communication are to act merely as intermediaries, passing the message on to the ultimate audience. And if we're going to be able to identify what, specifically, that ultimate audience needs to be told, we have to know the outcome we want from them.

'So, what do you want the staff to be doing, or able to do, as a result of having been told about the new layouts?'

This supplementary question (appropriately rephrased each time, of course) will get you the outcome required of the final audience. But does that render the 'telling' answer redundant? Certainly not. The intermediaries still need to do their job of passing on the message. We'll be discussing in the next chapter why it's fatal to have more than one audience for any communication. We therefore need two communications here: one for the intermediaries, and one for the final audience, each with its own outcome. If this sounds like it's just increasing your workload, it's worth considering a couple of things. Firstly, getting it right first time will mean that you won't have to do the job again. And secondly, the communication to the intermediaries will rarely need to be anything more than a brief covering note.

Other applications of outcome-focused thinking

This type of 'outcome-thinking' can apply just as readily to meetings (particularly the way you deal with the 'decision' and 'telling' phantoms). If you think about it, haven't you sometimes attended meetings that have no clear outcome in mind? I don't know anyone who hasn't. People tend to call meetings because they've got a current situation to sort out. And they leap to the conclusion that 'the answer's a meeting'. Without a clear outcome in mind though, how can they possibly know who needs to be at the meeting, or what to discuss. But this may not occur to them because, if you look at virtually any meeting agenda (if one is even written down) you'll find that it's worded in terms of the subjects that need to be *talked about*. This means it is focusing on the process of discussing, and not on the outcomes of having discussed. Before setting up or attending any meeting, therefore, you can now start using outcome-thinking to challenge its usefulness. And you can start producing **outcome-focused agendas**, that can make everyone aware of what you want yourself, and/or others to be able to do as a result of having discussed those issues.

Another useful time to use outcome thinking is whenever you're considering forwarding an e-mail to other people. All too often, e-mails get forwarded indiscriminately to entire departments, or teams, when they are only useful to one or two people. Perhaps you've received a few like that yourself in your time. If you stop yourself for a moment, and think:

'What do I want these people to be able to do as a result of having read this e-mail?'

You may well find that the number of people who will genuinely benefit from it is tiny – possibly even non-existent.

You can also apply this thinking when it comes to identifying training and development needs. Here too, people's focus can often be on the current situation, which can mean that they look for courses or other development programmes to move themselves or their staff away from that situation – without being clear about where they want any such development to lead to.

Indeed, any business project can usually benefit from having a clear outcome in mind. And it may sound crazy to say it like that, but I've known several multi-million dollar projects to be set up and run, often over a period of years, without any clear outcome in mind. Again, the focus has been on addressing a current situation, rather than being clearly focused on what people are doing, or able to do differently as a result of the project having been completed.

As one of my clients once put it, *'The beauty of this whole approach is that it leaves the outcome with nowhere to hide.'*

But even though the outcome can't hide, does it mean that the audience can't? Far from it. As communication problems go, disappearing audiences is a biggie. And it's where we need to focus our own attention next.

Chapter 8

Vanishing Audiences

'Do they mean me?'

Derek Jameson

In this chapter we will uncover:

➤ why audiences are not always as easy to identify as most people assume

➤ why communications fail when the audience isn't accurately identified

➤ the four questions you must ask to be certain that you've got your audience right

➤ how to ensure that the right hand knows what the left hand is doing.

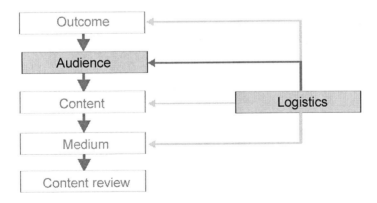

Have you ever had the experience of reading a communication, and finding yourself thinking, *'Is this talking to me, or is it talking to someone else? It feels like it's talking to someone else, even though I thought it was supposed*

to be talking to me.' It's rare to come across anyone in business who hasn't had that experience. But why does it happen, what are its implications and what can we do about it?

Naturally we have to identify an audience for every communication – partly to ensure that we talk to everyone we need to, and also to ensure that we're not wasting the time of people we don't need to talk to. This latter point is often missed by many communication owners, who feel it's better to tell too many people than too few. Although there may be some truth in this in the short term, it's much better if we can tell the right number, and not just for the sake of keeping down the cost of the audience's time. There's something considerably more expensive at stake.

For a communication to get people to respond, it has to make them feel that it's talking to them. Again this may seem obvious, but many business communications fail to do so, and instead engender that 'is this talking to me or someone else?' feeling. And if you've had that feeling yourself, what did you do next? My personal experiences, and my conversations with numerous friends, colleagues and clients over the years, have shown that people tend to respond in one of three ways:

1. They put the communication down, either back in their in-box (intending to look at it again if they have a free moment – which somehow never seems to arrive) or they just put it straight in the bin, virtual or otherwise.
2. They continue reading (or listening) through to the end, all the while feeling that the information they're receiving is for other people (not themselves) to take on board.
3. They continue reading it through until, at some point, they might find that it once again appears to be talking to them.

Given these three possibilities (of which the third is by far the least likely in practice) the communication in question will almost certainly fail to produce its desired outcome – from some or all of its audience. And given the vital link between money and communication, the consequences of this phenomenon can be quietly scuttling much business productivity and profitability. We therefore need to spend a few moments understanding just what's going on, in order to make sure we can identify an audience effectively.

Adopting different positions

What follows may sound a little odd, so I'll explain it by means of examples. People do something rather interesting in their minds, usually unconsciously (or perhaps semi-consciously) whenever they are reading communications: they adopt any one of three different perspectives, or 'positions', from which to read it. (With audio, video or live communications, it's usually only the second and third positions that are likely to come into play.) If you draw upon your own experience, I believe you may well recognise all three of these.

One position you can adopt is that of the 'Communicator': the person who's saying the words on the page (or screen).

This is something that a person might do if, for example, they were reading the words on the response coupon of a mailshot. The coupon might say something like:

'I would like more information about your special offer.'

And someone who would like to know more about that special offer is likely to pick up a pen and fill in their name and address. The same sort of thing would happen if they were filling in a questionnaire which said, for example:

'I believe this company communicates well.'

Here too, with pen in hand, or hand on mouse, they'd tick the 'Agree', 'Disagree' or 'Don't Know' box. When the words on the page are written in the first person – as if you had said them yourself – they're intended to put you into the Communicator Position. Many people have a low tolerance for having words put in their mouths, so it's a style of writing that works only very occasionally. Use it too much, or in the wrong context, and it can have the unfortunate effect of backfiring (more about this later).

Another position you can adopt is that of the 'Audience'. In this position, you don't feel that you are saying the words; instead you feel the words are being said to you.

So, when people are in the audience position (whether reading, listening to or watching a communication) they feel it is talking to them. And they therefore feel that any information in the communication is information for them to take on board. Any questions in the communication (unless obviously rhetorical) are questions for them to answer, any instructions are instructions for them to follow, and any calls to action are calls for them to act upon.

Not surprisingly, then, this is the position in which we need our audiences pretty much all the time if our communications are going to produce the outcomes we want, because if we don't have them there, chances are they'll be adopting the third position: that of a 'Detached Observer'. When you're in the Detached Observer Position, you don't feel that you're the one who's saying the words, nor do you feel that you're the one to whom the words are being said. Instead, you're acting more like a sort of fly-on-the-wall: eavesdropping, as it were, on the conversation between the communicator and the audience.

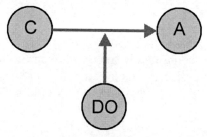

Maybe you've had such an experience yourself: reading a piece of communication and asking yourself, *'Is this talking to me? Is it talking to someone else? Is it talking to itself?'*

There are times when it's quite okay to have some people adopt the detached observer position. Let's say, for example, you've received a copy of an e-mail that's been written to a group of other people. You'll be able to read all the words on the screen, and understand everything those words are saying. But if you're on the 'copies list', you'll know that those words aren't talking to you; they are talking to the people on the 'distribution list'. So imagine that at the end of the e-mail it were to say something like:

'We need to discuss this further, so please give me a ring and we'll set up a meeting.'

Being on the copies list, you'd be unlikely to go picking up the phone at that point, to compare diaries with the communicator, because that instruction wasn't talking to you. And you'd know it wasn't meant for you. There are two key points here that have profound implications for your work. Together, they unearth a new and extraordinarily rich seam in your communication goldmine.

Why many communications fail

1. When people are in the detached observer position, they don't follow the instructions they may read, they don't answer the questions and they don't act on the calls to action – because they feel that those instructions, questions and calls to action are all being directed at people other than themselves.

2. There are nine different ways of writing communications that can push people out of the audience and into the detached observer position – unintentionally. Naturally it's unintentional on the part of the communicator – because the audience isn't going to respond from that position, so the communication is going to fail. Crucially, though, it's often unintentional on the part of the audience. Two of these turn-offs are conscious, and have long been known about. But seven are unconscious and have only recently been identified.

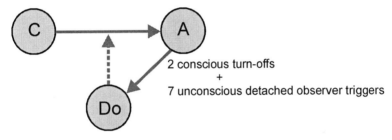

Conscious turn-offs: jargon and waffle

There's no question that both jargon and waffle have the ability to switch people off. That said, the question of whether or not a particular word, phrase or abbreviation is 'jargon' depends on the individual reader. If they don't understand it, it's jargon, and if they do, it's not.

The context can often make it easier or trickier to infer a meaning, and often it'll take more than a single piece of jargon to switch people off – usually it has a cumulative effect. With jargon, people can switch off either because they just end up just not understanding what's being said, or because they feel that the author is intentionally talking only to people who would understand it.

'Waffle' also has an attritional quality to it. Here it's not that the reader doesn't understand what the author's saying, but why they're saying it. Being switched off by waffle therefore has less to do with the audience's technical knowledge than it has with their patience. That said, a communication that's riddled with jargon may quickly seem to be waffling; a reader who doesn't understand what they're being told is less likely to know why it's relevant. (Appendix E looks at how to wipe out waffle).

Crucially, with both jargon and waffle:

- the audience takes a conscious decision to switch off
- there's a degree of subjective judgement going on.

The seven unconscious Detached Observer Triggers

With these seven triggers, the decision is, at best, semi-conscious, and usually happens unconsciously. And there's nothing subjective about them at all; they're objectively measurable. This unconscious quality, as we shall discover, is what makes them so damaging, and is one of the reasons they've gone largely unnoticed – until now.

But do these triggers really matter? Surely it's just a peripheral issue, isn't it? The evidence would suggest quite the opposite. There are two ways of measuring the impact of these unconscious triggers:

1. How often the they crop up
2. How many people are switched off each time

Measuring the first of these is simple; the second a little more tricky.

The scale of the problem

I first identified the existence of these triggers back in 1994. Since then, I have been analysing thousands of communications: electronic, paper, and scripts for live presentations. I've studied the triggers' presence in communications across numerous industries, from utilities to banking, government bodies to furniture manufacture, telecoms to retail, and across the full range of business departments: human resources, finance, customer service, marketing, IT, etc. The results are remarkably consistent.

Marketing communications tend to get off fairly lightly: an average of one trigger per 14 communications. Customer communications fare less well: here the figure is closer to one in five. But it's with internal communications that the picture is truly disturbing: 40 per cent of them contain at least one trigger, and in a random sample of any 10 internal communications, there will be an average of 11 triggers in all. So much for the volume, but what of the impact?

This is more complex, because not every person gets switched off by every trigger, so measuring it has meant getting people to read sample communications, and monitoring how they respond. My research here has thrown up three important facts.

1. For reasons I'm still researching, different people sometimes appear to have an immunity to one trigger or another.
2. Each trigger has a discrete structure, but the context in which it appears can sometimes affect its potency.
3. Even allowing for the above, each trigger will almost certainly lose between 50 per cent and 100 per cent of the audience any time it appears. In fact, most triggers will lose at least 80 per cent of the audience most of the time.

Why the problem has persisted

Unquestionably the figures are unsettling: 40 per cent of internal communications are losing at least half their audiences, and most of that 40 per cent are losing at least four people out of every five. Surely this can't be true. Surely if the numbers were that high, people would have noticed long ago – wouldn't they? Not necessarily. There are four perfectly good reasons for this problem to have remained hidden (and it can be useful to draw upon your own experience when thinking about this):

1. It's not entirely true that no one's noticed these triggers. Almost everyone, it seems, has noticed them – otherwise they wouldn't be being switched off. What they haven't done is consciously identified what's happening, and put two and two together. As a result, people's underlying awareness of these triggers' existence is unconscious.
2. When you get switched off (other than as a result of jargon or waffle), do you tell the person who sent you the communication that it's happened? Probably not. After all, the communication would now feel that it was supposed to be for other people. Therefore, if there was a problem with it, that would be for those 'other people' to take up with the communicator, would it not? Furthermore, if you trip out of the audience in this way, is it something you do deliberately? Or is it an unconscious reaction to what you're reading? In fact, for virtually everyone, the initial reaction is never more than semi-conscious. Of course, you would often become consciously aware that the communication felt like it was now talking to someone else. But what was it that caused you to have that feeling? In short, do you know what these seven detached observer triggers are? If not, and if your audiences wouldn't be letting you know that they've adopted the detached observer position when reading or listening to something you've written, could some of the communications you produce be failing – without you even knowing it? Might this explain, perhaps, at least one

of the reasons why some communications need to be repeated? Might it also explain why some staff may complain that they aren't kept informed – even when you know that they have been?

Although it's undoubtedly possible that some people may claim not to have been told something in order to cover their own backs, or because they're swamped with useless communications, it's equally true that these hidden detached observer triggers do exist. And when any one of them kicks in, it's not because members of the audience are deliberately making it do so. So no one's going to be letting you (or any other comms professionals) know they've switched off. You therefore won't find out about any specific instances of the triggers that the audience become aware of – albeit no more than semi-consciously. (In chapter 18 we'll discuss why authors and approval group members are unlikely to spot the triggers themselves.) And it gets worse.

3. These triggers are often very subtle, and audience members can frequently be switched off without even realising it's happened: they just kind of 'zone out'. They'll carry on reading, but do so as if they were being 'copied in' rather than addressed directly. As a result, even though they may read the communication, they will feel that the instructions are for 'other people' to follow, or the questions for 'other people' to answer. Often, then, the audience itself can be unaware of many instances when the triggers have kicked in.

4. For reasons we'll be discussing later, the triggers have no effect on communications in the recreational arena: newspapers, radio, television, theatre, etc. Nor do they affect academic communications. It's only business communications that suffer. Yet almost all the textbooks on how to write English have been put together by journalists or academics. As far as I am aware, therefore, until now no one has ever produced a book for business writers which discusses these triggers, so the business writing community in general has been unaware of their existence.

The consequences

It all means that business communications can be suffering wholesale failures without anyone being able to predict them, pin down when they're even happening – or why, or stop them at source. So, ever since people started compiling rules about 'the right way to write stuff', the business communication 'rule book' has had an enormous hole in it. And as we shall discuss, this hole doesn't affect only the rules for writing business communications, but also those for identifying whom those communications need to go to. This is a hole with serious commercial implications.

- ❏ Businesses are incurring communication failure costs on a potentially impressive scale – both in terms of number and size.
- ❏ Staff are complaining they aren't being kept informed – even though, on the face of it, they are being communicated with. This has long been documented as a major cause of both frustration and stress for employees.
- ❏ Ill-informed employees often make mistakes, often costly ones, as a result (and the cost may not be just financial: the health and safety implications, for example, can also be more than a little disquieting).
- ❏ Failed communications are having to be repeated, adding to the communication overload – and exacerbating the stress.
- ❏ Even the approval of communications is often a lengthier and more tortuous process than it needs to be.

Given all this, if money is the lifeblood of your business, the Detached Observer Triggers constitute one enormous haemorrhage. The good news is they mean your commercial potential may be a heck of a lot greater than you might previously have suspected. In fact, it's probably not going too far to say you've just uncovered the mother lode, because this book is going to show you how to wipe these triggers out. Your ability to dramatically speed up approvals, reduce communication overload, engage audiences as never before, wipe out huge tracts of communication failure costs at a stroke, and build your personal reputation – massively – are all contained in this one concept. Feel free to tingle a little if you want.

The first trigger: writing about an irrelevant subject

Of the seven detached observer triggers, six are linguistic. And in later chapters we'll look at what they are, how they work and what to do to disarm them. But the first trigger fires off when people feel that the very subject matter they're reading is irrelevant to them. And not because it's waffling or contains jargon, but because it's talking to more than one audience. This is something we need to address in the brief. Get it wrong and you may undermine not only the outcome of the communication in question, but those of future communications too. I say this because if someone receives a particular communication which isn't relevant to them, they'll get to the end of it (or possibly not bother getting to the end) and know that they've just had their time wasted – time which they could have used more productively doing other things. So what will happen if they receive another communication on that subject, or from the same department, or with the same branding on it? They might give it the benefit of the doubt and go through it, but it would perhaps be less likely. And suppose that second communication also proved not to be relevant to them. Would they bother with the third one that came along? It's less likely still, isn't it? But suppose that third communication was relevant. If they didn't read it, they'd then be trying to cope with that aspect of their job or their life without having all the information they needed.

In the case of internal communications, they'd be more likely to make mistakes (and incur those costs) and with customer communications, each intended member of the audience might well be on the phone to the customer service department, taking up staff time there, asking for answers they'd already been given. Multiply this by the dozens or hundreds or thousands of people who receive such communications and you're into some serious money.

That's why it's so dangerous for anyone to believe they're better off getting their message to as many people as possible. It's an idea that is critically flawed, and is almost certain to backfire. All too soon, they'll end up telling too few people, because some of those being communicated with won't be bothering to read what they've been sent. So what's the answer? Again, this is not an exact science – but it can be much more exact a science than most people use. So, it can get you more productive results.

The total potential audience

First of all, it's much easier to identify your overall audience from the outcome than it is from the process. Given that the outcome tells you what actions the communication is going to prompt and/or enable people to take or avoid, identifying the audience requires you to find out:

'Which people do you want to be doing, not doing, or be able to do these actions?'

This is simple enough. But it's not the whole story. It merely gives you what we could call your *Total Potential Audience*, and from here it starts to get interesting.

Just imagine that three tourists want to visit Buckingham Palace. They all have the same outcome in mind, but one of them is starting from Wimbledon, one from Stratford-Upon-Avon, and one from New York. Would the same vehicle get them to where they need to be? No. The Wimbledon tourist could hop on a bus or underground; the Stratford tourist would need to take a coach or train, and then a bus or underground; and the New Yorker would need to catch a plane first. So just because they all want to get to the same destination, the means of getting there has to take into account where they're starting from. Similarly, when it comes to communicating, even though you may have just the one outcome in mind, you may need to produce different communications in order to get everyone there.

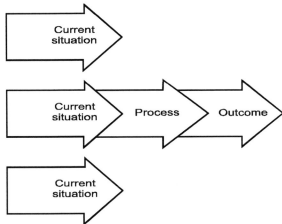

Your communication process needs to take into account not only where you want it to take people to, but also where those people are starting from: their current situation. And this means that, within your Total Potential Audience, you may have a number of 'Real Audiences' (i.e. groups of people who are starting from different current situations).

Real audiences

Let's say, for example, that a company is launching a new piece of publishing software. As a result of having got someone to read one of their sales letters, they may want that customer to be visiting a website to buy the new software. But the company may be writing to some people who've got an old version of this software, other people who have competitors' packages, and other people who don't yet use this type of package at all. Would the same communication be likely to work effectively with such different audiences? It's unlikely isn't it? They're all potential customers for this software but, initially at least, they're starting from a number of different current situations, and are therefore not all the same 'real audience'. And with any communication, if you're not going to push people into the detached observer position, you always need to ensure that you only ever have one real audience for each communication. Otherwise, at different points throughout the communication, it will become irrelevant to everyone.

If, for example, we were to try writing a single sales letter for the software package, we would be having to try to convince the uninitiated that it would be a good idea for them to use this type of package. The customers who are already using this type of package would be left thinking 'But I'm already using this type of package, and you're clearly talking to people who aren't – so you're not talking to me.' This letter would also be trying to convince people who are already using this type of software that they should upgrade or change brands. And someone who's never used this type of package before would be left thinking 'They seem to be talking to people who are already using this type of software, and I'm not – so they're not talking to me.' This example may seem obvious, but there's often a lot of subtlety involved in identifying real audiences accurately. Fortunately, having the outcome firmly in place will make it easy to identify, with three simple questions, whether you need to break down your total potential audience.

Identifying real audiences

To keep this clear, let's recap on what you should already know by the time you get to this point in the briefing process. You should know what the communication owner wants people to be doing or able to do as a result of having read the communication. And you should also know which people he or she wants to be doing or able to do that outcome. From here, you can ask:

1. Why aren't they doing/able to do it already? ('it' being the outcome)
The answer to this question may leave your total potential audience as one group, or may split it into two or more groups. If you've more than one group, you need to ask the following question separately for each group you've identified so far.

2. What are they doing instead?
At this point a number of things can happen.

    (a) You end up with the same group or groups as before.
    (b) The group or groups have split further.
    (c) Previously split groups have come back together into one group.

Whatever has happened so far, there's one more vital question for you to ask before knowing whether you have one or more real audiences to cater for. And, if your previous two questions seem to show that some people are starting from different current situations than others, you'll again need to ask the following question separately for each of these groups.

3. Why would these people want to stop doing what they're doing now, and start doing what you want them to do?

The answer to this question may again split a single group into two or more groups, or it may reunite a number of seemingly disparate groups. Reuniting these groups is fine, because it shows that in relation to the outcome they are starting from the same current situation.

The following example, taken from a live briefing I ran during a training session, illustrates how these questions can work in practice.

'*As a result of having received this communication, people are visiting our website to buy our new publishing software.*'

'*Why aren't they buying it already?*'

'*Some people don't currently use this type of software, and others don't know that we've updated it.*'

'*So those who don't currently use this type of software, what are they doing instead?*'

'*They probably don't even know that this type of software exists or what it can do for them.*'

'*And those who are using this type of software?*'

'*Well, some people are using completely different packages and some people are using the old version of our package.*'

'*So why would people using the old version would want to upgrade?*'

'*They'll be able to work more quickly and more flexibly, and produce better results than they can with the current version.*'

'*And how about the people who are using competitors' packages?*'

'*The same applies, greater speed and flexibility, better results, and it's simpler to use than competitor products.*'

'*Is it simpler to use than the current version of your own product?*'

'*Not really. In some respects it is, because it's more flexible, but we've added in more features, which makes it more sophisticated too.*'

'*So would simplicity be the single biggest reason why these people would want to switch, or would it be the greater speed and flexibility?*'

'*I think, if we're going to convert people, they need to know that it can do more than their current package, but we also have to reassure them that they're not going to have to spend ages struggling to learn a whole new package. So we're going to have to do both: give them a good reason for switching, and remove their reason for inertia.*'

'*And would that be true both for people using your old software and those using a competitor's package?*'

'*Yes, because people using a competitor's package would have done so*' *in preference to or ignorance of our old package. And if people who've bought ours are going to switch, they might consider looking at competitor products. So we're going to have to explain why this new version is not only better than the old package, but the competitor products too.'*

'And for the uninitiated in this type of software?'

'Oh, they're probably struggling along with WP packages, so they're only really going to be in the market for this if they need to be able to present information in a more professional manner. If that's the case, then this is the best package for them to go for.'

These answers tell you two things:

1. that there are, indeed, two 'real audiences', who will need different communications
2. that some of the issues we would need to address within these communications are already starting to emerge (these questions often start to nudge some of the content out into the open – particularly if there's more than one real audience involved).

Intentional detached observers

Before we move on to formally identifying the content, though, there's one more job we need to do: ensure that the right hand knows what the left hand is doing. The owner may need the communication to go to other people as well. For example, a sales brochure may need to be distributed to customer service staff, to help them field customer questions effectively. However, in their capacity as customer service staff, they are not the audience: you don't want them to read it in order to get them to buy the product, but to make sure that they know what the customers have been told. (This doesn't mean, of course, that they can't want to buy the product, but simply that this is not the purpose of sending it to them.) They are therefore, quite legitimately, detached observers (as is the case with people receiving copy e-mails). This communication is not being written to talk to them; it's being written to talk to customers.

Again, this may seem obvious, but some businesses make the mistake of writing sales brochures for their own sales staff, rather than for customers – or trying to get the brochure to talk to both groups at once (and therefore failing to talk effectively to either). It's an all too common mistake. If a communication is going to work, it can only ever afford to have one real audience. Anyone else who's going to receive it will be an 'intentional detached observer'. And to identify them, and ensure that they know why they're receiving a communication that isn't meant to be talking to them, you can use the following two questions:

1. Who else needs to know what the audience is being told?
2. What do you want them to be able to do as a result of knowing it? (Intentional detached observers usually – but not always – receive copies of a communication so they will be enabled to do something.)

These questions will help your communication owners to ensure that the left hand continues to know what the right hand is doing. The last question is important, as you need to check that there is a valid outcome to be gained from copying in these detached observers, rather than simply telling them 'because you can'. (Unnecessary use of 'cc' is one of the biggest causes of communication overload.) It will also mean that you'll usually have to do a brief for another mini communication to these intentional detached observers. The mini communication will let them know what the owner wants them to be able to do as a result of having read the primary communication. Only by doing this can you be sure that they will read the primary communication, rather than just binning it (because, quite rightly, it isn't talking to them). For example, customer service staff would be detached observers for the sales brochure, but the audience for the covering memo which tells them why they've been sent the brochure and what they're supposed to do with it.

Using this approach to identify your audiences will ensure that everyone who receives your communications will either know that it's talking to them, or know that it isn't meant to be, but that it's still relevant. At least, it'll almost ensure this. Even with an outcome, real audiences and intentional detached observers clearly identified, a communication owner can still include irrelevant content unless they're rigorous in how they identify it, so that's where we need to go next.

Chapter 9
The Unnecessary Leap of Faith

'It is good to express a matter in two ways, so as to give it a left foot and a right. Truth can stand on one foot. But with two it can walk and get about.'

Friedrich Nietzsche

In this chapter we will uncover:

➤ how to be certain that you're starting your story at the right point for the audience

➤ the five different types of content you'll usually need to use to complete your communication

➤ why communication owners often make erroneous leaps of faith about what to say, and how to stop them doing so

➤ how to avoid the possibility of audiences thinking 'Well they would say that wouldn't they.'

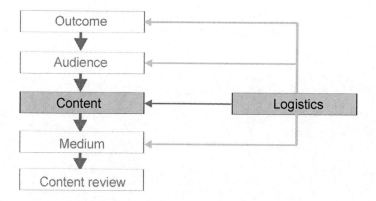

Working out what to say is a challenge that faces any business writer. How do you decide what's relevant and what isn't? It's all very well for some

smart Alec to say, *'Start at the beginning, work through the middle until you get to the end, and then stop.'* Yes, it makes sense. But how do you identify where the beginning is?

Discussing content is where many communication owners start their briefing process. And not surprisingly perhaps, when they start there they often struggle to know quite what it is they want to say, or what it is they don't like about what they see when the copy comes back for their approval. However, establishing the outcome and audience up front makes it relatively simple to identify what needs to be said.

After all, you know what the owner wants the audience to do, avoid doing, or be able to do as a result of having received it; you also know why the audience aren't doing or able to do these things already and what, if anything, they're doing instead. This already gives you the audience's current situation – so you know where they're starting from and therefore where you need to start from too. And the outcome is the end of the story. All you need to do now is to fill in the gaps, and using the following questioning techniques can make the subsequent drafting rather like painting by numbers.

The involuntary audience

Importantly, of course, we need to recognise that we're not working in the recreational environment, which has two crucial implications for us.

❑ The people we're addressing usually haven't volunteered themselves to be receiving the communication.

❑ If it's an internal communication, we often can't afford to have people self-select themselves out of the audience.

Some people, then, may be apathetic about reading our communications, and about acting upon them, while some may be actively hostile, and look for any reason not to do so. Clearly, then, we need to identify all the reasons why they wouldn't do what we want (or avoid what we want them to avoid etc) and knock them over one by one. From my research, these seem to be the main objections we need to overcome, and we'll need a different type of content to address each of them.

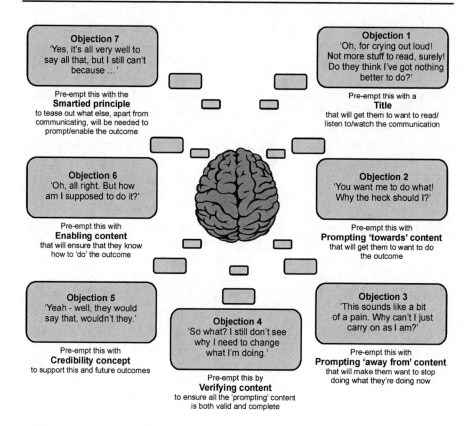

The following text appears within the diagram:

Objection 7
'Yes, it's all very well to say all that, but I still can't because ...'

Pre-empt this with the
Smartied principle
to tease out what else, apart from communicating, will be needed to prompt/enable the outcome

Objection 1
'Oh, for crying out loud! Not more stuff to read, surely! Do they think I've got nothing better to do?'

Pre-empt this with a
Title
that will get them to want to read/ listen to/watch the communication

Objection 6
'Oh, all right. But how am I supposed to do it?'

Pre-empt this with
Enabling content
that will ensure that they know how to 'do' the outcome

Objection 2
'You want me to do what! Why the heck should I?'

Pre-empt this with
Prompting 'towards' content
that will get them to want to do the outcome

Objection 5
'Yeah - well, they would say that, wouldn't they.'

Pre-empt this with
Credibility concept
to support this and future outcomes

Objection 4
'So what? I still don't see why I need to change what I'm doing.'

Pre-empt this by
Verifying content
to ensure all the 'prompting' content is both valid and complete

Objection 3
'This sounds like a bit of a pain. Why can't I just carry on as I am?'

Pre-empt this with
Prompting 'away from' content
that will make them want to stop doing what they're doing now

Titles

Crucial though this is, it's obviously not something to concern ourselves with when taking a brief. I've therefore covered it in Appendix E.

Prompting and enabling actions

Objections 2 and 3 suggest we need to add another insight to the purpose of all business communication. I said earlier that its purpose is to prompt and/or enable people to take and/or avoid actions. In practice, though, it will usually have to both prompt and enable actions. After all, there's no point in getting people all fired up to, say, buy your new product, and then not tell them how much it costs or where they can get it. Similarly, there's often little point in giving people all the information they need to be able to do something in a particular way, if you don't give them any reason for using that information. (Naturally, there are some exceptions: telephone directories, for example, don't really need to motivate people to use them.)

When identifying the content, then, we almost always need to identify:

- the content necessary to *prompt* actions
- the content necessary to *enable* actions.

That said, the way we go about identifying this content will depend on whether the primary purpose of the communication is to prompt actions or enable them (i.e. does the outcome say that people are doing something, or that they are able to do something. Whichever it is will be the content you need to identify first.)

Verifying the content

When commissioning communications, people often have an idea what they need to say if they haven't identified the outcome. But now we've got an outcome clearly identified up front, we can also verify the proposed content against that outcome, before sitting down to write it.

This is likely to lead to better results for two reasons. Firstly, and most obviously, if this content isn't going to produce the outcome, it's simply going to be a waste of time saying it. Secondly, I found that if I didn't verify the content against the outcome, it could slow down the approval process. When I presented the draft copy back to the owner, he or she would start making subjective judgements about whether or not they 'liked' what was in front of them, rather than judging it on the basis of whether or not it was going to achieve the outcome. And often, they wouldn't be sure about whether they were uncomfortable with the content or the phraseology, or both; they just didn't like it. Later on, I'll explain some of the reasons why people can feel uncomfortable about the vocabulary and sentence structure of the text in front of them – and how to deal with this problem. For now, though, I'd like to look at how to remove personal hobby-horses from the subject matter itself.

In principle, it's really simple. It's just a case of distinguishing between what it's *possible* to say and what it's *necessary* to say. What's possible to say doesn't matter a damn if it isn't what needs to be said. And we need to say whatever it takes to get the outcome. When the content is focused on achieving the outcome, then much of the subjectivity disappears from the debate. It's no longer a case of:

'I want to say this because ...'

'Well, I don't think you should because ...'

It's simply a matter of identifying what the owner needs to say which will make the audience want to do (or avoid doing) or be able to do (or be able to avoid doing) the actions stated in the outcome. But even when I knew this, I still found that some owners were reading from the hymn sheet they'd already worked out before they'd identified their outcome. That's why I started to check the validity of what I was being asked to write. And I discovered that if we verify the content while doing the brief, we can get three handy benefits:

1. We can check the validity of what's going into the communication.
2. We can often identify more detail – filling in previously unseen gaps.
3. In doing the first two, we can often speed up the approval process, and reduce the need for re-writes.

Something else I discovered was that when communication owners were going through the process of verifying their content, they often arrived at one or both of the following conclusions:

1. that what they had originally intended to communicate wasn't going to produce the outcome they'd subsequently identified
2. that communicating alone wouldn't be enough.

This second realisation has proved time and again to be particularly important.

Why 'communication' problems often aren't

Many people say that 'communication is to blame' for problems which it just can't solve on its own. One company I was working with had a security problem at the time (nothing to do with me) – and thousands of pounds worth of computers were walking out of its buildings every week. Security was the responsibility of the Facilities Management department, who were told they had to sort it out. And how did they do it? Posters. They got a whole bunch of posters printed and plastered all over the walls of every building, which said something like: *'You know who you are, but does anybody else? Make sure you wear your ID badge.'* And, surprise surprise, it didn't make the slightest bit of difference. (I'm not making this up, by the way – it really did happen.)

Resolving any business issue often involves a number of different changes, some (but not all) of which are people's ad-hoc behaviours, which you can influence through communication. Often, there also need to be changes in certain people's responsibilities or authority, changes in business processes, the installation of new equipment, or the sacking of the useless security guards and the employment of some who are actually awake.

If you verify the content of a communication, these other issues can become all too clear. And it can often cause a communication owner to get all dismayed and say things like, *'This isn't going to work, is it.'* There's therefore a useful question to have in mind any time you're identifying (and particularly when verifying) the content, which is this:

'What else needs to happen to bring about this outcome?'

Interestingly, when I get to this point in training sessions, someone usually has an awakening to the fact that the process we're looking at here is not designed to give you a brief for a communication. It's designed to give you a brief for an *outcome*. And getting outcomes often requires more than just communicating. It can often involve several aspects of what I call the **SMARTIED** principle. The SMARTIED principle was something I came up with when I was involved in a major culture change exercise, and it's intended to help identify what it takes to get people to do things. It would appear that in business (and in life generally) people often need any or all of the following in order to engage in a given behaviour:

Skills
  Money
    Authority
      Responsibility
        Time
          Information
            Equipment

All of these could be summed up as having the *ability* to act, on top of which, people also need **Desire.**
If all of these are in place, chances are that people will do what the communication owner wants. If not, it's much less likely.

Content to prompt actions

Taking a brief for communications whose purpose to prompt actions is more involved than for those whose purpose is to enable actions, so I'll start with how to identify the 'prompting' content. (For the sake of simplicity, the following questions will be using the word 'say'. However, as business communicating needs to be a two-way process, there can be plenty of instances when you may want to replace the word 'say' with the word 'ask'.)

There are two ways of identifying the content that's going to prompt people to engage in the outcome. It's a good idea to use both.

  a) Identify the content to move them towards the outcome
  b) Identify the content to move them away from their current situation

There are two questions to ask to identify the content to move the audience towards the outcome:

1. *'What can we say which will make them want to do what you want?'*
2. *'And what else?' 'And what else?'*

(Keep repeating this second question until you've exhausted all the possibilities).

This should give you some fairly big chunks of information, on which you can start gathering more detail by asking a couple of **verifying questions**. These verifying questions are designed to 'causally link' the content back to the outcome. Some people are a bit puzzled by the phrase 'causally link', so I'll briefly explain what I mean by it.

With a clear outcome to focus on, no one needs to make arbitrary decisions about what to say. Nevertheless, many people make leaps of faith, sticking doggedly to the content they'd identified before their outcome was even known. In effect, they're saying, *'If we tell people X, they will do Y'*. Well how can they be so sure? These verifying questions are designed to challenge such leaps of faith. I'd suggest using both of these questions, because each is designed to encourage a different quality of thinking. People are often astonished at the fact that these two questions can deliver such different information. The first is designed to draw out a finer level of detail:

'When we're telling people this (i.e. one of the big chunks of information you've just identified) what specifically will we be saying which will make them want to do...(the outcome)?'

'And what else?' 'And what else?'

When I introduce clients to this question, they often say that they think it's a bit awkward. But after they've used it a few times they usually realise how effective it is at extracting the information they need. One of the challenges with presenting such a question in a book like this is that I have to give you the generic version. But when you use it in a live briefing, you'll have a context for it, which will help it to make more sense. Perhaps an example would help here, so let's look at that security issue again. The outcome that the owner wanted was that people would be locking away their valuables and challenging strangers in the building. With this in mind, the 'content' part of the briefing could proceed along the following lines:

'What can we tell people which will make them want to do this?'

'One thing we can tell them is that we've had half a dozen computers pinched over the past three weeks.'

'When we're telling people that we've had half a dozen computers

pinched, what specifically will we be saying which will make them want to lock away their handbags?'

'Well we can point out that there are clearly people wandering about the place helping themselves to anything that's no nailed down, so our staff are likely to lose their own possessions if they don't look after them.'

And so on.

This verifying question makes owners drop their thinking down to the next logical level, so that they give you more detail about what to say in order to prompt the outcome they're after. For this reason, you may want to repeat the 'and what else' question a few times after they've started thinking at this lower logical level, to make sure that you pick up all the detail you need. Many people think this first verifying question is a bit of a mouthful when they see it for the first time. So if it seems that way to you, you're not alone. However, clients are constantly telling me how quickly they get used to it and understand how well it works when they use it in the context of a live briefing meeting.

The second verifying question is asking the same thing in a different way:

'How will telling them this make them want to do...(the outcome)?'

The phrasing of the first verifying question is designed to get people to search for a lower level of detail. This second question can also do this. But depending on the person you're working with, it can also send their thinking in the opposite direction, to a higher logical level. This can be useful if you're working with someone who loves dealing in detail, and hasn't yet connected that low level detail to the bigger picture. For example:

'What can we tell people which will make them want to lock away their valuables?'

'One thing we can tell them is that we've had half a dozen computers pinched over the past three weeks.'

'And how will telling them this make them want to do it?'

'It will make them realise that their valuables aren't as safe as they might have thought.'

Having these two verifying questions gives you different ways of getting information out of communication owners. Each brief is different, as is each individual's way of thinking. Because of this, I can't give you any hard and fast rule about the sequence in which to use these two questions. The idea is that you can use them not only to verify the original chunks of content, but also to drill down deeper into each other's answers – verifying what needs to be said, and how it's going to produce the outcome at finer and finer levels of detail.

People who are doing 'big picture' thinking may need their attention brought down to lower levels of detail, while people who are caught up in 'detail' thinking may need their attention pushed up to higher logical levels, in order to connect their detailed content with the final outcome they want. And the beauty of having both questions available to you is that you can use them in tandem, asking one in response to the answer you get from the other. In this way, you can shift the owner's thinking to get the information you need, until you can clearly see in your own mind's eye how and why the proposed content stands the best possible chance of working. And if an owner suddenly gets stuck, switching from one of these questions to the other will usually free up their thinking. This will help you to make the brief increasingly robust and concrete.

In both of the causal-linking questions, a key word is 'make' (How will this content make that outcome happen?). The owner's leap of faith suggests that they think the outcome will come from the audience receiving this content. And often it won't. These questions put that content on the spot, making owners aware that it isn't necessarily going to achieve the outcome on its own, and bringing into play that important 'SMARTIED' question: *'What else needs to happen to bring about this outcome?'*

Identifying 'away from' content

Identifying and verifying the content that's going to prompt the audience to move *away* from their current situation is, not surprisingly, a mirror image of the first set of questions. And it will mean that you may get a lot of the same information repeated. But because these questions are re-orientating the owners' thought processes, these questions almost always highlight information that had been missed earlier:

1. *'What can we say to them which will make them want to stop doing what they're doing now?'*
2. *'And what else?' 'And what else?'*
3. *'When we're telling people this (large content chunk) what specifically will we be saying which will make them want to stop doing...(the current situation)?'*
4. *'And what else?' 'And what else?'*
5. *'How will telling them this make them want to stop doing...(the current situation)?'*

Having got this far, there are two more jobs we can do before moving on to the enabling content. Firstly, we can bolster the communication's credibility, and thus its effectiveness, by presenting a balanced point of view. And secondly, we can help ensure that the owner is engaging in a two-way process, by encouraging feedback.

Closing the credibility gap

An internal business communication can often get people to do what the owner wants simply by telling them they've got to do it. But doing so is unlikely to have the audience acting with genuine enthusiasm. They may go through the motions, but is that what the business really wants? Surely it's going to be more productive if people are enthusiastically doing what the owner wants. And looking beyond the individual communication, if the business's policy is simply to pull rank every time it wants its people to jump, it's probably going to have a problem holding on to employees – or at least to the good ones. The following three questions are therefore designed to help identify the other side of the story, and enable you to present a balanced picture to the audience:

1. What's the benefit to the audience of staying as they are?
2. What would it cost them to change?
3. Why would they be better off changing?

The answers to these questions can identify content which will reduce the likelihood of sceptical members of staff thinking, *'Well they would say that wouldn't they?'* Marketing communications too can benefit from these questions. As consumers have become more sophisticated over the years, they've become both sceptical of offers that seem too good to be true, and more trusting of companies that are prepared to be up front about the limitations of their product or service.

Encouraging feedback

Although many people say that they understand communication to be a two-way process, it's rare to find it being treated as such in business. The following question is deliberately provocative in forcing the issue:

'What are you going to say to encourage feedback on this communication?'

Naturally this presupposes that they are going to encourage feedback: it's just a question of how they're going to do it. Many people may have no intention or desire to encourage feedback. And they are therefore unlikely to have considered what kind of feedback might be useful, to have set up any kind of process for dealing with it, or to have budgeted the time that might be involved in dealing with it. Clearly, then, this single question opens up a whole can of worms – too big a can, in fact, for this chapter. So while the question is wholly appropriate for inclusion in your briefing process, its wider implications warrant a chapter of their own, and are something we'll come back to later.

Enabling content

We can now consider the content that's going to enable the audience to do what the owner wants. Here again we need to identify and verify it. It follows the same pattern as before, and can often raise more issues of 'What else needs to happen?'

1. *'What do they need to know to be able to do what you want? (And what else? And what else?)'*
2. *'When we're telling them this, what specifically will we be saying which will enable them to do it? (And what else? And what else?)'*
3. *'How will telling them this enable them to do it?'*

And then, finally, we often need to close the loop by giving the audience a reason for doing what the owner wants in the way he or she has just suggested – hence these last two questions:

4. *'What's the benefit to them of doing it in this way?'*
5. *'What could it cost them if they didn't do it in this way?'*

Together, these questions for identifying and verifying the content will give you a truly robust brief, which will let you know how telling people this will make them want, and be able, to do that. And it'll highlight whatever else needs to happen to produce the outcome the owner is after. Thus, you may well find that you get to this point in your briefing, only to be told that the communication can't happen yet, because it won't work until something else has been taken care of first.

However, sometimes there can be logistical issues that only raise their heads when the communication arrives with the audience. So that's our next port of call.

Chapter 10

The Right Tool for the Job

'No, no. Sentence first, verdict afterwards.'

Lewis Carroll

In this chapter we will uncover:

➤ the two potential moments of truth in the life of a communication

➤ how to walk a communication owner successfully through these moments of truth

➤ how to check what the audience thinks of it.

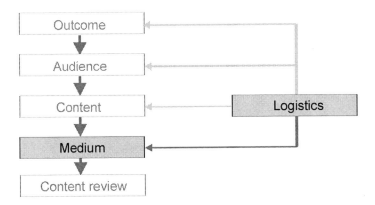

If one lesson has been brought home to me more than any other during my research, it's this: stating the obvious is one of the few ways of ensuring that you don't overlook it. And overlooking the obvious is something that communication owners do all too often when identifying the medium they want use. After all, they often begin their communication decision-making process by settling on the medium, without having considered the outcome for a moment. And they'll frequently begin a brief by saying:

'I want you to do an e-mail to staff about...' or *'We need a new web page about...'*

In effect, they're starting their thinking by telling themselves, *'The answer's a web page, now what's the question?'* A while back, of course, it would have been, *'The answer's a brochure...'* and while advances in technology may sometimes have changed the brought to the plumping process itself. Starting off by identifying the medium they want to use is, once again, back-to-front thinking.

That doesn't mean an owner's assumed medium is necessarily wrong. And with new media coming into play virtually every year, it would be pointless trying to give you a definitive list of which media are best for carrying out which job. But when you know the actions that the owner wants the audience to take or avoid, there are several questions you can use to identify and/or verify the most appropriate media. I say most appropriate because there will often be several possibles. And even if you don't feel you can identify a specific medium, the answers to these questions should provide a more than adequate steer for a graphic designer to come up with an effective solution. Of course, the logistical issues of budget and deadlines can sometimes limit your choice, but these are often set arbitrarily. And given the cost of the communication failing if the medium isn't right, it may be possible to get these revised if you can show it to be necessary.

At this point in the briefing process, we're dealing with the practicalities of getting the messages into people's eyes and/or ears. As such, this chapter is not so much about linguistics as logistics. It's quite conceivable, therefore, that you may already be using a variant on the approach I'm proposing, but I didn't feel I could leave out such a vital part of the briefing process. Furthermore, you may find some of the following anecdotal evidence useful to quote to anyone who won't set aside enough time to brief you properly, or insists that 'the answer's a web page...' without having thought it through rigorously.

It's almost impossible to come up with a definitive list of questions for you to use, as the answer to one question may make others necessary or redundant. But there are some questions that owners often forget to ask themselves, and which are almost universally useful. Even with this select list, some of the following questions can be redundant in certain circumstances. But when relevant, they have proved crucial in steering owners away from a pre-conceived idea which would never have worked, or showing them that they needed a second medium in addition to the one they'd already identified. I've therefore produced a list of principal questions, and a supplementary list of others.

Moments of truth

The principal questions focus on two key moments of truth in the communication's life. The first is the moment it arrives with the audience. In that moment, the people who are receiving it will make a decision about what they're going to do with it. Are they going to go through it there and then, save it for later? Ignore it? Delete it? Chuck it in the bin? They will make a decision – it just may not be the decision the owner wants them to make. The choice of medium may have a big impact on whether the audience makes the decision the owner would like.

The second moment of truth can be the moment that the audience uses the communication. Of course, if the communication is intended to be acted upon straight away, this will be the moment the communication arrives. But many communications are not intended to be acted on immediately, so there can be another moment of truth later on (which, with some communications, may be repeated a number of times). Although, sequentially, this may be the second moment of truth, it is the part of the equation that needs to be sorted first. A communication must arrive in a way which will enable it to be used effectively. We therefore can't identify how it ought to be delivered until we first know how the owner expects people to use it once they've got it.

Usage

1. When is the audience likely to act on/use the communication?

There are eight different timeframes within which an audience can act upon a communication. Take your pick:

1. Just do it now (an immediate, one-off action) e.g. ring me now to arrange a meeting.
2. Do it now and continue doing it ad infinitum – e.g. obey the new security rules every time you enter or leave the premises.
3. Do it on an ongoing basis from now until a certain date – e.g use the back entrance of the office until the building work is complete.
4. Just do it, as a one-off, by a certain date – e.g. reply to a seminar invitation.
5. Just do it on a certain date – e.g. turn up for an interview, or a blood donation session.
6. Do it from a certain date and continue doing it from then on – e.g. follow the new accounts procedures as of the beginning of the next financial year.
7. Do it between one future date and another future date – e.g. make

alternative arrangements for feeding yourself in the middle of the day during the second week of December, while the official Christmas lunches are going on in the staff restaurant.

8. Do it at some indeterminate time(s) in the future – e.g. use this telephone directory; follow the fire exit signs etc.

2. Where could they be at the time?

If there is a gap between the time someone receives a communication and the time they act on it, it's possible that the place in which they use it might not be the same as the place they receive it. We therefore need to know where they are likely to be when they are using it. We also need to recognise that, if they're going to use it more than once, they might not always be in the same place on each occasion.

I was once working with an HR department to help them improve the communications they were sending out around the business. The manager of their company car management team was bemoaning the fact that it was a waste of time communicating with any of the drivers, because they just didn't listen.

She told me that a few months earlier they'd had some time and motion people in, who'd identified that the team was using one and a half people just to answer calls from company car drivers about trivial matters to do with repairs, breakdowns etc. And it was always the same fifty or sixty questions that were being asked. The time and motion people therefore suggested that the team produce a booklet which could answer all these questions, send a copy out to everyone who had a company car and, hey presto, save the cost of one and a half members of staff. Thinking this was a great idea, she got the booklet produced and had it distributed six weeks prior to my conversation with her. And it hadn't made anything but the tiniest difference. The team was still getting almost exactly the same number of calls, with exactly the same questions.

I asked her how the booklet had been distributed and she told me it had gone out through the internal mail system. It had been accompanied by a covering memo, which had said something to the effect of: *'This is your new company car handbook. It tells you everything you need to know about how to run your company car, so keep it in a safe place.'* Apparently, they had monitored the calls for four weeks prior to putting the booklet together, to make sure that they picked up all the questions that people kept phoning in with. And they'd answered all those questions in the handbook. But there was a problem which, although obvious when it was pointed out to them, they'd clearly overlooked. The question I put to her was:

'If I were a company car driver, where would you expect me to keep my handbook?'

If, for example, I were to have an accident in Plymouth, it would hardly be of much use to me sitting on a shelf above my desk in, say, Birmingham. Similarly, if, a few weeks later, I had repair or insurance paperwork to deal with at my desk, the handbook would hardly be much use to me sitting in the glove compartment of my car, in a car park half a mile away.

I shan't trouble you with the Fleet Manager's response to this. Suffice to say it involved certain biblical references. The point is that communication owners need to have thought through the nuts and bolts of how they expect someone to use any communication they want produced. And they need to ensure, when they send it out, that the people they want to use it are equally clear about those nuts and bolts. When going through these questions, therefore, it's useful to keep an eye on the content of the communication, to ensure that it includes clear instructions (if necessary) on what the owner wants the audience to do with it. In short…

3. What actions do you expect them to take when using it?

This is what I call an environment check and is, perhaps, the most important question of all. And yet when I ask it of people, they often look at me as if I'm mad. To them it seems so childish to state the blindingly obvious about how they envisage someone 'sitting down in a chair, opening the brochure, reading it through' etc. And yet when they do so, they frequently find themselves pausing half way through their description and saying, in a rather crestfallen manner, *'This isn't going to work, is it.'*

I was once invited by a marketing director to discuss a 'crisis' that he said had arisen in a product launch. This happened in the days before mobile phones were commonplace. His company had invested heavily in a direct response ad campaign in a London evening newspaper. They'd set up a call centre to handle the calls. And after three days they'd received a total of two responses. I got him to give me a copy of the newspaper with the ad in it and then, in my mind's eye, took myself through what I'd be likely to do with the newspaper. The ad was appearing on page 9 of the paper, so it was highly unlikely that I would 'receive' it immediately I bought the paper. Indeed, having been a London commuter myself, I was aware that I would be unlikely to start reading it as I was walking along the road (far too many pedestrians to bump into for a start). Instead, like most people I'd wait until I'd got a seat on my bus or train home.

As I imagined myself sitting on the train, I started going through the newspaper and came across the ad. It was unquestionably striking, and the offer looked good. There was only one problem. In order to respond to it, I had to ring a freephone number. And as I was already on the train home and (like most people in those days) wouldn't have had access to a phone, I couldn't make the call. And so I moved on through the rest of the paper, got distracted by other items and could imagine only too clearly that, by the time I got to my station and had made my way home, the ad would have been long forgotten.

And even with mobile phones being as common as they are nowadays, there's still room for people to make huge mistakes of this kind. Every day, thousands of radio commercials give out telephone numbers. How many people listen to the radio with a pen and paper, or their mobile phone in hand, waiting to take down telephone numbers from advertisements? It just doesn't happen. If I'm in my car on my way to work, or to drop the children off at school, do they seriously expect me to stop the car and ring up to ask them about their carpet sale?

The environment test is therefore a vital check to do. Obviously so. And that's the problem. It's so obvious that most people, it seems, don't bother to go through it. And almost everywhere you look or listen, you can find evidence of this complacency. The business world is littered with communication investments going straight down the toilet, for the simple reason that the people responsible for those investments haven't answered this simple question (and checked that their answer makes sense, given when and where they expect the audience to be using it).

Screwdrivers

But what happens if you just don't know the answer – as can happen if the communication is being produced for a third party to deliver? For example, a product brochure may be produced for the sales team to hand out, or send to potential customers, and some of those sales people – being creative souls – may find myriad different uses for it. This happened with my former employer. I was working on a project with the graphic design manager to re-think the company's entire suite of sales and marketing materials. We asked the Product Directors where they saw their various communications fitting into the sales process. And they told us, unanimously, that they didn't know – because they couldn't predict when or how the sales force would use them.

My response to this may, at first, seem somewhat surreal (it certainly did to the Product Directors). What I said to them was, 'Screwdrivers'. It may seem a peculiar response, but think about it for a moment. What is the purpose of a screwdriver? What is it designed to do? Surely it's to tighten and loosen screws. If a screwdriver cannot tighten and loosen screws, is it worth buying? Of course not, so such a screwdriver would be worthless to a company dumb enough to manufacture it. But let's shift our attention to another aspect of DIY – painting. If you want to get the lid off a tin of paint, what do you use? It might be a coin, perhaps, but most people I ask say they use a screwdriver.

Screwdrivers are handy for all sorts of tasks. But just because you can use a screwdriver to open tins of paint, or as a makeshift chisel, or to retrieve a rogue sock that's been discovered inexplicably wedged down the back of a radiator, it still has to be able to perform its primary function of tightening and loosening screws – without compromise. And this same principle applies to any communication.

The Product Directors couldn't predict the many wonderful and whacky uses to which some ingenious sales people would put the product brochures, so they chose to abdicate responsibility for deciding how these brochures ought to be used. And in some instances they were getting through 60 brochures for each sale. Needless to say, these weren't very effective communications. It was a case of the tail wagging the dog.

Just as the manufacturers of screwdrivers need to be clear about how they intend their tools to be used, so too must communication owners be clear about how they intend their communication tools to be used. If they're not clear about this, you won't be able to ensure that these tools are designed to be used successfully in that way.

Another reason for considering the actions the owner expects the audience to take when using it, is that it may influence how you organise the content of the communication itself. On several occasions, I have received training brochures or catalogues from various organisations (one of them, from a prestigious institute, was some 80 pages long). And they've all made the same mistake. They organise the content alphabetically, by course title. And the information about each course is usually organised on the basis of when and where it's being run, what it covers and how much it costs. That may sound like a sensible way to do it, but let's just think about how someone is likely to use such a brochure.

It is unquestionably meant to be used as a reference document, as different training needs can arise over the course of a year. And when such needs to arise, a manager is likely to think: 'Well, James seems to be having a problem understanding his clients, I wonder what training courses could help him with that?' And so they'd take the brochure off the shelf and find themselves having to wade through 80 pages of descriptions of courses, trying to find a description that matches the skills shortfall that they want to address. The brochure isn't starting where the audience is starting. The audience has a performance problem, and the communication has got an alphabetical listing of courses. And there's no index of performance problems to point the manager to the right course. It's about as useful as a telephone directory would be if it were organised in numerical order rather than alphabetical.

4. What will remind the audience to use it when and how it should be used?

If a communication isn't going to be used straight away, it might be filed somewhere and forgotten. So what's going to stop that happening? It may be that there's nothing you can do about it – or is there? If it looks like this could be a problem, it could be that the owner's suggested medium isn't going to work (or at least won't work on its own). This is where some creative graphic design input may be invaluable in order to stop the communication becoming out of sight and out of mind.

5. How are you going to get feedback from or through this communication?

This question, like the 'content' question on feedback, is dealing with that potential can of worms, which we'll look at in a few chapters' time. For now though, I'd suggest that it's always worth making the assumption that the owner is looking for feedback from every communication. In the event that there aren't feedback systems in place in the business, this question will have to be handled piecemeal: does the owner need a mechanism built into the communication, that can bring back the audience's opinions or questions? And has the owner budgeted the time to handle this feedback?

Delivery

If the communication is going to be used just once (and that 'once' is the point at which it's first received) you should have no need of the following three questions, and can move straight on to question 9. If not, you need to think about what you want people to do with the communication when they first get it.

6. When are they likely to receive the communication?

This question is necessarily ambiguous. In some situations, it might refer to a time of day, or day of the week. In others, such as a 'statutory right to cancel' notice on a bank loan, it might be that a person will receive it within a certain number of days of signing the application form. There seem to be three different possibilities to consider:

1. Is the timing of communication something the owner can control directly?
2. Is its delivery quite unpredictable because, for example, it's going to be delivered by a third party?
3. Is its delivery dictated by an external body (if, for example, it's a legal requirement).

If the communication is fulfilling a legal requirement, clearly the owner's hands are tied. But in other circumstances, what would their ideal choice be? This question may make the owner decide that they'd like to give the audience access the communication through more than one route. Whatever their answer, you may find that you want to cycle round both of the following questions a couple of times to identify the best 'fit' for the owner's needs.

7. Where could the audience be at the time they receive it?
Again, this may be something that's out of your control (e.g. if the communication is being delivered by a third party). However, you may find it useful to take a best guess at the possibilities. Alternatively, it may be something you can predict. Or it may even be an environment which your previous answers have told you that you need to create – e.g. setting up a conference.

8. What specific actions do you want them to take with it when they receive it?
This is a second environment check question. And again you need to ensure that this answer fits in with how the communication is going to be used. I was once working with a charitable trust who thought they wanted to produce a leaflet. It was intended to go to Citizens' Advice Bureaux (CAB) to help the people who worked there to fill in the Trust's application forms (which were almost always completed incorrectly).

We had already decided that this communication (leaflet or otherwise) would have to be used by the CAB staff when they were sitting with a client, filling in the form. Yet when it came to identifying what was likely to happen when these leaflets first arrived at the bureaux, the Trust's staff realised that they expected each leaflet to be individually inserted inside the front cover of each application form. They further realised that these forms were already sitting in filing cabinets in unknown CAB admin offices somewhere, or perhaps in the briefcases of numerous CAB staff. They therefore couldn't know if the leaflets would find their way to the right places, or how many application forms each bureau would have in stock at the time, and therefore how many leaflets to send them.

The logistics of getting the communication to work – as a leaflet – were so numerous, diverse and unpredictable that they realised they were backing a loser. What they really needed (and ended up producing) was a totally redesigned application form with clear instructions already built-in.

With the answers to all these questions, you ought to be able to know whether any proposed medium will do the job effectively, or if an alternative or additional medium will be required. And it leaves you with one final point to bear in mind.

9. What will make or enable the audience use it as you want them to?

You can tell the audience what to do with the communication when they receive it, or you can leave them to work it out for themselves. And rather than leave it to chance, it can sometimes be useful to include instructions, either in the body of the communication itself or in a covering memo or letter, which tell them what you want them to do with it. If, for example, the fleet admin manager had thought to ask herself this question, it might have shown her that one booklet per car driver wouldn't work, and have saved her a lot of bother.

Supplementary questions

These questions may have already been answered, or be self-evidently redundant for the communication on which you're working. But they're listed here, just in case:

10. Does some or all of this communication need to be tailored to individual recipients?
11. Do you need a guarantee that everyone has received it?
12. Do you want to know who has chosen to receive it?
13. Is some or all of the information confidential or sensitive?
14. If confidentiality is important, is the content of a personal nature, or can it be shared with a discrete group?

Logistics

The logistical considerations of budget and timescales may be one of the first things owners mention when they come to you, or it may crop up at any other time while they're briefing you. If it hasn't cropped up by now, though, these final supplementaries can put this piece of the puzzle in place.

15. How many people are you intending to communicate with?
16. How much can you afford to spend?
17. How far away is your delivery deadline?

Content Review

Together, the answers you get to all these questions may make it necessary to go back to the content and add to, subtract from, or play around with the order of, whatever the owner had decided to say.

The outcome-focused briefing process is an extremely powerful tool that many people have used to bolster their confidence and increase their business value whenever they sit down to take a brief from a communication owner, or put together a communication of their own. It can save time and money, and increase the effectiveness of virtually any individual business communication. But what of the bigger picture: communication planning and strategy? Surely that's where a lot of the action is – and where many decisions are taken before you ever get a look in with your briefing skills. So it's clearly an area we need to look at now.

Chapter 11

Looking Beyond the Label

'Dispose of the difficult bit in the title.
It does less harm there than in the text.'

Sir Humphrey Appleby

In this chapter we will uncover:

➤ the limitations of the briefing process

➤ why the very term 'communication strategy' can cause problems

➤ five events that can drive the development of communication strategies

➤ a new way of thinking about three distinct types of strategic communication plan.

Before proceeding, I feel I ought to make something clear. It is not my intention to go over ground covered in other books about communication planning. Instead, I'd like to extend into the 'strategic' arena the ideas we've already discussed, to uncover some new ideas for making such planning more powerful. It's possible, of course, that communication strategy may not be something you get involved in yourself. Nevertheless, I believe you'll find it useful to understand where any such strategies may be coming up short. You may even wish to get this section read by the people who do put such strategies together.

Even when communication strategies seem to be working well, there may still be ways in which they could be improved – not least in terms of their sustainability in the face of personnel changes, either at the top of the business or among the communication team itself. Over these four chapters, we'll be:

● getting under the skin of the more common challenges involved in putting together and sustaining communication strategies
● revisiting the very purpose of any such strategy, and establishing what it really needs to be

- examining the best phraseology to use when composing a communication strategy
- distinguishing between strategic communication plans and strategic communication policy – and understanding why the former will always struggle eventually unless the latter is in place (which it hardly ever is)
- tackling the thorny issue of integrating two-way communicating into every business system
- a simple, manageable way of measuring what you're doing.

(The number of communication strategies that can be running concurrently in any single business often depends on the size of the business itself. It's quite common within large corporations for different divisions of the business to have their own communication teams, each with its own 'strategy'. For the sake of simplicity, though, I'll look at the problem as it affects a corporate communication function sitting right at the heart of the business, as I believe this will embrace any issues facing peripheral teams.)

The problems

Lots of people like to talk about communication strategies, a lot. A communication strategy is an important 'thing', and you ought to have one. Oughtn't you? Erm... hang on a minute. What are we talking about here? The word 'strategy', like the word 'professionalism' is another of those abstract concepts. And just as no one is likely to argue with the idea of being 'professional' in their work, so too will most people agree with the idea of having a communication strategy. But what the heck is everyone agreeing to? For a start, how strategic ought a communication strategy to be? Most people seem to distinguish between 'strategy' and 'tactics' by means of logical levels. A strategy is at a higher level than tactics: the tactics explain how you're going to achieve the strategy. But if that's true, then what is 'the right logical level' at which to pitch a communication strategy? If we're honest with ourselves, it seems that the answer has to be, 'It depends' – one man's strategy could be another man's tactic. So what does a strategy need to look like and sound like? Does anyone dare hold their hands up and say, *'Excuse me, but what is a communication strategy?'* Or is it like the story of the Emperor's New Clothes, and no one wants to raise their hand for fear of being thought a fool. Could this mean that, just maybe, some communication strategies have got no clothes on? And could it be that, just maybe, many people have already been thinking along these lines themselves?

When I first mention to people the concept of the Detached Observer Triggers, almost everyone recognises what I'm on about. Instantly. Indeed, most people tell me that they had suspected the existence of these triggers. After all, the triggers do (as we shall study shortly) result in unconscious gut reactions that something's not right. Interestingly, it seems that many people also have a similar sense of uneasiness when it comes to communication strategies. Even if they have a strategy in place that appears, on the whole, to be doing a pretty good job, they can still have nagging gut feelings that there's something missing – possibly a big and important something – if only they could identify what it was. Once I'd put together the Outcome-Focused Briefing Process, a number of big, important somethings became all too clear.

The limitations of the briefing process

Outcome-focused briefing is designed to ensure that no one gets communications produced that aren't needed, and that the communications they do decide to produce are as effective as they can be. But it still means there's a crucial piece of the decision-making puzzle missing. However robust and effective it is, a briefing process can only ever kick in once an owner has decided to communicate something. And they may make no such decision (or at least fail to make it in good time) – with three possible results:

1. things that need communicating may go un-communicated
2. these things may not get communicated soon enough
3. they may get communicated on time, but in a rush.

Clearly, to have a watertight approach we need to take care of this. It would appear that in addition to an outcome-focused briefing system, some sort of proactive planning process also needs to be in place. Or, as some people like to call it, a communication strategy.

After I had been working with various corporate clients for a while, I began being drawn into discussions about communication strategy. Each time I would ask what they expected their strategy to do for their business; how it was measured, reviewed and updated. And I discovered why I'd always been a little unsure what anyone meant by the term 'communication strategy': it never seemed to be the same thing twice. Communication strategies varied massively from business to business, and even among different divisions of the same business. The label may have been the same, but beyond that the similarities began to fall away.

Some strategies would be little more than media plans. These plans set out which medium would be used for what type of message to which audience; some also identified how frequently such messages would be produced and who was responsible for making them happen. Others went further still: being linked to objectives in the business plan, and even including specific measures. Of course, having any such plan is infinitely preferable to not having one, but calling it a strategy sounded a trifle grandiose – rather like calling a dustman an 'Environmental Enhancement Executive'. But then again, why not? Does it matter what you call something as long as everyone knows what it means?

A false sense of security

When it comes to communication strategy, the label matters rather a lot, because it can often lead to that most insidiously destructive of business attitudes: complacency. It's as if senior managers can heave a huge sigh of relief, blow out their cheeks and tell themselves, *'Well we're okay now! Our communications used to be in a mess, but now we've got something called a 'Communication Strategy', so we don't have to worry (or, more disturbingly, to think) about it any more.'*

But are they right? Given that the same label is being applied to so many different types of plan, can senior managers really afford to rest on their laurels, just because someone has produced some sort of plan which they call a communication strategy? Because the very term 'Communication Strategy' is entirely abstract, it certainly isn't enough that everyone understands what it means. Not by a mile. Firstly, as with any other abstract term, it's foolhardy to believe that any one person's understanding is the same as anyone else's. And even if everyone's understanding were the same, would it necessarily be the right understanding – or could they all be agreeing upon an inadequate definition. What if the strategy doesn't do everything it should? What if it falls short of delivering what your business really needs?

It seemed clear from my conversations with numerous communication professionals, that rarely did their bosses seem to know in advance what they expected from a communication strategy. And on reflection, given that these bosses would usually be unclear about the very purpose of business communication, it's perhaps inevitable that they wouldn't be entirely sure about how to fulfil that purpose strategically. The result is that business leaders often seem prepared to content themselves with whatever they get – provided it has the title 'Communication Strategy'.

None of this means that media plans which go under a grander nomenclature aren't either well thought through or extremely valuable – as far as they go – for they are invariably both. But do they go far enough? Are many businesses missing not just a trick, but an entire magic show? And might there be a way of thinking about communication strategies that could:

- ✓ make it easy for everyone to know in advance what communication strategies need to look and sound like – every time
- ✓ ensure that long term strategies have the legs to stand the test of time.

I believe there is, provided we are again prepared to go back to the beginning, and start our re-think with a couple of logical insights that may sometimes be overlooked.

Back to the beginning

Firstly, if a communication strategy is going to have any impact at all, the person who comes up with it isn't going to keep it to him or herself; it's only going to make a difference when other people know about it. And this in turn means that a communication strategy (whether we're talking about the whole strategy itself: its procedures, processes, production calendars etc; or any overview documentation which summarises the strategy for approval by people higher up) is itself a series of communications. And both individually and collectively, these communications must be focused on moving an audience away from a current situation and towards an outcome.

Secondly, the very label itself: 'Communication Strategy' is used for numerous different types of plan, for moving people away from different types of current situation and towards different types of outcome. And the criteria for making a communication strategy work are likely to vary accordingly. Isn't it likely, then, that we could make life easier for ourselves by identifying the different types of current situation. This could enable us to identify different types of plan, give each type its own distinct label, and identify its outcome – in concrete terms. We would then be in a position to know what content we would need to put into the strategy to achieve that outcome.

What, then, are the circumstances (current situations) that can give rise to someone instigating a communication strategy? From my research with numerous clients, it's become apparent that the development of communication strategies can be driven by five principal situations:

1. Campaigns or other major events

Various events crop up from time to time, whether it's a new brand launch, or major regulatory change (or even a corporate restructuring programme) which require a plan of campaign – much of which involves communication of one sort or another.

2. Staff survey results

If these results show, as they often do, that staff are unhappy with internal communications, someone somewhere – usually high up – may say 'something must be done about this!' And someone else (possibly you) will be charged with the task of working out what that 'something' should be. That 'someone else' then produces a plan to generate new or different communications, which may be coordinated in a new way. And, that plan gets called a communication strategy.

3. A new broom

When new managers take over internal, corporate or marketing communication departments, they often want to make their mark. Added to that, their new bosses will almost certainly have given them objectives to achieve, so plans of some sort are almost inevitable. A similar situation can arise if a business gets a new CEO who is 'keen on communicating' and wants to see a corporate communication plan.

4. New corporate structure

Once the dust has settled on a corporate restructuring programme, it's not uncommon for someone to decide that they need a new communication strategy to meet the needs of the new structure (this is often, but not always, because a new broom has taken over).

5. A new round of business planning

Some communication strategies are put together as part of the business planning process, and may be intended to run only for the lifetime of that plan, at the end of which time the whole process is gone through again.

Three types of strategic plan

These five 'situations' suggest three different types of communication strategy:

Project strategy – campaigns and other major events are single issues with finite timeframes.

Perpetual strategy – with the new broom, survey results and new corporate structure, the strategy will need to be open-ended, because it will be dealing with multiple issues and have an indefinite lifespan.

Business plan strategy – this scenario is harder to nail down. It will have a finite lifespan, but with some business plans this can be anything up to five years – longer by far than the average job tenure these days – and it may be a rolling plan that is updated every 12 months, always looking five years ahead. Furthermore, what such a strategy would cover could also vary dramatically from business to business. In some businesses, the communications department reports directly to the CEO, and may be asked for a strategy to enable the implementation of the whole plan. In other businesses, the communications department is tucked away as a minor function of HR or Marketing, and its so-called strategic contribution to the business plan may, in fact, be wholly parochial.

For example, if the business wants to cut its cost base by 10% over the next 12 months, the communication team may get treated like any other department. Rather than being asked how they're going to help other departments to produce better results for less money, through helping them to communicate better, the communications team may simply be asked for a 'strategy' to produce the same old communications with a 10% smaller budget. (A spectacular waste of their potential, if I may be so bold.)

It's therefore impossible to say that a communication strategy for supporting a business plan will always be the same beast. All we can say is that it will probably fall somewhere between the other two types. And if we can take care of those two ends of the spectrum, it may be possible to combine these approaches to support the demands of a business plan. That said, whatever the type of communication strategy, it's often the business plan that's driving it. And to convert a business plan into a communication strategy we need to look again at our language.

Chapter 12

Translation, Translation, Translation

'We have first raised a dust and then complain we cannot see.'
George Berkeley

In this chapter we will uncover:

➤ four benefits of translating a business plan into communication planning language

➤ a four-step process for creating a clear, transparent link from an individual communication outcome to the business's mission statement - and vice versa

➤ the role of communication in addressing the demands of the SMARTIED principle.

As I see it, one major problem with strategic communication plans is the very way they're worded. More often than not, they appear to be couched in 'corporate speak': the language of the organisation's business plan. And this is not altogether surprising because, whatever the type of communication strategy, it may well have to talk the same language as the business plan, otherwise no one would be able to see how the two related to each other. And therein lies the problem.

Business plans tend, at least in places, to be both abstract and impersonal. (The same is usually true for any attendant SWOT analyses, which cover other possible contingencies.) Even those with extensive commentaries rarely, if ever, express themselves in terms of audience behaviours (except, perhaps, when the Directors are using the Balanced Scorecard approach). They don't talk in the terms that we can now recognise as communication outcomes: i.e. what people are doing, not doing or able to do, that will bring about the business results. And it's that missing piece of translation that's so crucial.

Communication planning language

Rather than produce a strategic communication plan in language that matches the business plan, the process needs turning on its head: the business plan needs translating into communication-outcome terminology, before anyone attempts to put together a communication plan for producing those outcomes. After all, business results tend to come from the actions of the business's audiences. Put simply, you can look at all anticipated results within the business plan (and SWOT analysis) and, for each one, ask the following question of the people who've put it together:

'What do people need to be doing, not doing, or able to do in order to make this outcome happen?'

Of course I'm not for one moment suggesting that you'll generate each of the business plan's desired results by producing a single communication. The business plan results will be at a higher logical level – most likely that of a business issue (as we discussed in chapter 7). From there you may need to plan individual projects (e.g. a brand launch) and within each project there will be individual communications.

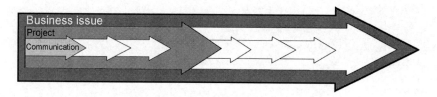

And there are some projects that may even straddle more than one business issue.

But you can use the same linguistic rules for expressing results at every logical level. I would also suggest that if you do so, you will be able to produce better results – not just on paper, but throughout your business. There are at least four reasons for this:

1. With the language of the business plan already expressed in terms of communication outcomes, it would be more difficult for anyone to get caught up in process-focused thinking when planning projects or individual communications.
2. When any project plan or individual communication brief is being put together or submitted for approval, its outcome will always be clearly traceable back to the business plan.
3. It should be possible for each communication to be better and more quickly produced (and, of course, engender the outcome therefrom) because everyone who's involved in the briefing, writing and approval

will be able to see immediately what its purpose is.

4. Crucially, phrasing the business plan results in terms of audience behaviours won't in any way compromise the accountants' ability to do the sums. In fact, if anything, it may make it easier, because what they'll be looking at will be that much more concrete. Indeed, business planners often do their sums on the basis of audience outcomes, and then translate those figures into corporate speak for the benefit of investors (so you may not have to do much translating anyway – just get hold of the original numbers).

Indeed, one could even take this thinking in the other direction from the business plan, i.e. upwards to express the business's overall strategic direction. Doing this could help ensure transparent business planning from top to bottom. And with the business plan itself written, as far as possible, in terms of human behaviours (which need not be instead of, but in addition to, the way it's being done at present) strategic communication planning could finally take its logical place as an integral part of the business planning process itself.

How to do the translating

The amount of translating you'll need to do will, of course, depend on how the business plan/company vision/project plan is worded to start with. Wherever you're starting from, though, I'd suggest that the final translation consistently uses all four of the following linguistic criteria, because they will ensure that it is talking in exactly the same language as that of communication outcomes:

1. **Make it concrete** – making the wording as concrete as possible makes it easier for you and other people to see in your minds' eyes what it means. For example, 'Increasing our market share by 4%' is an abstract concept. If that means '350,000 more customers are buying our products when they go shopping this year', then say so.

2. **Make it personal** – this means that what you can see in your mind's eye involves the people doing the outcome. It's possible to express actions personally or impersonally. For example, the increased market share idea could be expressed as '350,000 more of our products are being bought this year.' It doesn't tell you who is doing this, though, and not only will impersonal language make the expression less concrete, it will also stop you from fulfilling the third translation criterion.

3. **Focus on the 'end audience'** – it's quite possible to make the increased market share statement both concrete and personal, and to overlook the

ultimate audience whose behaviour will make it possible. For example, you could say, 'We are selling 350,000 more products this year.' This is focusing on the business, rather than its customers. Remember, the reason for doing this translation is to allow you, and everyone else who's involved in business planning or communication ownership, to be able to follow a consistent, transparent, logical thinking process from the top of the planning process to its final execution. The final execution is going to be carried out by the end audience, so they have to be in the picture throughout the process.

That said, it's worth bearing in mind two things.

(a) The end audience is not going to be the same for every aspect of the business plan. If you're looking at product sales, for example, the end audience is going to be the customers. But if you're looking at the introduction of revised working practices, in response to new Health & Safety legislation, the end audience will be employees.

(b) As you move down the logical levels of thinking, from the business plan to individual projects, and from projects to individual communications, your end audience is likely to change as the outcomes become more specific. With a brand launch, for example, a business may want to set up a mini project plan to get its own staff up to speed, and another one for its distributors, even though the end audience for product sales is, of course, the customers. Clearly there would be no point in setting up a seminar for your own sales people and then talking to them as if they were customers. So it's always going to be a case of focusing on whoever is the appropriate end audience for the logical level in question.

If you focus on the end audience, any intermediate audiences will immediately become apparent when you start thinking about 'what has to happen to bring about this outcome?' My research has shown that people who start off focusing on one of these intermediate audiences, sometimes miss the end audience.

4. **Make it dynamic** – The business environment is dynamic, not static, so it's useful to reflect this in your language when describing what you want to be *happening*. (Remember, the continuous tenses – those ending in *ing* – tend to get people making dynamic movies in their minds' eyes and, interestingly, tend to cause people to see more detail in their mental images – which helps make their thinking more concrete still).

A hypothetical example

For the sake of discussion, let's look at how this new strategic language might work in a motor car manufacturer's business. Such a manufacturer could set its direction as being:

'To be the biggest motor manufacturer in the world.'

In order to build any effective communication plans, we need to translate this statement into the language of communication outcomes. The question then becomes:

'What behaviours will let this business know that it has achieved this or, once there, that it's continuing to achieve it?'

And a logical answer might be, say:

'People are buying more of our cars than those of any other manufacturer.'

When we then look at the Audience question of 'Who do you want to be doing this?' the answer, obviously enough, is customers – who represent just one of the company's stakeholder groups. And if this is the direction we want this group to be moving in, what of the other stakeholders: staff, suppliers, distributors etc? We can just as readily express a direction for them in the same, outcome-focused language. The specific answers I'm giving you here may seem pie in the sky. That's not the issue for the purposes of this example, where what matters is not so much what's being said, but how it's being expressed. If we were to ask the question: *'What are these stakeholder groups doing which will make customers want to buy more of our cars than those of any other manufacturer?'* the answers might look something like this:

'Employees are supporting each other in continually developing and building the world's most customer friendly cars, as efficiently as possible.'

'Suppliers are providing, at the most competitive prices, only the best quality goods and services which will enable our employees to develop and build the world's most customer friendly cars as efficiently as possible.'

'Distributors are making it as easy and pleasurable as possible for customers to buy and run our cars.'

These directions may still seem a little abstract, but they are expressing some pretty high level thinking. What's important is the direction that they provide for the business plan (where the business planners get down to specifics, and the thinking can become much more concrete). Following this same linguistic approach, a business plan result on the subject of car sales might say:

'People in the UK are buying 750,000 more of our cars this year than last.'

Moving down a level, a brand launch project outcome could be expressed as:

'In the first three months, people are changing 200,000 old cars for our new ones.'

And dropping down again, to the individual communication level, a press ad outcome could be:

'People are ringing our showrooms to arrange a test drive.'

As I said, it's not the specific content of these answers that matters, but the fact that you can see the same, outcome-focused language being used throughout. The outcome of every communication can be transparently tracked back to the business's overall direction. And from the top down, the direction is always clearly provided for the next level below.

I believe this approach is essential for identifying appropriate outcomes for any kind of communication strategy – whether it's a project strategy, a perpetual strategy, or one to support a business plan. But will it go far enough?

Truly strategic communication planning

With outcomes expressed in the same way throughout, you'll be able to ask the same logistical questions throughout as well:

1. Who, specifically, do you want to do how much of this outcome, when and where?
2. What has to happen to get them to do it?

The first question is more one for the accountants and business analysts. But answering the second question brings us back once more to the SMARTIED principle, in most aspects of which communicating plays a major part. Gathering and disseminating **Information** is the most obvious way in which it does so, but it also comes into play with:

Skills – training and coaching are communication activities

Authority and **Responsibility** – job descriptions, individual or departmental objectives, organisation charts, policies and procedures are all communications. And business systems and processes always involve communicating to a greater or lesser extent.

Desire – again, formal and informal communications can play a major role in helping to motivate people.

Even, it seems, **Money**. Many's the time I've worked with managers who've had financial reporting as part of their roles, and who've bemoaned the fact that the finance division would keep asking for the same information four times, because they'd changed their minds about how they wanted it presented. (This has even happened when the client in question was a bank.) And the managers have said to me, *'If only you could teach the people in finance to understand that before they ask for any figures, they should get clear about what they want to be able to do as a result of having received them. It would save each of us about two days a month.'* All of these aspects of the SMARTIED principle therefore need to be included in a communication plan if it's going to be truly strategic.

Of course, in planning business results, there are many other things to consider in addition to communication. But in virtually every aspect of moving a business forward, communication has a vital role to play. And your business can choose to have effective communicating built into not only its business plan, but into the very planning process itself – provided the planners themselves know how to make that happen. And for that, we need a different type of strategy altogether.

Chapter 13

Another Kind of Strategy

'He took the "was" of "shall", and finding only "why"
smashed it into "because".'

e e cummings

In this chapter we will uncover:

➢ why you should never intend your communication strategies to
enable the business to communicate as effectively as possible

➢ what a communication strategy ought to do for you and the
business, and what could stop it doing so

➢ why your business needs not just strategic communication plans,
but a strategic communication policy

➢ what it will take to get a strategic communication policy off the
ground.

When I've talked with communication professionals about perpetual
communication strategies, and looked at what they've produced and had
signed off by their senior management, every one seems to have had pretty
much the same stated purpose:

'To enable the business to communicate as effectively as possible.'

On the face of it, this may seem perfectly reasonable, but in fact it's
critically flawed in two ways. For a start, how effective does anyone
consider 'as effectively as possible' to be? Compared to what? This phrase
is hinting at the idea of achieving an objectively measurable 'highest high'.
But in no communication strategies have I ever found a statement about how
that altitude is to be determined. As best as I can understand it, the method
of working it out seems to go something like this:

1. Here is a current situation, which isn't good enough (in terms of naff
communications and/or adverse audience opinions)

2. Here are some causes of that current situation (in terms of flawed processes

by which communications are produced and end up in front of audiences)

3. Here are some new, better ideas which will stop the horrors from continuing. They cover:
   a) what we are going to continue to do because:
      - it works as well as we believe it can, or
      - we're already committed to doing it
   b) what we are going to change, in terms of the communications we produce and/or the processes by which we produce them
   c) who's going to be responsible for doing what
   d) how we're going to measure 'a' and 'b' (or possibly only 'b').

4. If we put these processes in place, we can tell ourselves that we're communicating as effectively as possible (given that it's the most effective set up we can work out for ourselves at present).

When this is the kind of thinking that's going into perpetual strategies, it means that people are focusing only on the *current situation* and the *process* of communicating, not the outcomes. These strategies are all about how to change the current situation, by getting the process of producing communications under control and running better. Of course this will be useful. But it's again mistaking the process for the outcomes, so such a strategy is unlikely to give the business anything more than an efficient system for producing communications that may not even need to exist. Similarly, that process may still not generate all the communications that do need to exist.

And that's the second problem with having a communication strategy whose purpose is 'to enable the business to *communicate* as effectively as possible.' The very purpose itself is focusing on the process of communicat*ing* – and not on the outcomes of *having communicated*. Worse still, because it's not looking at outcomes, the word 'effectively' is dangerously misleading. Business communications are only effective when they produce the outcomes the business needs. And if no one ever identifies those outcomes, they can't possibly know that their communicating is effective. They can only know that the process they're using to produce and distribute those communications is an efficient one. Clearly, then, we need a more useful purpose for perpetual communication strategies. How about:

'To enable the business to produce communication outcomes as effectively as possible.'

When I've suggested making this linguistic shift, some people have looked at me as if to say, *'Ah, c'mon, now. You're just splitting hairs.'* Surely such a simple change of emphasis couldn't make that much difference to what the strategy needs to do, and what it needs to include – could it? Don't you believe it; those two purposes are as different as chalk and chinos. To understand why, let's consider how a perpetual strategy might be expected to make life better for the comms team, the communication owners and the business's audiences.

Anticipated benefits

My research suggests that most communication professionals want it to achieve some or all of the following:

1. enable them to plan in advance
2. stop audiences from being swamped with ill-thought-through communications arriving from just about anywhere
3. save money
4. ensure the communications that need to happen actually do so
5. ensure that people don't get left out of the communication loop
6. ensure that communication is two-way.

This is all very fine and dandy. But how realistic is it? In many cases, strategies either fall short of delivering these at all or, if they do deliver, they frequently struggle to do so for long. It seems that when focused only on the process, perpetual strategies can, like individual communications, be subject to dangerous leaps of faith in terms of *how* this strategy is going to *make* those things happen.

1. Enabling communication professionals to plan in advance

Naturally, planning in advance will mean that you can be more proactive and less reactive. So you should have longer lead times to produce your communications which, in turn, can both reduce your stress and frustration, and improve the quality of the finished products.

But how is a strategy going to enable you to do this? It seems that whatever plans you put in place, you will only reap the benefits of longer lead times if the more senior people are also thinking ahead. This means that no such strategy will produce this benefit unless it also changes these people's day to day thinking. (But few communication strategies ever manage to do this effectively, long term.)

2. Stopping audiences being swamped with ill-thought-through communications

Many communication strategies are introduced because the production and distribution of communications has got out of hand. This is particularly the case in a business which simply allocates pots of money to its departments, and gives total discretion to the department head as to how it's spent. In such situations, anyone with a budget can appoint themselves as a communication owner, and start producing their own newsletters, web pages and so on – without any valid business reason, and with no outcome in mind (other, perhaps, than those that go with any other form of vanity publishing). Web pages may need to go through some kind of 'gatekeeper', but that process may not be as rigorous as it could be.

Indeed, having controls on any widescale publications, by means of a central conduit through which all communications to a given audience must go, can certainly go a long way to reining in the insanity. But it also faces a number of challenges. Firstly, introducing such a system can often lead to resentment among those who've just had their personal mouthpieces muzzled. Secondly, it's often the most senior managers who want to get involved in deciding what goes out and what doesn't, which makes the system both costly and not necessarily effective. On the whole these people, although senior and conceivably of above average intelligence, have nonetheless had no more training in communication ownership than the people on whose communications they are sitting in judgement. Thirdly, the system is rarely sustainable over the long term and almost inevitably starts to deteriorate over time.

Other issues start to crop up for senior people, and attending communication management meetings becomes less of a priority. And even with such a system in place, all too often someone takes it upon themselves to use some of their budget to start producing a communication of their own – without consulting the 'official' communication management team. Or they start quietly producing their own logos and developing a separate 'corporate identity' for themselves – going to outside agencies and thus bypassing the central controls. And then other people start copying them. And bit by bit the whole fabric of the strategy falls to pieces – until someone senior takes it upon themselves to say, once again, 'Something must be done about this' and so a new strategy is spawned.

But, and here's the rub, the new strategy only goes back to the same place that the last one started. It doesn't address the source of the creeping erosion. Even if it has the most robust processes in place to stop people going off and doing their own things, there always seems to be someone high enough up who decides to ride roughshod over the agreed protocols, in order to get something produced for him or herself. And in so doing, they set a precedent that others can (and over time assuredly do) follow. And so the strategy breaks down.

3. Saving money

Reducing the sheer volume of communication will inevitably reduce the direct costs of print and distribution (or web-page design) and the indirect cost of the audience's time. And when non-electronic media are being used, pulling various disparate communications together into one place is likely to reduce the number of pieces being printed and distributed. Furthermore, being able to plan in advance will lead to fewer rush-jobs, with inevitably lower costs. But this all means that saving money is only possible if the previous two issues of planning and central control are taken care of – and it's therefore subject to the same practical challenges (and the same creeping erosion).

4. Ensuring the communications that need to happen actually do so

This is far more likely to happen with a short-term strategy that's being put together as part of a specific project plan. Such strategies tend to look at what needs to be communicated to whom and when, in order to make the project happen. It seems obvious enough, and yet it tends not to happen with communication strategies that have a broader or longer-term focus than a single project. With perpetual strategies, it seems that there are simply too many communication owners involved. And no such strategy can hope to be better than the awareness and communication ownership skills of all of those people. There may be rules for them to follow, but what if it simply doesn't occur to them to let you know they need something communicated? The system will always be subject to the lowest common denominator.

5. Ensuring that people don't get left out of the loop

Some communication strategies are instigated to ensure that the business's communications are more inclusive. This is more often than not driven by employee survey results, which have suggested that people currently feel left out. Certainly, having a media plan which shows what sort of messages go to which audiences, through which medium and when, makes it easier to know that those messages will be leaving the communicators. But it doesn't necessarily guarantee that they will be being received by the intended audiences. Sometimes, communications are intended to arrive with people via a cascade process, which relies on the communication savvy and commitment of individual line managers (something that is notoriously unreliable). Furthermore, the impact of the Detached Observer Triggers can leave people giving up early on many a communication intended for their consumption (because they don't feel that it is so intended). And even if people do continue to read, watch or listen through such communications to the end, they are still likely to feel that what they've heard was actually for someone else's consumption rather than their own.

Furthermore, although many people blithely talk about keeping people in 'the loop', they often overlook the fact that a loop is supposed to be circular. And without an effective feedback system in place, communication owners are unlikely to be aware of what the audience really need to hear, nor how well (or how badly) the messages are getting through – until it may be too late.

6. Ensuring communication becomes two-way

Many senior managers talk about how their people are their most valuable asset. They often claim to be committed to two-way communication. And yet, for reasons we'll discuss in the next chapter, feedback systems rarely seem to deliver the goods.

Whatever people's expectations, then, it seems that perpetual strategies rarely stand up to the slings and arrows of outrageous business decisions.

So if it's not going to lull people into an inappropriate state of complacency, what ought a communication strategy to be? Can it be simply a media production plan, or, given the symbiotic relationship between communication and money, does it need to be something that underpins the very mechanisms of running the business? Or both, perhaps?

Strategic communication policy and strategic communication plans

Certainly it makes sense to have a plan for managing the production and distribution of communications that deal with the everyday business of the organisation. But beyond that, surely, there also needs to be an overall way of:

1. deciding who it is that does the planning, and how they go about it – and
2. ensuring that those people always have the skills, authority, time and information necessary not only to produce the plan, but to execute it effectively?

So, in addition to any Strategic Communication Plans, that can unquestionably have value in their own right, it would also be useful to have a Strategic Communication Policy. Such a policy would need to transcend individual events, departments, business units or even business plans, in order to permanently guarantee the quality of communications and communication planning – even if the entire business were restructured. And it would need to be founded on a recognition of both the disciplines and the commercial impact of the following:

1. communication ownership
2. consistent, effective communication planning practices
3. two-way communicating.

(This may seem like a very short list, but in fact it takes care of all the shortfalls we've just discussed.)

Communication ownership

Whenever I work with Boards of Directors, I always explain to them the concept of communication ownership and then pose them the following question:

'Should you be a skilled communication owner?'

This almost always splits the room. Some say, *'Yes, of course I should. I wouldn't be doing my job properly if I weren't.'* The others say, *'Well, of course not; it's totally unrealistic. How can you expect me to be skilled at something that no one's ever shown me how to do?'* And, of course, they're usually both right. Some Directors may, through years of trial and error, coupled to some natural aptitude, have developed a certain amount of communication ownership skill. It may not be as great as it could be, and it may have cost the business hugely along the way, but at least it's something. However, many communication owners – whether at board level or further down the food chain, don't have much in the way of communication ownership skills, even though communicating may be virtually all they're doing nowadays.

We've already discussed the commercial implications of ineffective communication. But in many businesses, virtually anyone can become a communication owner, if they keep on being promoted for attributes that may have little or nothing to do with communication ownership. Thus, for example, a Finance Director or an IT Director, or any one of their senior managers, can end up owning communications without anyone evaluating their ability to perform that oh so critical job. (These are merely examples, and not a dig at anyone who works in Finance or IT; the problem can arise in any department.) Sometimes they might call upon, and be prepared to have their hands held by, a communication professional – from in-house or from an agency. But often, particularly if they go in-house, they can end up pulling rank, and insisting on things being done their way – even though they may not know how to make effective decisions. And if they go outside, they don't have the skills to evaluate the quality of advice they're being given.

Wouldn't it be sensible, then, for an organisation's overall business strategy to include a policy on communication ownership? In most businesses, the idea that communication owners have an adequate level of skill to discharge that part of their jobs is taken for granted – by both the business and the communication owners themselves. When challenged, many people will even take offence at the very suggestion that maybe they could be better at communication ownership. As we discussed earlier, they may have excellent skills in both social and academic communicating, but these are not business communication ownership skills.

It's time to face facts: communication ownership is not the same as writing, listening or talking. Although it involves all three, identifying what needs communicating to whom, when and how in business is an arcane discipline in its own right. And relying on someone do it properly, without them having had any appropriate training, is like expecting someone to drive a heavy goods vehicle competently when they've only ever driven cars. Sure, like a lorry driver, communication owners would be bringing to bear many of the skills they already possessed. But as I hope I've demonstrated throughout this book, there are unquestionably other skills involved – and greater levels of skill. And as with driving an HGV, anyone who tries doing the communication ownership job without developing the necessary skills is almost certain to (a) get it wrong at some point, and (b) make a much bigger and costlier mess when they do so.

To avoid making such a mess, and ensure instead that the necessary messages reach their destinations on time and intact, your business needs to accept the fact that communication owners – however senior – need adequate training, support and management. Currently that just doesn't happen in most businesses; instead they tend to adopt a sink or swim policy. The business assumes its communication owners can swim, and provides no swimming lessons. It also does nothing to check how any of them are getting on (other, perhaps, than a vague question or two in an annual staff survey). And with no one to tell them otherwise, the communication owners may assume they can swim too – when at best they're merely treading water. The ramifications are far reaching indeed.

Communication ownership is not a recognised skill set. Little or no account of the need for these skills is taken into account when people get a job that will involve communication ownership. That aspect of their role is often not explicitly included in their job profile, so there are no performance measures, and if someone is no good at this part of the job it's unlikely to be picked up. It therefore won't stop them from being promoted into a position where they also have responsibility for managing other communication owners: for evaluating their performance and maybe even providing hands on coaching. In short, this is a malaise that can (and in most businesses surely does) reach right to the top. Is it any wonder that, in many businesses, communication is an accident just waiting to happen? But surely it can't be as bad as all that, can it? Or if it is, it can't make that much difference to a business's performance – otherwise it wouldn't survive. This would be a fair point if it weren't for the fact almost all businesses are in pretty much the same boat. Any business can survive, even though it may be awful at communicating, if its competitors are just as poor.

Budget ownership

How different this situation is from financial management. If people get allocated a budget to manage, you can be sure that:

- they get clear procedures to follow
- their performance as a budget owner is monitored
- they receive the necessary training and coaching, and
- if they can't cut it, the budget gets taken away from them and/or their upward progression suffers as a result.

Apart from the fact that there are robust systems in place for budget management, there's also a very clear personal incentive for every budget owner to learn how to get it right. If they want their careers to progress, investing the necessary time and effort is not an option. And yet, as the ten communication costs make clear, if someone screws up on their communication ownership, they're likely to cost the business loads more than they ever could by making a mistake as a budget owner. So why have inadequate communication ownership skills gone unchecked for so long?

Firstly, up until now, a budget error has usually been much easier to identify and attribute than a communication cock-up (we'll shortly be looking at how to change this). Also, becoming a budget owner tends to be a relatively formal process when compared to that of becoming a communication owner. One day someone is not a budget owner, the next they are. But communication ownership rarely has such a clear dividing line. Email has given many people a tool with which they can communicate to huge audiences. And there are many similarities between the thinking skills required to put together an email to a dozen people and a conference presentation or cascade communication to ten thousand. Indeed, I would suggest that the questions you need to ask are identical both times. The differences lie in the fact that:

- the answers are likely to be more complex as the audience gets bigger
- a communication owner will probably be getting other people involved in production and approval
- they may now be spending some hard cash
- the commercial implications of the final communication's success or failure will be greater.

But given the similarities, it's maybe not surprising that people can be assumed, by the business and themselves, to know what they're doing when it comes to communication ownership. Indeed, had they been shown what questions to ask, and what answers to look for when they were just writing e-mails, this assumption wouldn't be that misplaced. But they weren't. So it is.

The logistics

When you consider the number and size of the unnecessary communication costs, this state of affairs could be said to fall somewhere between crazy and scary. But, and I don't think it's possible to over-emphasise this, it's no one's fault. People don't lack the necessary skills because they're stupid or lazy – but simply because the discipline of communication ownership, and its commercial consequences, have never been adequately understood before. And changing the status quo in your business is not something you can do on your own. Introducing a strategic communication policy is a decision for the Board. But what would they need to sign up for? Here we need to turn our attention once more to the SMARTIED principle. Your business's strategic communication policy would need to ensure that anyone who has, or is in line for, a communication ownership role would have the necessary:

- ✓ SKILLS to identify what needs communicating in the first place (and what doesn't)
- ✓ MONEY to communicate it
- ✓ AUTHORITY to ensure it happens when and how it needs to
- ✓ RESPONSIBILITY for getting it out there and actioning the feedback
- ✓ TIME enough to devote to this aspect of their job
- ✓ INFORMATION upon which to decide what, when and how to communicate (which is yet another reason for developing two-way communication)
- ✓ EQUIPMENT necessary to do the job
- ✓ DESIRE to give it the priority it needs.

This is likely to require a wholesale rethink of the role of communication ownership, involving the HR department in setting up performance measures for assessing both the requirements and value of the role – and the mechanisms by which people acquire it. It would mean them looking at the reward and recognition structure necessary to incentivise communication owners to get the job right, evaluating their current skills and those of the people who are managing them – even to the very top of the business. Finally, it would mean introducing training and development to bring everyone up to the necessary level of competence. How high that competence would need to be would depend on whether your business wanted to go for a hands-on or hands-off policy.

Hands-off or hands-on

The difference between the hands-on and hands-off approaches lies principally in the matters of Skills, Authority and Responsibility. A hands-on approach would require communication owners to gain a greater level of skill, so they could decide what needed to be communicated and ensure that it happened. In short, they would need to understand – really understand – at least all the principles covered in this book. They could draft in help from you and your fellow communication professionals to do the leg work, but the owners would be able to run the show, as it were.

With a hands-off policy, the owners could take more of a back seat, freeing up their time for other activities. They would need some training, but this could be simply to get them to a point of 'conscious incompetence' (so they realise that they lack the expertise to identify what needs communicating, and have to rely on you and your fellow communication professionals to come in and do the job). Without such training two things are likely to happen. Firstly, the owners may leave it too long before calling in help. And they may instead stumble on making ineffective decisions, which are too far gone for you to reverse by the time they get you involved. Secondly, whether or not it's too late, many owners may become so strongly wedded to the decisions they've arrived at, that they pull rank and insist on having their ineffective instructions carried out. And naturally this could be hugely expensive for the business.

Indeed, even with this hands-off training, it's possible that some owners may simply not think to ask for help until too late in the day. In an ideal world, the best solution of all would be to have owners trained to the point where they could adopt a hands-on approach if needs be, and then have them utilise expert help to the full. They would then be not only better versed in the disciplines necessary to provide effective briefs; they would also appreciate the value of getting experts involved as early as possible. In fact, having better communication ownership skills would enhance their interpersonal skills and their general thinking, planning and management ability. In any event, a hands-off policy would need to result in communication professionals having a pretty hefty slab of authority; it simply couldn't work otherwise.

Identifying communication owners

It would be difficult within any book to be too specific about how to go about identifying who is, or ought to be, a communication owner. As a general rule of thumb, in any business with over 200 employees, it would probably be safe to include everyone in the top two tiers of management, plus anyone who has a communication budget against his or her name. And probably each section head in the HR department itself (HR, of course, being a source of loads of internal communications). Making such a policy really work – long-term – would also mean having succession and/or contingency planning in place for communication owners, just as one might for, say, the management of departmental budgets.

All this may seem like a lot of work but there are two important reasons for pursuing this policy – both of them financial. Firstly, if you refer back to the ten costs of communicating, and consider what it would cost your business if it didn't do this – indeed, what it is costing your business right now – I think it would be difficult for any senior management team not to see this work as a worthwhile investment. Secondly, it may not be that much work after all. Your business may already have in place many of the mechanisms for managing the appointment of communication owners, through the way it manages people's appointments as budget holders. If someone has a communication budget, you know they're effectively a communication owner, or have line management responsibility for one. And if budget holders are simply allocated a lump sum, with discretion to spend it as they will, the same still applies. It just means spreading the net further to ensure that everyone with the financial resource to start producing communications, has the skills, performance measures and management support to go with it.

After all, your business wouldn't think twice about ensuring that these people know how to manage the budget itself. And given the exponential commercial impact of communication, the introduction of the strategic communication policy is simply a logical extension of what it's already doing. Indeed, if the top level managers were to sit down and do the sums, I'm pretty sure they'd find not doing so to be commercially indefensible.

Chapter 14

Bringing the Process Full Circle

*'It is the province of knowledge to speak, and it is the privilege
of wisdom to listen.'*

Oliver Wendell Holmes

In this chapter we will uncover:

➤ four reasons why annual staff surveys don't work as well as many
people like to believe

➤ the three key pieces of the feedback puzzle

➤ a system for measuring communication effectiveness

➤ how to produce outcome-focused survey questions.

In the same way that many people can come unstuck when they talk about
communication strategies, so too can they do so when discussing two-way
communication. Yet again, the very expression itself is focusing on the
process, rather than the outcome.

Although by no means always the case, a feedback process is sometimes
little more than a sort of appeasement exercise: it exists so the senior
management can be seen to be listening, rather than because they actually
intend to do anything differently as a result of having received the feedback.
Even with the best of intentions, other business priorities often take
precedence over responding to staff feedback because, it would seem, doing
so is not considered an integral part of the business planning and
development process.

That seems to be not only a waste of an extraordinary wealth of ideas, it's
also going to be counter-productive in the long term – as people see their
contributions being ignored.

The outcome of a strategic communication policy

Rather than thinking in terms of two-way communication, then, perhaps it
would be more valuable to think of two-way business development. With
such a mind-set, the purpose of a feedback process would not be simply a

PR exercise. Instead, it would be to continually bring forth ideas for business development from any and every part of the business. And if we bring that idea together with the training and managing of communication owners, and transparent communication planning, perhaps we can at last arrive at a truly strategic outcome for a communication policy to produce:

'Everyone in the business is communicating, at the best possible time, only whatever and with whomever they need to, in order to:

1. deliver the planned business outcomes and

2. develop the business's ability to do so increasingly.

And they're not communicating anything nor with anyone they don't need to.'

This outcome may seem a little restrictive at first. But by 'communicating' we're talking about what we could call formal communicating, i.e. through meetings, websites, email, newsletters and so on. It doesn't mean informal communicating, such as goes on with your workmates by the water cooler. Leaving out the restrictions would give everyone license to communicate everything to everyone, which would be no better than having no strategy at all.

The limitations of staff surveys

With a business plan (and any attendant SWOT analyses) couched in terms of communication outcomes, your business could start developing a watertight process to determine, in advance, what communication owners needed to be communicating, so they could be prompted to brief a comms professional in good time. The strategic communication policy should be ensuring that communication owners have the Skills, Money, Authority, Responsibility, Time. Equipment and Desire to do the job. And together, the business plan and SWOT analyses should provide a useful chunk of the Information that a communication owner would need, in order to identify what to communicate to whom and when. But they can't provide it all. For the rest, we need to ensure the feedback systems are firing on all cylinders.

Call me perverse, but I would suggest that there's something seriously wrong with a business's communication systems if it needs to conduct a survey of its staff's opinions every year (or, in some cases, every two years) in order to find out how people feel about things. We live in a business environment which is not only changing faster than ever before, but whose very rate of change seems to be increasing with each passing day. And the senior managers are only bothering to check in on their people once a year? I'd say they're going to be woefully out of touch – and not just because of the length of time between surveys. That's not to say that annual staff surveys are a waste of time. They can sometimes provide a useful snapshot of people's attitudes, and it can take time to implement changes in response to those attitudes. It can therefore be useful to check in again a year later to find out if the changes have made the desired difference to the attitudes. But there's often a danger of senior managers believing that such surveys are enough to ensure that they really understand their staff, because these surveys can suffer from up to four fatal handicaps:

1. currency over importance
2. out of date agendas
3. lack of self-regulation
4. ineffective purpose.

Currency over importance

Sheer time pressure ensures that annual staff surveys are limited in the scope of information they can acquire. Much of it is quantitative – usually designed to provide benchmark figures that can be measured year on year to monitor progress. And although these surveys do leave room for qualitative input, it's often fairly limited. Not only that, but such qualitative input as a survey can pick up may involve only the biggest issues in people's minds at the time the survey happens.

In 1999, there was a major national survey carried out in the UK, to find out whom people considered to be the greatest musical talents of the millennium. And, surprise, surprise, Robbie Williams came higher than Beethoven. Now there's no gainsaying the fact that Robbie has a great voice, a beguiling personality and an outstanding ability to strut – whereas Beethoven shuffled around with a certifiable haircut and an ear trumpet. However, at the time of the survey, Robbie had no recognised talent for playing musical instruments, and he wasn't composing the music for his songs. But in 1999, he was in the charts and Beethoven wasn't. Had the survey happened 25 years earlier, no doubt Beethoven would have had to battle it out with David Cassidy and Donny Osmond – neither of whom, needless to say, would get a mention by the turn of the century. And therein you have a key problem with any survey: people may not focus on what's most important, long term, but what's most current.

Out of date agendas

The second problem lies in the quantitative feedback. On the face of it, setting up these surveys to measure progress over time seems a perfectly logical idea. But it also necessitates using the same agenda every year. Who sets that agenda? And how long ago was it set?

While I was still a corporate employee, my employer started running an annual staff survey. And in the first year it was run, the general consensus among the numerous people I spoke to was that many of the questions were either meaningless, ambiguous or irrelevant. Given my job, I thought I ought to point this out to the HR Director – which I duly did, suggesting that it might be prudent to consider making some changes to the next year's survey. This, he informed me, would be impossible. They needed to ask the same questions again, otherwise they wouldn't be able to track how people's attitudes had changed. He seemed unable to comprehend that he wouldn't be able to do that anyway, or at least not reliably – not in a way that would have any real business value. Much of the information he would be getting from the first survey would be based upon a combination of apathy and guesswork, and would therefore be unreliable to the point of being worthless. Without changing the questions, the following year's feedback would be equally worthless. So he would be able to do nothing more than track the movements between two equally useless sets of figures. But once the thing was set up, he felt compelled to keep throwing good information after bad – ad infinitum.

I know from conversations with clients that such blinkered corporate obduracy is by no means unique, but it may not go on in your business. However, even if most of the questions in a staff survey are unambiguous, meaningful and relevant to everyone who answers them, the principle of having to follow exactly the same agenda each year is fundamentally flawed. It cannot help but limit your senior managers' ability to be really in touch with how people feel about issues that weren't pertinent when the survey was originally set up. And even if a few new questions are introduced each year, the agenda is still being set by the people who are running the survey. In short, virtually every annual staff survey is designed to find only the information that the surveyors are looking for (and quite possibly decided to start looking for several years ago). And it won't necessarily be looking for the ideas that the audience would like to contribute – and which could be of considerably greater business value. And the fact that the audience may not even understand the statements or questions on which they're being asked their opinions gives rise to a much bigger and more insidious problem.

Lack of self-regulation

Many surveys use statements to which people can respond by ticking one of a selection of boxes. These boxes usually say something like:

- ❏ Strongly agree
- ❏ Agree
- ❏ Disagree
- ❏ Strongly disagree
- ❏ Don't know

Sometimes they also include a 'Don't Care' box as well. This may seem to cover all the bases, but it doesn't. Not by a mile. If these are the only options available to people, they can't tell you something crucial about the survey itself. What if a statement is (as can often be the case) either incomprehensible or ambiguous to some or all of the audience? How are they going to tell you? They may just leave it blank, or tick the 'Don't Know' or 'Don't Care' boxes, or even take one of the 'Disagree' options. And you're never going to know that their true answer would have been 'Don't Understand'. If you don't give people the option to tell you that they don't understand the statement (or question) – or are at least unsure about it, you'll never know whether they're clear about what they're being asked to give an opinion on. And you won't be able to rely on the opinions themselves – ever – because you won't discover that you need to change the wording next year to make every bit of the survey unambiguously comprehensible to the respondents.

Ineffective purpose

An employee survey is a business communication. And like any other business communication, it has to fulfil the purpose of prompting and/or enabling people to take and/or avoid actions immediately and/or eventually. With a survey, of course, it's the communication's owners who are the audience for the eventual answers. And just as they do with other communications, these owners almost always focus on the current situation or the process, not the outcomes. Or they get stuck in the emotional or intellectual responses. They want to 'know' X, 'understand how people feel about' Y, or 'assess' or 'evaluate' Z.

But they never get to the point of identifying what they want to be able to do as a result of knowing, understanding, or having assessed. And if they don't know what they want to be able to do as a result of having received and evaluated the answers, how can they possibly tell what answers to look for? And if they don't know what answers they're looking for, how can they possibly know what questions to ask?

Once again, we need to get clear about our purpose. What is the purpose of canvassing employee opinions? What does the communication owner want to be able to do as a result of having canvassed them? Surely it's ultimately about ensuring that those being surveyed have the desire and ability to fulfil the business's *raison d'etre*, is it not? It's about finding out whether they have that desire and ability and, if not, discovering what has to happen so that they do have it, and taking whatever actions are necessary to ensure they have it. We'll look at the questions that can elicit this information shortly.

An additional approach

Given the limitations of annual surveys, it would certainly make sense to take an additional all-year-round approach to canvassing employee opinion. And to make such an approach work, my research with clients has shown that there are three pieces to this particular puzzle. You may already have some or all of these in place, but even then there can be subtleties in the way they're used which can make them more or less effective.

Firstly, there has to be a mechanism in place for audiences to use whenever they have questions to ask or ideas to contribute. Many businesses do have an equivalent of a 'suggestion box', through which staff can contribute ideas. But such feedback systems often fail, for several reasons:

(a) The feedback isn't forthcoming
(b) It is forthcoming, but it isn't acknowledged and disappears into a black hole, never to be seen again (so it's less forthcoming next time around).
(c) It's forthcoming, acknowledged – and then disappears into a black hole.
(d) It's forthcoming, acted upon, but not acknowledged, so the person or people who came up with the ideas don't feel valued (and are less inclined to provide feedback in the future).
(e) It's forthcoming, acknowledged and acted upon, but the reasons for the changes it has wrought are not communicated to the wider audience, so all they see are changed priorities without any explanation as to why.

These issues again call into question whether the business leaders are taking communication seriously enough. If they were, surely the processes would be in place to ensure that feedback is:

✓ always received by the relevant person or people
✓ instantly acknowledged
✓ acted upon, and the reasons for those actions explained to everyone affected by them.

141

And this brings in the second part of the feedback puzzle: encouraging feedback on every communication that goes out.

Some people are horrified by this suggestion. Every communication? Well why not? For example, team brief can include team debrief. (Such a debrief would involve rigorous, monitored processes for gathering ideas, information and questions at each Team Brief session, for upward and/or sideways dissemination.) And with written communications, you could create a standard sentence, to appear at the end of every communication. Something like:

'If you've any questions, concerns or suggestions about what you're being told here, or any ideas about how I could improve the way I'm communicating it to you ...'

... and then you can include details about the process for providing feedback. An intranet site would be a perfect mechanism for staff who have access to one, as it could enable you to gather loads of useful management information, and even show – where appropriate – the questions and suggestions, and the subsequent responses coming from all over the business. And because it would be being promoted with every communication, it wouldn't disappear from people's minds.

Of course, simply encouraging feedback blindly – just for the sake of doing it (or being seen to be doing it) is of little business value; far better to seek it purposefully. And this again raises the question of, *'What does the communicator want to be able to do as a result of having received feedback on this communication?'*

Whatever the communications, do the owners want to achieve their outcomes or not? And if they do, wouldn't it be useful to know, sooner rather than later, if something is going to stop that happening? And if this would be useful, there seem to be two ways in which getting (or at least encouraging) feedback from each communication could help them. Firstly, it would enable them to keep up to speed with staff attitudes and creative ideas in real time, as opposed to retrospectively once a year. Secondly, with the right questions, it could help develop the effectiveness of the communication process itself. I'll explain how shortly, as soon as we've taken care of the third part of the feedback puzzle.

Measuring communication effectiveness

People sometimes ask me about measuring internal communication effectiveness. For a long time it was one of those issues I felt somewhat unsure about. How the heck are you supposed to do it? And why would you want to? It was only when I'd put together most of the Communication

Goldmine ideas that I started to understand the answers to these questions. And I would say that measuring communication effectiveness can be done – up to a point – and that there is value in doing it – up to a point.

First of all, it would be useful to be clear about what we mean by effectiveness. It would ultimately mean the effect of communication on stakeholder value. And in a commercial business, given that one of the stakeholder groups will be shareholders, one measure would be the bottom line. There has been quite a bit of work carried out over the past few years into 'econometric tests' which, while they cannot provide absolute causal proof of the bottom line impact of communications, can show a very strong correlation between improving communications, staff satisfaction, customer satisfaction and income generation.

The reason you can never provide an absolute causal link is because of the SMARTIED principle. Quite simply, it's rare for communications to produce an outcome on their own. Often, they rely on people having the necessary *Money, Authority, Equipment* and so on. So you can't say that a communication is necessarily to blame if a given outcome doesn't happen and, equally, that it is entirely responsible if that outcome does happen. Not only that, but the effectiveness of some communications may be being scuppered by the ineffectiveness of others. Your team briefing may be terrific, but be let down by the fact that, perhaps, the training necessary to give people the *Skills* they require isn't up to scratch, or the extent of many people's email overload is such that they don't have enough *Time*.

Therefore, measuring communication effectiveness solely on the basis of the outputs (i.e. audience behaviours) while doable, is not necessarily going to give you an accurate steer. That's not to say that it isn't worth doing, of course, because it can enable you to see how the overall business development process is working. It's simply unwise to lay all the blame or credit at the door of communication.

Measuring inputs

But suppose you were also to measure the inputs, *and* to link both the input and output measures? At the beginning of this book, we discussed seven unnecessary business communication costs, at least some of which could be calculated with a fair degree of accuracy – and tracked over time. You could supplement this with an audit system to achieve the following:

1. Check that all major communications (e.g. those over a given audience size) have a written brief, which includes a clearly defined outcome, audience, intentional detached observers, causally-linked content and verified media.

2. If the business plan has been translated into 'communication outcome language', you can check that there's a communication plan in place into which any given communication fits. And you should be able to trace its outcome back logically to the business plan and/or company vision.

3. At a more strategic level, you can know whether all the business's communication owners have been trained to an appropriate level, and that the necessary performance measures are in place and being used.

4. You can know that the necessary feedback processes are in place, and are being used.

5. Coming down to individual communications, there may be other input measures you might want to use (the application of appropriate graphic design templates, for example, or the following of any writing style guidelines).

6. You can also check the content for any of the linguistic Detached Observer Triggers, which we'll be discussing throughout the rest of this book.

Keeping tabs on all these inputs can let you know if the communication part of the puzzle is operating as well as possible. They can also provide the basis for the performance measures of the communication owners, and thus spotting errors could be as easy and as clinical for communication ownership, as it is for budget ownership.

Furthermore, you ought to be able to track improvements in the input measures against movements in the unnecessary costs. For example, what percentage of communications are having to be sent out twice, or three times, compared with this time last year? How much time are employees saying they're having wasted with useless communications, compared to 12 months ago? And if communication owners are still having problems getting their required outcomes, and if the input measures are showing that the communication process is working at maximum effectiveness, the problems must logically reside elsewhere. And you can use your genuinely two-way communication processes to tease out exactly where those problems are – provided you're asking the right questions.

Making surveys outcome focused

If communication owners want to be more proactive still, the option is always there to run surveys – whether ad-hoc on a particular communication or campaign, or an annual employee survey. And whatever the mechanism for feedback, the key thing is to make sure you're asking questions that will give communication owners the information they need in order to get the outcomes they're after.

Logically, it seems, they ought to be looking to find out:

1. What else they have to do to get the outcome they were after from the communication/ campaign/business plan
2. How they can reliably (or more reliably) get the outcomes they want in the future, should they have similar issues to address.

For example, with a health and safety campaign, they may have produced a video to help teach people about a new series of regulations. In such a situation, some people might be tempted to ask a question like:

'Do you feel you understand the new regulations?'

But that's not going to tell them whether the audience are either capable of following those regulations (if, for example, they don't have the necessary equipment or time) or have any desire to do so. Again, given the purpose of business communication, it's far better to use the following two questions:

'Are you now able to do Y?' (Y being whatever the intended outcome was)
'Do you now want to do Y?'

And if the answer to either of these questions is 'No', you can then ask:

'What has to change for you to be able to do Y?'
'What has to change for you to want to do Y?'

This will tell you what, from the audience's perspective, is stopping the outcome from happening. And, importantly, it will enable you to then ask the audience to 'causally-link' this feedback, in much the same way that I suggested when we looked at identifying the content for a communication. I believe it's important to do this, because the answers to the above questions will give the communication owner a 'causal equation'. In simple terms, the answers they will have received thus far will be telling the owner that the audience believes the following:

'If X changes, then I will do Y.'

The unspoken implication here is that changing X will cause Y to happen. What it doesn't tell the owner, though, is how changing X will cause Y to happen. And as long as it remains unspoken, it's easy for people to make erroneous leaps of faith. I'd therefore suggest that you also include the following supplementary questions, in order to achieve two rather useful outcomes:

1. Validate the audiences' leaps of faith, so they're not just going to be asking for things that won't make the necessary differences to their behaviours
2. Help the communication owners to understand what the audience's

expectations are of any changes they're recommending in their feedback. This will make the suggestions that much more concrete, and make it easier for the owners to know how to go about making the necessary changes. The supplementary questions that I believe could accomplish all this would be:

'*How would any such changes **make** you want to do Y?*'
'*How would any such changes **make** you able to do Y?*'

The information these questions can deliver will probably highlight one or more aspects of the SMARTIED principle that need to be attended to. And if, for example, it's the **Information** that's lacking, it will have shown the communication owner – in good time – that a new communication is needed. These questions should therefore make it that much easier for owners to know what to do next, and make their communication, project and general business planning that much more assured. But your business can only rely on this to work if the final piece of the puzzle is in place: a process for handling the contributions, and responding to those who've provided the ideas.

If it's not simply going to be a pointless and costly cosmetic exercise, getting feedback requires three things to happen. Firstly, the people for whom it's intended need to receive it. Secondly, they need to do something useful with it. And thirdly, they need to let the originators of the feedback know what they're going to do as a result. This takes time, effort, and reliable processes. Without them, the feedback will surely dry up pretty quickly, for it will be seen as not worth providing by the audiences themselves.

Pulling it all together
As I see it, then, an effective communication strategy is one which ensures that:

1. No one gets to 'own' communications in your business without first having the skills (or receiving the necessary training) and the management support to do so, the time built into their job remits to perform the necessary tasks, and the performance measures, and reward and recognition structure to go with it.
2. All of the business's planning and management communications, from the mission statement, down through business plans, project plans, policies and procedures, are expressed, if not exclusively then certainly inclusively, in terms of desired audience behaviours.
3. Not only are communication plans an integral part of the business plan,

but communication planning is one of the key methods of business planning.

4. The business has rigorous processes in place for continually encouraging, using and responding to audience feedback, as an integral part of its ongoing business planning and development system.

5. The key inputs to communication effectiveness are being measured.

With all that in place, together with an outcome-focused briefing process, how could your communications ever go wrong? Unfortunately, the answer is 'very easily indeed', because even the best laid plans can come unstuck if your audiences switch off. And there are still six linguistic Detached Observer Triggers lurking in the English language, just waiting to undermine everyone's hard work. It's time to root them out and disarm them.

Chapter 15

A Linguistic Minefield

'Pronouns are the devil aren't they? ... breezing gaily along, you suddenly find you've got everything mixed up.'

Monty Bodkin

In this chapter we will uncover:

➤ the identity of the six linguistic Detached Observer Triggers

➤ how some of these triggers can gang up on you, causing you to trip over one in your attempt to side-step another

➤ why people may miss these triggers when they're writing or approving communications

➤ how to identify and disarm the first trigger.

I was once explaining the idea of the detached observer position to a friend in the pub (what an exciting life I lead, huh?). He seemed fascinated by what I was telling him, and pressed me for more information.

'How do you get people into the audience position then?' he asked.

My reply disappointed him.

'It's quite simple. Once you've identified your audience correctly in the brief, all you have to do is make sure you don't push them into the detached observer position.'

'That's daft. It's like telling someone with an electric drill that the best way to use it safely is not to drill through any part of their own or anyone else's anatomy.' (which may not be an altogether unsound piece of advice – if somewhat incomplete).

But what I'd meant was that with written business communications and (provided the speakers are doing their jobs properly) live presentations, it seems that people will automatically adopt the audience position from the start (unless explicitly positioned as detached observers, by having their names placed on a copies list.)

Starting in the audience position seems to be less common with video and audio communications, when it seems that many people start out as detached observers. I'm not certain quite why this should be. Maybe it's got something to do with the fact that audio and video media were principally developed for recreational purposes. And if you think about your own experience of listening to the radio, you may be able to identify with the following. If it's a talk show, in which people are having a discussion, they're talking to each other and you're eavesdropping on that conversation. Similarly with a pop music programme, from which position would you listen to, say, Joss Stone singing:

'Yeah! I'm digging on you. Your love is super duper.'

Would you consider yourself to be the 'You' that's being sung to? I would guess not. So here too, bizarre though it may seem, radio audiences aren't actually in the audience position at all. And this raises the question of how radio advertising works (which it undoubtedly can do). It appears to do so in the same way as a copy email. As long as people start off by positioning themselves as detached observers, they seem quite capable of picking up on the information that they unconsciously feel is for a real or imaginary group of others (it's a bit like overhearing a piece of juicy gossip). But when people start in the audience and then feel themselves being excluded, they're likely to switch off completely – often ditching the communication then and there – and feeling disenfranchised. And when reading written business communications, or attending business presentations, it seems that people usually do spontaneously start themselves off in the audience position.

As written and live communications make up the majority of those that go on in business, we need to ensure that we don't do anything to disrupt people's sense of being in the audience position because, if we do so, they will slip out of it and become detached observers. Of course there are exceptions, because everyone has their own way of responding to communications. Some people seem able to remain immune from one or more of these linguistic triggers. But the triggers unquestionably exist, lurking in the English language, ready to send the audience off to do some detached observing. And these triggers can kick in even if you've identified the audience accurately in the brief.

A huge unseen menace

I feel it's worth restating that one reason no one seems ever to have identified these triggers until now seems to be because – from an academic perspective – there's nothing grammatically or syntactically wrong with the English. It just doesn't work for a business communication. Therefore the remaining chapters of this book are devoted to helping you understand the structure and implications of these triggers, how to disarm them, and how to influence others to do so as well. When you get on top of these triggers, your personal reputation and business value can take a quantum leap forward.

Interestingly, many professional business writers already know the content of these chapters – instinctively. It's quite possible that you would never dream of tripping over any of these triggers. But often, that's not enough. I've worked with professional copywriters in marketing and advertising agencies who, although they would instinctively avoid at least some of these triggers, have never been able to explain to anyone what they were up to. And problems were often arising when clients wanted to change the text. Without the explicit knowledge contained in this and subsequent chapters, these writers were powerless to defend their particular style – even though they instinctively knew their clients had got it wrong. The rest of this book will help you to understand why some people don't appreciate that particular phrases can undermine an entire communication. And it will enable you to argue your case not merely on the basis of a subjective gut feel, but objective commercial expedience.

The six linguistic triggers

People adopt the detached observer position when they're no longer sure that what they're reading is talking to them. But to whom do they think the communicators are talking? In fact, there are four possibilities:

1. No one at all
2. Another audience
3. The communicator is talking to him or herself
4. If the communication is coming from a group of people, that group appear to be talking among themselves.

Different triggers lead to different responses, but all six triggers involve the use or absence of personal pronouns:

- Trigger 1 kicks in because no personal pronouns have been used when they should have been. We'll look at it later in this chapter.
- Triggers 2, 3 & 4 involve the pronoun 'you'. We'll discuss them in chapter 16
- Trigger 5 involves the pronoun 'I'. We'll discuss it in chapter 17.
- Trigger 6 involves the pronoun 'we'. We'll discuss it in chapter 19.

Importantly, these triggers – particularly the first four – are able to gang up on unwary writers. In an attempt to avoid one of these triggers, it's all too easy for someone to trip unwittingly over one of the others. Picking your way between them is rather like trying to make your way through a linguistic minefield. My intention is to provide you with a route map. We'll look at each trigger in turn, understanding how to spot it, and how to subtly change the phraseology to disarm it – without setting off one of the others. But why should this be necessary? Surely if someone's instinctive gut reactions can steer them away from one trigger, why not all of them?

Why people miss certain triggers

There are several reasons and I believe you'll find it useful to know what they are, as it may help you to understand why some of the people you work with may not 'get it'.

1. We need to recognise that not everyone responds in the same way to the same words. When I've shared these ideas with clients, I've discovered that some people get turned off by all of these triggers, while others can be immune to one or two. It's therefore possible that some people you deal with may not realise that they're asking you to rewrite a piece of text in a way which is likely to fail with much of its audience.

2. The sort of people who might challenge the way you've written something are likely to be either communication owners, or members of an approval group. And from which position: communicator, audience, or detached observer, are they going to read the text in front of them when they're approving it? The truth is that they may adopt any one of these three positions. But detached observer triggers push people out of the audience position, so it's only those who adopt this audience position who could have the gut reaction that tells them something's gone awry.

3. I've also discovered that experienced, senior business people can often be affected by the triggers less than people who are less experienced and more junior. This puzzled me for a while, as it didn't seem to have anything to do with educational attainment. Graduate entrants could be just as readily turned off as people with no academic qualifications. My studies into this issue haven't been exhaustive, but they have led me to suspect that the key lies in the motivation of senior people.

   It seems that they can get switched off by the triggers, but that they carry on gallantly anyway. And, importantly, some seem determined enough to go back over the bits they'd been switched off from, and make themselves read those passages again until the message goes in. My guess is that, either second or third time around, they are anticipating the trigger, and so actually start their re-reading from the detached observer position. In this way, they are able to numb themselves to the impact of the triggers. The trouble is that not everyone is as committed as this to make a communication work for them; and many just don't have the time. Rather than rely on the commitment of the audience, it's much more effective to make life as easy for them as possible, by disarming the triggers up front.

4. Even those who think they're in the audience position may not be. Many people say that they put themselves into the audience's shoes when they're writing or approving text. But there are two quite different ways of doing it: objectively and subjectively. The distinction between objective and subjective experience is a subtle one, and a little tricky to explain. But it can make an enormous difference to the way someone responds to what they're reading, so I feel we ought to address it. And the easiest way to do so is by means of a little visualising.

Objective experience

Imagine that you're at a fun fair – at the dodgems. If you look down at the dodgems from the edge of the arena, watching the cars whizzing around, you may be able to spot yourself sitting in one of them. Watch yourself for a few moments, being crashed into, and charging about after the person who'd just bumped into you. As you do so, you may be able to see yourself shoot away to the far end of the arena, and be able to see the back of the dodgem car in which you're sitting, and the upper part of your back, your shoulders and your head protruding above it. What you're witnessing is an objective experience of yourself.

Subjective experience

Imagine, now, that the ride has come to an end. From that vantage point at the edge of the arena, watch everyone, including yourself, getting out of the cars and wandering off out of sight. A new ride is going to start in a minute or two, so go up to the cash desk, pay some money over the counter, and then go down and sit in one of the cars. Feel the hardness of the seat as you sit down. Reach out and take hold of the steering wheel. This is a subjective experience of yourself. You can see the backs of your hands on the wheel, but unlike the objective experience, you can't see the back of your own head.

These two types of experience not only give rise to quite different mental images, but different feelings as well. I've discovered that many people, when they say that they put themselves in the audience's shoes, do so objectively (which actually means they're in the Detached Observer position. It's only the subjective experience that's going to give them a chance of experiencing the communication in the way that the audience will.

Getting technical

Given that many of the people you deal with may not realise that the triggers are even there, we may have to get technical in order to convince them that a given piece of text needs to be reworded. This means looking at different aspects of the English language. And although the words involved are commonplace, many people don't know their technical names. Unfortunately, there seems to be no way of avoiding the odd technical label here and there, especially if you want to be able to fight your corner when someone else is trying to change the way something's worded – or insists that you stick with their ineffective wording. Time and again I've found that having the technical names for different words at my fingertips has made it that much easier to convince people that I know what I'm talking about.

But to avoid getting bogged down, I'm going to keep technical explanations to a minimum – even if it means stretching the odd grammatical category here and there. What matters to me is that you get the logical distinctions between how different types of words work, and if this means I run the risk of inducing apoplexy in an ageing grammatical purist or two, so be it. If any of what follows is unfamiliar to you, and you want to know more about the meanings of the technical names, there are plenty of books on English grammar that can help you out.

Linguistic Trigger 1:
Using too many impersonal verbs and abstract nouns

The first linguistic trigger – using too many impersonal verbs and abstract nouns – can give the impression that the communication is talking to no one at all. (Many abstract nouns are impersonal verbs in disguise):

Gratitude is expressed for the reading of this book. It is to be hoped that the book proves enjoyable and stimulating. The ideas being shared provide new ways of thinking about the writing of business English. Thus it is anticipated that learning will ensue, and the subsequent implementation of the ideas contained herein will result in more effective communication.

You may think that this example is unrealistic. When I present this trigger to people, I'm often greeted with cries of, *'But surely no one in their right mind would write anything like that?'* To be honest, I don't consider myself qualified to comment on any possible mental instability among business writers. What I can say, though, is that some people (and numerous committees) do churn out communications worded like this.

If you adopt this style of writing, you won't be talking to your audience at all, but merely making an academic observation for them to read. That said, I've found it nigh on impossible to come up with a hard and fast rule about how many consecutive impersonal verbs and abstract nouns you can get away with before alienating an audience. However, in some contexts I've found that many people switch off when just two impersonal verbs appear in succession. Getting around this trigger is easy enough: you just need to write personally whenever possible:

Thank you for reading this book. I hope it proves enjoyable and stimulating. It may give you some new ways of thinking about how you write business English. I hope you'll learn some new ideas which, if you put them into practice, will help you communicate more effectively both with communication owners and their audiences.

This solution is so simple that, initially, I was left wondering why people would ever write impersonally. I've now come up with four reasons:

1. They haven't identified their audience effectively in the brief, and so aren't entirely sure whom they're addressing.
2. They're copying a style that they've seen elsewhere, believing that they need to write in this way in order to 'sound professional'.
3. They are trying to hide behind impersonal language, so that no one in the communicator group is committing themselves to anything.
4. They instinctively feel (without being consciously aware of why) that, if they write personally, they're likely to alienate the audience by tripping over one of the other detached observer triggers.

This fourth scenario is not as unlikely as it may appear. Professional copywriters are not alone in being instinctively aware of these triggers. The very fact that these triggers switch people off means that anyone can notice, consciously or unconsciously, that something's amiss. But when someone is writing, editing or approving communications, not only may they adopt the communicator or detached observer positions, they can also flip between them, and the audience position too – quite unconsciously. And this can mean that they'll not be as sensitive to these triggers as they would be when they're members of an audience. (We'll be discussing the impact of these triggers on the approval process in Chapter 18.)

Nevertheless, some people may instinctively shy away from the other triggers, and choose impersonal verbs as the least damaging option. Unfortunately, impersonal verbs can do as much damage as the other triggers. As a starting point, then, I'd suggest writing with personal verbs at every opportunity, and never to use two impersonal verbs back to back.

While this will avoid the first linguistic trigger, it may sometimes cause you to trip over the others, for which we evidently need some alternative solutions.

Chapter 16

You – Who?

'You will softly and suddenly vanish away, and never be met with again.'
Lewis Carroll

In this chapter we will uncover:

➤ three different uses and abuses of the word 'you' that cause people to switch off

➤ why one of these triggers can work retrospectively, undermining not only what follows it, but what's preceded it as well

➤ how to tread a path safely between these triggers to keep people in the audience

---

It's with the pronoun 'you' that the linguistic minefield becomes most tricky to negotiate. Because there are three 'you' triggers, it's all too easy to side-step one of them, only to tread inadvertently on one of the others.

The three triggers are:

● Trigger 2: Presupposing the audience's attitude or situation
● Trigger 3: Writing about 'the reader(s)'
● Trigger 4: Quantifying the audience

Some people seem able to thread a path instinctively between these triggers without any difficulty, while others often come unstuck. Whichever camp you fall into, this chapter will enable you to consciously understand how the triggers work, and how to make the solutions do likewise. And in doing so it'll give you the explanations necessary to convince others about the need for changes – or the need to avoid changes.

Linguistic trigger 2:
Presupposing the audience's attitude or situation

Some authors use impersonal verbs because they don't want to imply that what they're saying necessarily relates to everyone in the audience. This may be because they're instinctively trying to steer clear of this second trigger, or simply to avoid being lynched. Unfortunately, this particular trigger has the capacity to get up people's noses in no uncertain manner. And if you'll excuse me while I dive for a convenient bunker, I'll demonstrate how it does so with the following example. (I don't mean the next bit, it's just to illustrate the point, okay?)

Thank you for reading this book, which I know you're finding both enjoyable and stimulating, even though you're obviously finding it difficult to follow. I know you've been struggling to grasp these ideas, but don't give up. It will be worth all your effort in the end.

How can I possibly know anything I'm claiming to know? I don't know who you are. I don't even know what part of the planet you're on. This being the case, how likely is it that the text in that example was talking to you? Everyone's different. Even people in the same audience, who may be doing the same job for the same company, are different. Their attitudes are likely to be different, their personal situations are almost certain to be different, and their motivations for doing or not doing things may well be different too. Anyone whose writing ignores this and suggests instead that everyone reading it has the same attitude, or is in the same situation, is almost certain to make some readers feel that they aren't being spoken to. In fact, such writing may turn an audience not into neutral detached observers, but actively hostile ones. And even though you may never write like this yourself, perhaps you can imagine how others might, or recall having read communications written in this way. Many people believe that everyone sees the world in the same way they do. I once came across a piece of internal promotional material issued by a company's training department which included the phrase:

Naturally, you want to keep learning throughout your career

But some people may not be interested in learning, or even in having a career at all. They may be happy with just a nine to five job – in which case they'd be quite justified in feeling that whatever the author said after this statement applied only to other people. Even if you feel that the statement applies to everyone, many people object to having their attitudes taken for granted, or seemingly dictated to them by others:

e.g. We know you care about company security.

There are two potential problems here:

1. It may be true that many people care about their company's security, but not at the expense of their right to think for themselves. (Even if you have been finding this book enjoyable and stimulating, it's still possible that it may have jarred on you to have been told a couple of paragraphs back that I knew this to be the case.) I've often heard employees say of communications that make such blatant assumptions, that they feel the authors can only be addressing people who are prepared to be talked down to.

2. The example suggests that the authors are sure of their facts: that they've checked their information. And anyone who hasn't been asked about their attitude to company security could quite naturally (albeit unconsciously) feel that this statement was being directed only at those who had. And if this statement were just a guess on the part of the author, and no one's views had been canvassed, it could quite conceivably switch off a large segment of the audience.

I'm not saying that these will definitely be the reactions of everyone, merely that they're possible with some. And given that there are loads of ways of avoiding these potential problems – which don't require you to use impersonal verbs – they are risks that no one needs to run.

How to disarm this trigger
In order to avoid presupposing people's attitudes or situations, the first thing to recognise is that you can talk *to* an audience and you can talk *about* them. This trigger kicks in when someone is trying to talk about **the whole audience** in circumstances where doing so isn't going to work. Using impersonal verbs does get around this problem, but it goes too far in the other direction. However, there is a path you can tread between the two extremes. It's a path which enables individual readers to feel that you're talking *to* them, by allowing them to decide for themselves whether or not you're talking *about* them. In short, it gives people a bit of psychological 'wiggle room'. There are at least half a dozen linguistic techniques you can use to achieve this.

Flexible and Inflexible language
There are various types of 'flexible' words that can give your audiences the wiggle room they might need, and a similar number of 'inflexible' words that will deny it to them. By looking at the following examples, you may be able to see immediately the impact they're likely to have.

Word type	Inflexible examples	Flexible examples
Adjective	impossible/absolute	possible/occasional
Adverb	definitely/always/never	possibly/sometimes/often
Article	the	a/an
Conjunction	as/because	if
Quantifier	all/none/every	some/many/most
Verb Auxiliary	will/must/can't/have to	could/may/can/might
Verb	know/is/are	hope/believe/think/feel

Sometimes, the question of whether a word is flexible or inflexible depends on how you use it. For example, if I say, *'I believe this makes sense,'* the word believe is flexible. If, however, I say, *'You believe this makes sense,'* I'm guilty of presupposing your attitude, so I'd need to use a verb auxiliary, such as 'might' ('You might believe this makes sense') in order to make the expression flexible.

Used correctly, then, flexible language allows people to decide for themselves whether or not the words that are talking to them are also talking about them. Inflexible language denies them that choice, with the result that, if they feel they are not being spoken about, they also cannot be being spoken to. The impact of changing from inflexible to flexible language is easy to see if we return to the earlier example:

Inflexible
Thank you for reading this book which I know you're finding both enjoyable and stimulating.

Flexible
Thank you for reading this book, which I hope you're finding both enjoyable and stimulating.

The flexible version isn't insisting that you are finding it enjoyable. And oddly enough, this means that people can still feel this expression is talking to them even if they aren't enjoying reading it.

Direct and indirect statements
Sometimes, making the language flexible isn't enough and it can be useful to go down a different route, making what are sometimes called 'indirect' statements. The distinction between direct and indirect statements is a simple one, which the following example will illustrate:

Direct
It's possible for you to become a better communicator.

Indirect
It's possible for people to become better communicators.

In this example, even though the direct sentence has used the flexible term 'possible', it's still suggesting that whoever has written it knows something about each and every individual reader. And it doesn't even matter if what they're saying is true (given that there's no limit on how good a communicator anyone can become). For many people the very suggestion that someone, who's never met them, dares to tell them what they're capable of, will often be enough to turn them off. Changing the personal pronoun 'you' for the more general term 'people' overcomes this.

Sometimes, then, you may want to make your language indirect rather than direct. And it's often useful to combine both flexible and indirect language, because simply leaving out a flexible word will frequently make an expression inflexible. This, I have discovered, is a subtle but significant point which, unless I make a bit of a song and dance about it, many people don't notice. So, obvious though it may appear, I want to illustrate how this works. Let's take one of our earlier examples:

You want to keep learning throughout your career.

We can turn this into an indirect statement:

People want to keep learning throughout their careers.

Because the term 'people' has not been quantified in any way, this statement contains at least the suggestion that it is intended to apply to all human beings. Avoiding this is simple enough if we also make the statement flexible:

Many people want to keep learning throughout their careers.

Thus the presumption about the individual reader has disappeared.

Making your language flexible and indirect can take care of the most damaging aspects of this trigger. But it doesn't necessarily take care of all the problems in every situation. And there are other techniques you can employ in different circumstances depending on what the situation seems to demand.

Playing around with the attitudinal references

Your job is not only to stop people tripping out of the audience, it's also to prompt them to take some kind of action, so referring to people's attitudes can often be useful – even necessary. After all, you could say, *'Many people want to keep learning throughout their careers,'* and someone could look at that statement, shrug their shoulders and say, *'Yeah, So what?'* This puzzled me for some time, until I started to look more closely at which specific audience attitudes, when presupposed, would cause this trigger to kick in. And it seemed always to be the same two:

1. their attitude towards their current situation

2. their attitude towards engaging in the behaviours identified as the communication's outcome.

But there's a third attitude which it might be safe, even useful, to focus on:

3. their attitude towards the benefits they could get from engaging in the 'outcome' behaviours.

E.g. People who want to increase their earning potential find it useful to keep learning.

Of course there's always a danger that this may turn off people who aren't interested in increasing their earnings. But if that's what you've identified as a key reason why people would want to do what the communication owner wants, it's unlikely that anything you say to these more obdurate folk is necessarily going to switch them on.

Crucially, the attitudinal reference (in this example 'want to increase earning potential') is being made with an indirect statement, so the communication will still be talking even to those who don't want to increase their earnings. As such, they will still be in the audience, and something later on in the communication (a different benefit perhaps) may still be able to click with them.

Shifting tenses

Another technique available to you is to play around with the tenses of the verbs you're using. The present tense often suggests an all-encompassing generalisation, whereas the past tenses can again give more room for manoeuvre. This is somewhat subtle, but if you give yourself a moment to reflect on the meaning of the following examples, you may get what I'm driving at.

When asked about the secret of his success, he placed his feet on his desk, and scratched his ear reflectively.

When asked about the secret of his success, he places his feet on his desk and scratches his ear reflectively.

Using the present tense suggests that this is a habitual behaviour, something that you can rely on every time, whereas the past tense is citing a single example. (The future tense can also create a generalisation, suggesting knowledge of how someone will behave.) When talking about people's attitudes, shifting into one of the past tenses can often be useful, for two reasons:

1. A generalisation written in the past tense must, by definition, be historically based, which means it doesn't have to apply to the individuals reading it today.

2. It also enables you to cite historical knowledge, which may add credibility to your argument.

E.g. People who've continually increased their earning potential have found it necessary to keep learning.

Together, these techniques can give you enough options not only for side-stepping this rather nasty trigger, but also getting people to want to feel that you're talking to them. There may be many other techniques you can discover but, for now, here are a couple of others that you may wish to play around with.

Quotations and questions

Citing or quoting a widely respected individual can often get some people feeling they want to follow suit.

E.g. Winston Churchill said that he always kept learning throughout his life.

Questions demand answers – even if only unconsciously, and can often be a powerful way of connecting people with the benefits you want them to focus on.

E.g. How much more could you be earning if you were to continue your learning?

There are reasons to be cautious about using questions, which we will address when we look at the fifth linguistic trigger (the pronoun 'I'). For now, though, it's time to turn our attention to the third.

Linguistic trigger 3:
Writing about <u>the</u> reader(s)

Given that I'm presenting this information to you through the medium of a book, this trigger is slightly tricky to communicate as clearly as I'd like, because it seems that book authors, particularly those who write non-fiction or academic books, often fall into the habit of writing in this way. (But they can get away with it, given that a book is, according to the definitions we came up with earlier, a recreational or academic communication.) As such, the impact of this trigger may not hit you as readily in this medium as it might were it to appear in a newsletter at work, or an email. Nevertheless, I'd like you to notice how you feel as you read the following.

When going through this example, you may start wondering who is being spoken to. This would be perfectly understandable, given that the reader has already been exposed to a couple of detached observer triggers before getting to this one. The Business Communicator is therefore likely to be familiar with what to look out for.

Isn't it a somewhat bizarre experience to be reading a communication that's talking to 'you' and then coming across someone called 'the reader'? At the very least, it suggests that 'the reader' is someone other than 'you'. So who is 'the author' talking to there?

This trigger baffled for a while – not its solution, but the very fact that anyone would even think of writing like this. Could it simply be a hangover from their reading of academic treatises, which often use this linguistic device (for reasons I've never fathomed). Is it that, when writing, they imagine themselves explaining things to one of their colleagues and forget that they're actually writing for someone else entirely (more of this later). Or could it be (at least when they use the plural form 'readers') that they're again trying somehow to avoid presupposing the audience's attitude or situation?

Whatever the reasons, and whatever the specific nomenclature (reader, employee, applicant, listener, customer etc) and whether singular or plural, I would always start by reverting from the third person label – e.g. 'the reader(s)' – to the second person pronoun 'you'. And if doing so looks like it will presuppose the audience's attitude or situation, well we've already dealt with that. But it may be that it could also cause the fourth trigger to kick in.

Linguistic trigger 4:
Quantifying the audience

This trigger may not be unique to the English language, but it's certainly true that many languages are unable to create it. The French language, for example, has the words 'Tu' and 'Vous' to distinguish between the singular and plural forms of the second person pronoun but, in English, we've just got 'you'. If a piece of writing starts off by using the word 'you' to mean an individual, and then changes it to mean a group, that piece of writing will effectively split the identity of the audience. And this can leave each individual wondering if he or she still belongs in the audience or not. For example:

This book is presenting you with a whole bunch of ideas about business communication, and some of you may be wondering how easy it will be to get to grips with them. This is hardly surprising as many of you will never have come across them before.

Other than this illustration, you're unlikely to find ideas expressed like this in a book. But it's all too common to come across such linguistic foibles in business communications. There seem to be three situations in particular which give rise to this type of writing:

(a) when the communication is being written for more than one audience
(b) when the communication is a script for a presentation
(c) when the communicator is trying to avoid presupposing the audience's attitude or situation.

And at the risk of getting a mite technical again, there are four different ways to quantify the audience and set this trigger off:

1. with flexible quantifiers
2. with inflexible quantifiers
3. with plurals
4. with certain adverbs.

Flexible quantifiers

This means quantifying the word 'you' with words such as *any of, some of, many of, more of, most of,* or even *those of.* To explain how the problem works, I'd like you to read the following:

When you read a communication, you can decide whether or not it's talking to you.

In this example, the word 'you' has appeared three times. And each time, it's referring to you as an individual. You're therefore able to recognise yourself as the individual being addressed, and feel (albeit unconsciously) 'this is talking to me'. But when 'you' is quantified with a term like 'some of', the word 'you' can no longer be referring to an individual; so you can no longer feel 'this is talking to me'.

When you read a communication, any of you can decide whether or not it's talking to some of you.

The idea of a communication talking to 'some of me' just doesn't make sense. You therefore have no choice but to change the meaning of the word 'you' from the singular to the plural: from me to us. So the text which you might have thought was talking one on one with you, is now talking to a group. Who is this group? Do you belong in the group or not? After all, where did it suddenly spring from? Why weren't they being spoken to before? Or were they being addressed earlier and you just didn't realise it? All of these subtle, unconscious questions can arise when the meaning of 'you' changes unexpectedly from singular to plural. They're questions to which, often, no one can be certain of the answers. But what people can be consciously aware of is a simple gut reaction which makes them feel unsure that the text is talking to them. This being the case, it's always possible that when you read certain communications, many of you may wonder whether if they're talking to any of you. (There is an exception to this. If you're writing to a couple, you can get away with the terms 'both of you' and 'each of you'. As there are only two people involved, neither of them can question whether or not they are in that 'both', or to whom the 'each' applies.)

There are three simple solutions to this problem. The first is to remove the quantifier, e.g. **not** *'Many of you may find this easy to learn,'* **but** *'You may find this easy to learn.'*

Alternatively, you can change the statement from a direct one to an indirect one: from 'of you' to 'people', e.g. **not** *'Many of you may find this easy to learn,'* **but** *'Many people find this easy to learn.'*

A third way of dealing with it, which is more appropriate in some situations (particularly if the inference is a potentially uncomfortable one, or if you're referring to historical evidence) is to make the sentence flexible, by using the word 'if', e.g. **not** *'Many of you may have found this difficult to learn...'* **but** *'If you have found this difficult to learn ...'*

However, this is a solution that needs to be treated with caution. The key question to consider is how long an explanation you're going to have to give to those people to whom the 'if' applies (in this example, those who have found it difficult to learn). You've flagged up the fact that you're now addressing a select part of the audience, so everyone knows where they stand. But if the explanation starts to drag on, those people who haven't found it difficult are going to switch off. Inevitably, there's no way of giving you a hard and fast ruling on this, but I would be wary about addressing a 'sub audience' for any more than two sentences. If the explanation needs more space, I'd write it separately and direct those who are interested to the appropriate page or section.

Inflexible quantifiers

The quantifiers *all, each, none* and *every one ... of you* can also push people into the detached observer position. Even though they are all-inclusive terms (or all-exclusive in the case of none) they still force people to change the meaning of 'you' from singular to plural. When this happens, each individual has to accept that 'this is talking to a group'. And when an individual feels that it is a group that's being addressed, it's always possible for that person to leave any actions (i.e. the communication's outcome) to others. This may seem strange, given that the quantifiers are all inclusive, but there are three reasons why they can still result in some members of the audience opting out:

1. The quantifier appears early on in the communication, and is then not used later, when the call to action is being discussed. If the group has been identified as 'each of you' and then the call to action just refers to 'you', an individual may feel that they've been given a let out. *'After all,'* they may be able to tell themselves, *'if the communicators had meant each of us, they'd have said so, because they did earlier on.'* This may seem simply a convenient way for lazy people to think, but there is a kind of inescapable logic to it. Why, after all, was the term 'each of you' used earlier, if it wasn't trying to convey something different from the word 'you' on its own? Chances are it wasn't trying to do anything of the kind. But the doubt has still been raised nonetheless.

2. Often, communicators use such quantifiers when they know they have to appeal to the conscience of their audience, and can't check up on each individual. In such circumstances, they often use phrases such as:

    'It's up to all of you to make sure this happens.'

    This sort of language is often a dead give-away – making it clear to those who want to opt out, that no one's going to know for sure if they do so.

3. The third reason why inflexible quantifiers can turn people off applies particularly to communications that people are reading, rather than those they receive through a presentation. It's somewhat subtle, and is easiest to explain to you by means of demonstration. I say this because I'm sure you'll appreciate the problems of inflexible quantifiers as soon as you're all standing up. So if you could all stand up for me now, before reading any further...

    If you're now unsure about whether or not you need to be standing up to read this sentence, the chances are you're not alone. (You don't need to be standing by the way). The end of that last paragraph may not have fazed you at all – but some people get thoroughly confused by it. And yet all I did was again shift the meaning of 'you' from singular to plural. So once more, you could no longer feel 'this is talking to me'. How, after all, could I expect only part of you to get to your feet? So even if the quantifier ('each', 'every', 'all', or 'none'... 'of you') is explicitly meant to include everyone, it still creates problems by forcing people to feel that they are part of a group that they hadn't previously realised they were supposed to belong to.

In all three scenarios, losing the quantifier will remove the problem, because even though the communication is going to a number of people, each of them can be addressed as an individual, e.g. **not** *'We need all of you to understand an important change in our procedures.'* **but** *'We need you to understand an important change in our procedures.'*

Using plurals

This crops up a lot in presentations, and often when someone has been offered the following piece of advice: 'write as you speak'. Colloquial writing is generally more digestible than the kind of formal, arid style of business writing prevalent throughout much of the 20th century. However, it's also true that reading is a different experience from listening, which means that writing as you speak is not always going to work. Generally, the communications we're talking about in this book are not going out to single individuals, but to groups of people. In such circumstances, suggesting to authors that they write as they speak may prompt them to use expressions such as this:

'You need to keep your laptops safe.'

And how many laptops, plural, does each individual reader have? This particular use of the plural can have one of only two effects – both of which are damaging.

1. It is changing the meaning of 'you' from singular to plural – incurring the consequences we've already discussed
2. It could suggest to its readers that it's talking only to people who have more than one laptop each.

Either way, it's likely to set off that trigger. In these circumstances, the solution is simply to drop the plural. But there are other circumstances in which you need to take a more circuitous route. Plurals often crop up when communicators are responding to feedback, or saying thank you. In such instances, it's common to come across an expression such as this.

'Thank you for your calls.'

Again, just how many calls – plural – did each individual make? This statement again leaves each individual reader feeling that the communicator is either addressing a group, or an individual who made multiple calls to the communicator. Even those people who did make a call may still be unable to feel this is talking to me, because each individual probably made only one call, not several. This may seem like I'm splitting hairs, but even if it doesn't switch everyone off for sure, it's still chipping away at the rapport between communicator and audience. And it's a problem that simply doesn't need to be there at all.

There are a couple of ways of dealing with this. Certainly, it wouldn't work if you made the sentence singular – 'thank you for your call' – as this would still lose all those who didn't make one. And in many circumstances, it would also be likely to lose even those who did. It's an oddly perverse thing, but although you always need to address an individual (at least when communicating in writing) you can't afford to be too obvious about it.

Imagine, if you will, that the HR department had sent out a proposal of some kind, asking for people to ring in with suggestions. I think most staff would be likely to instinctively assume that not every single person would have expressed an opinion (some would likely have been off sick or on holiday for a start). And if the HR department were then to send out a blanket follow up communication to all staff, saying, 'thank you for your call', even those who had called would probably be left wondering who it was supposed to be talking to, given that not everyone made a call. And knowing that those who hadn't made a call were being thanked for something they hadn't done, the rest of the communication would likely ring hollow. Of course, if it were sent only to people who had called, you could get away with it. But only if it arrived personally addressed to each of those individuals.

A better way of dealing with plurals in these circumstances is either not to mention the feedback at all, or to mention it but not say thank you (which doesn't need to sound as rude as some people might imagine), e..g. *'We received 217 calls, which have helped us to refine our original ideas.'*

An alternative is to thank the audience obliquely, by saying something like, *'We received loads of calls, which we're really grateful for, because they've helped us tremendously to refine our ideas.'*

Or you may be able to use the 'if' word to make it flexible – *'We received loads of feedback and, if you took the time to get in touch, thank you.'*

To be honest, I don't consider any of these to be ideal; I see them performing a kind of damage limitation exercise, and I'd be inclined to keep such expressions as brief as possible and move on.

Quantifying the audience with adverbs
Paradoxically, perhaps, you can split the audience's identity if you accentuate the individuality of each reader. I once received a letter from one of my tutors. It was obviously a standard letter, as the salutation read, 'Dear graduate.' It ran for two pages, during which he used the word 'you' half a dozen times. And then, in the closing paragraph, he wrote, *'I will therefore be writing to you individually to canvas your views.'*

By including the word 'individually' he had blown all his previous uses of 'you' – turning them from singular to plural. (The words separately and together have the same effect.) These adverbs imply that the communicator hasn't been addressing the reader individually all along, but has been talking to a group.

As with the inflexible quantifiers ('all of', 'each of' etc) the words 'individually' and 'separately' are unnecessary in this context, and you can just drop them out, e.g. *'I will therefore be writing to you again shortly to canvas your views.'*

Significantly, unlike the other triggers we've looked at, the effect of this trigger seems to be retrospective. The other linguistic triggers can make people wonder if the text is talking to them any longer. They usually feel that it has been talking to them up to the point the trigger kicks in, but that they are no longer sure about it beyond that point. But this fourth trigger gets people questioning whether the text has ever been talking to them. Suddenly, the very meaning of the word 'you' has changed from the singular to the plural and they are left feeling that, even though they may not have realised it when they began reading, it was likely to have been plural right from the start.

Clearly, the way people use (or avoid using) the word 'you' can cause numerous unnecessary problems. The way they use the word 'I', by comparison, can cause only one. But it's a single problem that lifts the lid on a whole can of others, which can crop up with distressing frequency when communications are being approved. It's time to understand what happens when people have words put in their mouths.

Chapter 17
The Ventriloquist's Dummy

'When people say they hear voices in their heads ...
as opposed to where, exactly?
Hearing voices in your legs: that's proper mental.'

Jimmy Carr

In this chapter we will uncover:

➤ why 'Question and Answer' formats are almost always doomed to failure

➤ why any audience's favourable opinions of Q & As are redundant

➤ how to disarm the fifth linguistic trigger.

I have a confession to make. I don't like Question and Answer formats. Actually that's not quite true. I loathe and detest them. I always have done, although for many years I didn't know why. Despite being a gentle soul who was kind to animals, old people and traffic wardens, I seemed unable to read the words 'Your Questions Answered' without wanting to hunt down the person responsible, and set about their more sensitive portions with a meat tenderiser. Or a garlic press.

Okay – that's maybe overstating it a bit, but I know I'm not alone in having an emotional response to Q & A formats which is similar to that induced by the sound of a dentist's drill. Many people I've spoken to over the years have been in hearty agreement with me. 'Condescending' is a word that often springs to their lips. Yet the Question and Answer format has remained a popular way of presenting chunks of business information for as long as I can remember. Popular with communicators at any rate. But does it work? Many communicators like to think so. However, when we consider the potential of 'Q & As' to push an audience into the detached observer position, we might be wise to call their efficacy into question. And see what answers emerge when we do. (Even if your business doesn't use Question & Answer formats, I believe you'll find this discussion worth following, as it has profound implications for the writing, editing and approval processes.)

I think it would be as well to start with a real example, so at the risk of having you feeling that I'm talking to someone else, I'm going to give you a short Question and Answer section to read. It's quite possible that at some point during this example, you may start to wonder whether or not it's talking to you. It's also possible that you may do nothing of the kind, and feel you're in the audience all the way through. There is no right or wrong reaction to this exercise; just have an open mind, and go with whatever happens.

Your Questions Answered

The fifth linguistic trigger kicks in when people misuse the 'communicator' position. At present, its implications may not be entirely clear to you, so it wouldn't be surprising if you had some questions about it:

Q *'What if I don't understand the concepts you're covering?'*
A Explanations will be given in full to cover all aspects of this detached observer trigger.

Q *'How can I be sure that you'll cover all of my questions?'*
A The discussion in this book has come from many years' experience of working with dozens of companies across a wide range of industries.

Q *'Will I be able to easily convince other people to stop using Question and Answer formats?'*
A Some people are strongly wedded to this format, but there are many convincing arguments which suggest that it may not be effective.

So, was it talking to you all the way through or not? Like I said, there's no right or wrong response to this exercise. And it's quite okay if you currently feel it was talking to you and then decide to change your mind later on (some people don't change, but many do). We'll dissect it shortly. But first, let's consider why Q & A formats are so popular.

Many communicators cite two main reasons for liking Questions and Answers. Firstly, they say that it means they can raise issues which the audience might not have thought of. And secondly, they can break the information up into nice little bite-sized chunks. Frankly, I've never understood either of these arguments. After all, if they can raise these issues by writing Questions and Answers then clearly they're capable of writing about these issues. The format itself is immaterial. Similarly, these communicators are evidently capable of producing bite-sized chunks of information. They don't need to head up each chunk with a question. But then again, why shouldn't they? What's the problem with the question and answer format?

Although Questions & Answers may be popular (even with some audiences) my studies have shown them to be probably the most ineffective writing format ever devised, as they can trip over at least one, and often as many as three detached observer triggers. (Indeed, I've known one question and answer section to include six of the seven triggers – a mighty impressive feat.) There are several reasons why. Some of these may sound like I'm pushing it a bit. However, the following observations come not only from my own reactions, but from years of talking with people in many different types of business about their attitudes to Questions and Answers. Much of the following is implicit and subliminal, but no less troublesome for all that.

The Heading

Sometimes, Question and Answer sections are headed up as follows: 'Your questions answered'. This very heading is presupposing the audience's attitude or situation. For a start, it suggests that everyone in the audience even has questions (and many may not). Furthermore, hardly ever is there a situation in which Q & As are used, when everyone in a business audience has been asked what their questions are (it can happen, but it's rare). And each reader knows that their opinions have not been canvassed, and they also know that the communicators are not psychic. It's hardly surprising, then, if they feel that the communication is talking only to those who have been asked what their questions are (which is often no one).

Questions and non-answers

Looking critically at numerous question and answer communications over the years, it's become clear that the questions often aren't being answered at all. Closed questions in particular, to which the answer is either Yes or No, often have answers which run on for several sentences (and end up saying neither yes nor no). Although this may again seem like I'm nit-picking, this issue is more insidiously damaging than it might appear.

It suggests that the communicators either don't know the answer to the question, aren't prepared to give it or, perhaps even more worryingly, they don't know what the question is they're trying to answer. And this leads on to a second problem, which is that many people have told me they skim the questions to see if there are any that they consider relevant. And they don't read the answers to the irrelevant ones. So, if the answer isn't answering the question, it may contain vital information which the audience needs, but which they don't read because they feel that the question doesn't concern them.

Missing questions

Anyone who uses question and answer formats is also making themselves a hostage to fortune. Often, a member of the audience will have a question and will lose faith in communicators who don't include that question and its answer. Not unnaturally, many people will feel that their question is an obvious one (it occurred to them after all). And if it doesn't appear, it can raise in their minds the question of 'Why haven't they asked this question?' Very often, it seems, audiences can be just as affected by the missing questions and answers as they are by those that are included. Missing questions can damage the credibility of communicators, making them appear incompetent, out of touch, or somehow a bit shifty ('what are they trying to hide by not addressing my question?'). Or they can make some members of the audience feel foolish, and believe that perhaps the question hasn't been asked because everyone else already knows the answer. And again, not wishing to appear foolish, they don't dare to ask the question themselves. So the communicators remain unaware of some real questions that the audience do indeed have.

All of these problems serve to undermine the effectiveness of questions and answers. But they can pale into insignificance when compared to the potentially destructive power of the following phenomenon.

The mind's voice

The term 'your mind's eye' is a common one, and I've never known anyone to look bemused when it comes up in conversation. It was one of the many terms coined by William Shakespeare which have now made their way into common parlance. Interestingly, though, the Bard never mentioned your mind's mouth or your mind's ear, even though they are every bit as real as your mind's eye, and every bit as important for your overall mental functioning – especially when it comes to reading.

A few people have learned to speed read, but if you're like most people you'll probably read in the way you were taught as a child: sounding the words out in your mind. (And even if you can speed read, you can probably also read by sounding out the words. There is a tiny percentage of people who use a visual process for reading. As I don't know how to use it myself, I can't comment on it. If you are among this tiny group, the following may seem strange to you, but it really is how almost everyone reads. You may want to ask other people to do the exercise that follows and tell you how they respond.) When you are reading, it is, in effect, your mind's mouth saying the words to your mind's ear. And this means that there's a mind's voice that you can hear. Over the years, I've learned that the mind's voice can have a profound effect on how people respond to what they're reading.

Choices of voices

Most importantly, the mind's voice is not just one voice. In fact, whenever you read something, you're likely to have a choice of up to three different types of mind's voice. Some people's range of mind's voices is more extensive than others, but over 97% of people seem to have access to all three types:

1. your own voice
2. the voice of the communicator (although naturally enough, you'll be able to use this voice only if you know who's written the communication you're reading, and what that person's voice sounds like)
3. an imaginary voice (any voice which is neither your own, nor that of the communicator – it could be the voice of someone else you know, a famous person's voice, the imagined voice of some unknown person, or even a mechanical or synthesised voice).

Now that I've brought this to your attention, you might like to spend a moment to become aware of which mind's voice you've been using while reading this book. Is it your own voice, or an imaginary one? Neither is wrong and neither is right. No mind's voice is any better than any other; they're just different. And whichever voice you're using, it's the one that's naturally right for you – in this moment and with this communication. And it's also quite natural for your mind's voice to change when you read another communication – which has been written by a different person, or arrives through a different medium or on a different day, or is about a different subject. And it's equally natural for it not to change. There is no right or wrong about this.

Some people think that the idea of using voices other than their own is nonsense. When they read business communications, they find that they use their own voice all the time. If you feel that you belong to this group, you might like to consider what happens when you read a novel, which has different characters in it. What happens when those characters are having a conversation? Do they all have the same voice then, or are you able to notice that they have different voices? Almost everyone is able to appreciate that they can, in fact, experience different mind's voices. (There is a small percentage of people who even hear different characters all using the same voice. And if you are in this tiny special group, I would again suggest that you share this chapter with other people and let them tell you how they respond. If my experience is anything to go by, their responses may startle you.)

Implications for Q & As

The reason for raising this whole issue is that some interesting things may happen to your mind's voice (albeit unconsciously so far) when you're presented with a bunch of Q & As to read. Now that you're aware of which mind's voice you're using to read this text, we can return to that earlier set of Questions & Answers, and notice how they affect your mind's voice, and your ability to stay in the audience. In doing this, you may find it useful to listen out for four pieces of information:

1. Does the voice change?
2. If so, when does it do so (it may well happen more than once)
3. If it changes, which voice does it change into (it may change from your own into an imaginary voice, from an imaginary voice to your own, or from one imaginary voice to another)
4. Most importantly, who is the new voice now talking to?

It may seem like I'm labouring the point, but I must stress there are no right or wrong ways of responding to this exercise. Whatever you do is right for you.

Your Questions Answered

The fifth linguistic trigger kicks in when people misuse the 'communicator' position. At present, its implications may not be entirely clear to you, so it wouldn't be surprising if you had some questions about it:

Q *'What if I don't understand the concepts you're covering?'*
A Explanations will be given in full to cover all aspects of this detached observer trigger.

Q *'How can I be sure that you'll cover all of my questions?'*
A The discussion in this book has come from many years' experience of working with dozens of companies across a wide range of industries.

Q *'Will I be able to easily convince other people to stop using Question and Answer formats?'*
A Some people are strongly wedded to this format, but there are many convincing arguments which suggest that it may not be effective.

Over the years I've found that there are dozens of different ways in which people can respond to this exercise. (You might find it interesting to show it to your friends or colleagues and discover what their reactions are.) Some people feel it is talking to them all the way through. Others feel that it starts talking to someone else, or to itself, or even to a group of people. For many people it flips back and forth talking to different people. And of those who feel it's talking to a group, some feel they are inside that group, while others feel they are outside it. One person I worked with even had it in stereo, with two different voices talking at once. If you had the same voice going all the way through, it's likely (although by no means certain) that it was your own voice. If this was the case for you, you might like to go through it again, this time starting with an imaginary voice, and notice what happens.

Interestingly, when I first expose people to this exercise, an average of about 70% of them believe that it is talking to them all the way through. By the time they've understood their mind's voices and been through it a second time, that number has dropped to about 15%. I believe this tells us a number of things:

1. That the detached observer position can be somewhat difficult to spot at times; people can be pushed out of the audience without even realising it's happening.
2. This in turn means that an audience's opinion about whether or not they like the Question & Answer format is somewhat redundant. Popular or not, Q & As simply don't work with most people – and by and large the audience aren't even consciously aware of this.
3. Even if some members of the audience do have some of their questions contained in the Q & A section, they often find that they wouldn't phrase those questions in the way in which they appear in the text. The words on the page (or the screen) simply don't fit comfortably into their mind's mouth. And, rather than feeling that it is he or she (the reader) who is saying the question (which is what's intended, given that it's written in the first person) it feels like it must be being said by someone else – someone who would phrase a question in that way. As such, the question is being asked by someone other than the reader.

    The only way they can stay in the audience, then, is by becoming the person who is being asked the question. Otherwise, people must feel that the question is being addressed to someone else. In this second scenario, the individual reader has no choice but to become a detached observer. And if the reader becomes the person who's being asked the question, what happens when the question comes to an end? They may find themselves, bizarrely enough, in the position of the communicator – answering the question to this unknown person. Or they may feel that the author is taking over again to answer the question. This means that the reader again has two options – the first is to pop back into the audience (albeit that audience is now probably a group containing the mysterious person who asked the question. And we've already seen the kind of problems that can arise when a communication starts talking to a group.) The other alternative is to feel that the communicator is now carrying on a conversation directly with the unknown person who asked the question.

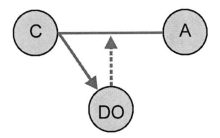

In fact this is the more likely scenario, as it would make more sense for the communicator to address their answer to whoever asked the question. And again, the reader has nowhere else to go but the detached observer position. (See what I mean about Questions and Answers being about as ineffective as it's possible to be?)

4. The mind's voice may be influencing people's reactions to what they read in other circumstances as well – most notably in the writing, editing and approval processes. We'll be looking at this in the next chapter, as soon as we've tidied up the problems created by Questions & Answers.

Disarming this trigger

Putting words into readers' mouths forces them to phrase things in a way which they probably wouldn't normally do. Rather than use Questions and Answers, therefore, you can use statements and explanations instead.

Rather than saying, *'What if I don't understand ...?'*
You can simply write, *'What to do if you don't understand ...'*

Using 'You' questions

At this point in a training session, some people ask me if it's okay to use questions if you use the second person rather than the first, e.g. *'What if you don't understand...?'*

This would seem to get around the problem. But it can be treacherous. We'll be discussing in the next chapter how the mind's voice can influence not only how people read, but also how they write: how they can often unconsciously copy the corporate style they see (or, more truthfully, hear) around them. When you change your style, therefore, you're likely to influence others to follow suit. And when you've got your head around these triggers, you may want to enshrine your understanding in some writing standards (whether the business currently has any or not). Either way, many people may copy what you're doing – without necessarily having your understanding of why you're doing it. And the question and answer format can often backfire with the second person – if you're not careful. For the sake of simplicity, I've presented this as the 'I' trigger, because that's how it usually works. But you can also put words in people's mouths with 'you'.

To illustrate this, here's an example from one of my clients' communications about a new IT security system:

'We're upgrading the system to ensure better customer security.'

'Are you saying that the system hasn't been secure up to now?'

'No, the system has always been secure, but as hackers become more sophisticated, we have to stay one step ahead of them.'

'Will you have to switch off any of the security systems during the upgrade?'

And so on. Even by using 'you', then, you won't be able to guarantee that people won't end up putting words in each other's mouths. Statements and explanations can achieve the same ends as questions and answers, but without being contrived and without the dangers. There are, however, three notable exceptions.

1. Within a Statement and Explanation format, it's sometimes useful to include an occasional impersonal question, if a statement would sound tortuous, e.g. **not** *'What a unit trust is,'* **but** *'What is a unit trust?'*

   Here, the question is impersonal (i.e. doesn't include I, you, they, etc) so it won't involve readers personally. And provided you use them sparingly, such questions won't push people into the detached observer position.

2. If you are writing a letter to answer someone's questions, you may wish to use their questions as headings, to enable them to find their way around the letter easily.

3. You can quote genuine readers' questions. I have seen this work in businesses which have an active policy of eliciting and publicly responding to staff questions, but the authors follow two strict guidelines to ensure that it does so. They always quote the questions exactly, and they always either name the person who asked the question, or state that it has been posed anonymously. Having at least some of the questioners

named gives the whole thing that ring of authenticity which enables people to know where they stand all the time vis a vis the audience and detached observer position. Most importantly, by quoting real questions which have been posed by people whose names can be recognised by their colleagues, it means that readers know they are meant to be detached observers. They adopt that position intentionally, rather than being pushed into it involuntarily.

Using questions within the text itself can sometimes be quite a handy technique. It can often be powerful to make an indirect statement and then ask a direct question, e.g. *'Everyone who values their quality of life needs to ensure they'll have enough money to retire on. Are you sure you will have?'*

All these are useful for keeping the audience in the position you want. But what about those who are approving the communication before the audience gets to see it? There are numerous ways in which the mind's voice can impact upon the writing, editing and approving of communications, so much so that they warrant a chapter of their own.

Chapter 18

Implications and Applications of the Mind's Voice

'You sometimes find that a thing, which seemed quite thingish inside you, feels quite different when it gets outside and has other people looking at it.'

A A Milne

In this chapter we will uncover:

➤ why people want to change text unnecessarily during the approval process, and how to stop them

➤ why someone can have an unnecessary crisis of confidence in what they've written, and how to solve it

➤ how people can even use the mind's voice to improve their grammar.

In many businesses, high profile communications have to be approved by a number of people. And it's not unusual for some approval group members to want to alter the text without really changing the substance of what's being said. Often people correct each other's corrections, or get into debates about 'the right way to write it'. All of this can affect the business in three ways.

1. These people (who are often senior and very expensive by the hour) are almost certainly wasting their own and each other's time unnecessarily.
2. Deadlines can be missed completely, or pushed to the limit (requiring some people to put in absurd hours just to get the communications out, and often pushing up the print costs as well).
3. The finished article is often of a sub-standard quality, partly because of the rush, and partly because of unsatisfactory compromises on the content and phraseology.

But perhaps we can now understand where at least some of the problems lie – and sort them out.

Positions and voices

Having a clear, robust brief can help enormously. And as we discussed in chapter 15, people in approval groups can adopt any one of the three positions: *Communicator, Audience* or *Detached Observer* when they are approving communications. This means that different people in the same approval group could be reading the same communication from different positions. And this in turn is likely to influence how they feel about what's being said. We now also need to consider which mind's voice they will be using. Again, it could be any one of the three, which can have a huge impact on how comfortable or otherwise they feel about the words in front of them. (The issue of one person's words not fitting comfortably in another person's mind's mouth is particularly pertinent here.)

I was once invited to work with a large financial institution, where there was a particular writer (let's call him John) whom I was asked to help. He kept getting his text rejected by the directors whenever it went up for approval. His boss felt that the problem was there because John was, as he put it, 'a very stylised writer'. Having read samples of John's work, I was baffled; his writing was excellent.

But when I came to explain the different mind's voices in a group workshop, John was incredulous. He only ever heard his own voice (or so he claimed). But when I asked him about what happened when he read conversations in novels, he realised that the characters did, indeed, have different voices. With business communications, though, it was only ever his own voice he heard – whether he was reading or (and this was the important bit) writing. Immediately, I saw what could be causing the problem.

One of the impacts of the mind's voice on a person's writing is the way it can affect how they express themselves, both in terms of their vocabulary and their syntax. John was using his own voice when he was writing, so the lexicon and sentence structures he employed were idiosyncratic to himself. And as it turned out, the directors were using their own voices, not John's, when (dis)approving the stuff he had written. The result was that John's words didn't fit comfortably in their mind's mouths. They didn't consciously know why it was they didn't like what they were reading; they just couldn't get comfortable with it. I suggested to him that when he was writing in future, he simply change the mind's voice he was using – from his own, to the voice of the individual director for whom he was writing. I knew from my own experience that doing this made me spontaneously start using the vocabulary and syntax of the person whose voice I had adopted. Although John was somewhat sceptical about doing so, he agreed to give it a go. And hey presto, problem solved. Instantly.

I've shared John's story with people I've subsequently worked with, many of whom have tried it for themselves (after being made aware of the following caveats) and found that it works like magic. Before charging ahead with this approach yourself, though, it's worth bearing in mind the following points.

Firstly, there are three different positions from which people can approve a communication, three different types of mind's voice they can use, and, within the third type, an infinite number of imaginary voices to choose from. Not surprisingly, then, whether you have to write things for other people to approve, or you have to approve text that others have written, or both, this whole process has plenty of potential to come unstuck.

An emotional powerhouse

I've looked into (well, listened into) the mind's voice for several years now, and taught many people about it and got their feedback on the subject. And there's something that has become abundantly clear: it's powerful. I don't think words can do justice to the awesome ability of the mind's voice to impact on people's emotions. With my own eyes I have witnessed someone's emotional response to a piece of writing change from a desire to beat its author to a pulp, to an urge to race over and hug her with gratitude, simply by changing the voice with which they were reading that author's words. Indeed, I've seen it happen with several people on different occasions. Tears of frustration and anger have changed to looks of relief, even enthusiasm – in moments. Admittedly, these responses happened in non-business contexts, and the subject matter in question was personal and highly emotive. No matter; it wasn't the words on the page that had changed – only the mind's voices that the readers were using to absorb those words.

Yet despite its breathtaking emotional influence, the mind's voice seems to have remained virtually unobserved by business communicators ever since businesses started communicating. It silently (or perhaps not so silently as it turns out) sways people's emotional responses to the words in front of them, pretty much from the moment they stop reading out loud (usually at about the age of five or six). So, even though it may not have been something you've given much thought to before, and may not be discussed by business communicators, the mind's voice's influence can be spectacular.

Indeed, when it comes to the process of getting business communications approved, I think it's appropriate to misquote a famous advertising slogan: Never underestimate the power of the mind's voice. Its ability to undermine any approval process is enormous. Yet virtually all it takes to disable it potentially destructive influence is a realisation of the very fact that it's there. Here, then, are the key issues to be aware of (or at least those I've unearthed so far).

What's going on in the approval process

Just as you can't see into anyone else's mind's eye, so too is it impossible to hear anyone else's mind's voice. More important still, you can't feel the impact that it has on their emotions. It's therefore impossible for anyone to know:

- in what way someone else will be emotionally affected by their mind's voice, or
- how strong that emotional impact will be.

I therefore can't hope to tell you how anyone will react to what they're reading, only how they could do so, given what I've discovered through a decade's research into the mind's voice's capabilities.

Perhaps most significantly, the voice you use when you're writing will tend to drive the vocabulary and syntax you use. To a certain extent it may even influence the angle you take on the content. Once you've written the text, your choice of vocabulary and syntax is likely to influence – to one degree or another – the mind's voice of each reader.

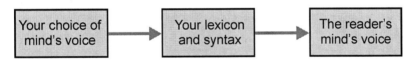

When it comes to the approval process, one of the simplest ways of dealing with the problems caused by the mind's voice is simply to make approval group members aware of how these problems work. Appendix G summarises both this chapter and chapter 8 (which introduced the concept of the three 'positions'). If you share it with approval group members, they'll then be able to understand how they may be making themselves feel unnecessarily uncomfortable with what they're reading. And from there, they may be able to reach an agreement about the position from which they'll read draft text, and maybe settle on a mind's voice they're all comfortable with. If they can't agree upon a particular position, at least they'll know that they can change positions if they're not comfortable with the words in front of them.

To return for a moment to the story of John's problems with getting Directors to approve his text, the solution I offered him (i.e. using the mind's voice of the communication owner) was one which frequently works when writing something for one individual to approve. It is often effective, but not always. I realised fairly quickly that, if I'm the author, communication owners may be just as likely to use my voice as they are to use their own. But if they do so, my writing could sound to them like I was trying to do a bad impersonation of them. And because this would be happening unconsciously, they might feel that I was taking the micky. Even if they weren't personally affronted, they could certainly feel uncomfortable with the text, and not know why.

This is one of the reasons why some people will ask an author to go back and do it again (giving them that oh so helpful input, *'I don't know what I want, but I'll know it's what I want when I see it'*). But if you've got a robust brief, based on the principles we discussed earlier, this statement will be a dead give-away, confirming that owners aren't consciously aware of their mind's voice. In truth, they won't know it's what they want when they see it at all. They'll know it's what they want when they hear it – and when they feel it. This unawareness of the mind's voice can also result in many senior managers believing that they can't trust anyone else to write things for them, and end up completely rewriting the text they're given – almost every time.

Speeding up approvals

Bearing all this in mind, I would recommend the two approaches. The first you can use if you have to write something for one other person; the second if you yourself are approving text that's been written by someone else.

1. You could save yourself a lot of time and frustration by finding out which voice the owner uses when approving text – before you start writing. If it's their own, or yours, then you can know which voice to use yourself when writing. If it's an imaginary voice, then it may be the voice of someone you both know (e.g. the CEO or the Managing Director) or it may not. If it is someone you know, then again you can use that voice. If not, you're somewhat stymied as far as using that voice is concerned, but at least the owner will know that he or she can change their voice if they're finding your words uncomfortable. Indeed, it's better still if you can agree up front on a voice you'll both use.

2. If you have to approve someone else's text, you can advise them of which voice to use when they're writing. But beware; there's so much more to the mind's mouth and ear than meets the eye.

It's also possible that some people may use a variety of voices for different communications, or even for the same communication. Just making them aware of their mind's voice should help you to work through the problems that much more quickly. But just what is it that they need to be aware of?

Why authors can sometimes lack confidence

I've come across numerous writers, whose abilities have ranged from the perfectly competent to the truly gifted, and who have suffered from a quite unwarranted lack of confidence. Interestingly, their uncertainty about their ability is often inconsistent. Sometimes they're quite happy to bash words out, and on other occasions they can spend ages staring at a blank or half-filled page or screen, chewing their knuckles, and with a look in their eyes that's part despair, part panic. Their confidence meltdown often seems to come upon them when they have to write for a particular person (or for a particular group). And talking this through with them, it appears that their mind's voice is at least partly responsible. Many problems come from inadequate briefing, so taking care of the brief will do much to make this problem fall away. But even when the brief is clear and robust, problems can still linger. (This is going to get a little involved – not because I like making things difficult, but because we humans are so gloriously sophisticated – so please bear with me.)

The following applies to you or anyone else who's writing text. It also applies to anyone who's approving the text that someone else has written. For the sake of illustration, I want you to imagine that a male senior manager has asked you to write a communication for him. Imagine that you've written the text and that he's sitting down to approve it.

As he does so, he can have any one of the three types of voice going on in his mind. And he can also position himself as the communicator of what's being said, or imagine himself as a member of the audience, or read it as a detached observer. This means that there's a total of nine combinations of voice and position available to him (as shown overleaf).

And, most importantly, these nine options were also available to you when you were writing the communication. So already there's potential for a mismatch between your choice of voice and position and that of the owner. And maybe you've always known this – albeit unconsciously. I've never shared the idea of the positions and mind's voices with any professional

1 His own voice *Communication position*	**2** His own voice *Audience position*	**3** His own voice *Detached observer position*
4 The author's voice (i.e. yours) *Communication position*	**5** The author's voice (i.e. yours) *Audience position*	**6** The author's voice (i.e. yours) *Detached observer position*
7 An imaginary voice *Communication position*	**8** An imaginary voice *Audience position*	**9** An imaginary voice *Detached observer position*

writer who hasn't immediately realised that they kind of knew it all along – they just hadn't been consciously aware of it. It's therefore quite natural for any business writer to feel that they need to try second-guessing how the owner is going to read the text. And it would appear that many business writers find it easier to second-guess some owners than others – hence a sporadic nose-dive in confidence.

Tonality and the mind's eye

Getting this second-guess right is more involved still, because the nine combinations of position and voice represent only the tip of the iceberg. There are two more ingredients for us to add in, which can increase the potential mismatches exponentially. First of all, there's the rather niggling fact that even when you've settled on one particular voice, you haven't. One person's voice isn't just one voice; it can be their smiley voice, or their corporate voice, or their sarcastic voice, or it can be angry, obsequious, comforting, namby pamby, condescending, excited and so on. Importantly, it is often this tonality that can be affected by an author's choice of vocabulary and syntax.

Therefore, even if some members of an approval group only have access to their own voice, that single voice can still be influenced by the author's. And on top of that, there's another part of our mental processing which we've been ignoring up to now, but is about to take centre stage and really muck things up for us good and proper. I'm referring to the mind's eye. Or more specifically, to the fact that someone can not only hear a particular voice, but can picture someone else using it.

For example, let's imagine you were writing something for, say, a senior female IT manager. Let's also imagine that you've chosen to write the text using her voice. Let's further imagine that you've now written the text (or even part of it) and are reading it back to yourself. Could you, in your mind's eye, see a cynical member of staff doing a sarcastic impersonation of the IT manager, while reading out those words to their colleagues? How much confidence are you going to be able to maintain in those words? Or, to take another scenario, what if you were to see the IT manager reading your words out to her own colleagues, while doing a sarcastic impersonation of your voice?

Some people might say that the above scenario would be little short of paranoia but, as we shall be discussing shortly, it can often be rather useful. Indeed, my research has shown that one reason why people (however senior or junior) can produce awful communications, is that they don't check out their text with different voices or from different positions. The mind's voice can be an extremely valuable tool when you are consciously aware of what you're doing with it. However, being only semi-conscious of it does explain why, if you or one of your colleagues gets stuck, it may well be because you just don't know how to make a communication sound right for either the person who's commissioned it or an imaginary member of your audience. And the communication owner (or any member of an approval group) can lack confidence in what you've written for exactly the same reason.

Just as you might be able to imagine your words being read with derision by someone else, so too can the person you're writing for. If the communication is going out in the IT manager's name, she could easily imagine the text that you've written being read in her own voice by members of the audience – including, perhaps, the CEO, or the MD. And what if she were to hear the CEO using her voice in a namby pamby tone? Might her gut reaction to your words be somewhat different to that which she'd have if she were hearing your voice, and without picturing anyone else using it? You bet it could.

To recap, then, both you and the communication owner have each got:

1. three positions you can adopt
2. three types of mind's voice to choose from, of which the imaginary voice has an infinite number of possibilities
3. an almost infinite number of tonalities for each of those voices, and
4. the possibility of those voices being used by an almost infinite number of imaginary people.

Furthermore, much of this complex intellectual processing is going on unconsciously. And if neither you nor the owner are consciously aware of which position, voice, tonality (and possible imaginary user of that voice) the owner is running, it's certainly possible that there could be problems. You may never experience any such problems yourself. But perhaps you can appreciate how someone else could. Worse still, these problems can remain unresolved through many communications, damaging both parties' confidence in your ability. (And, remember, all this mismatching can go on when just one person is doing the approval. Multiply it by however many members there are in an approval group, and perhaps the odd niggle here and there is only to be expected.)

How to handle the problems

There are several things you can do to speed up the approval process. Much will depend on how you do things already. In essence, the changes fall into two categories:

1. changing procedures.
2. improving people's skills.

In many organisations, approval problems arise because people are arguing not only about how things are written, but also what needs to be talked about in the first place. It seems crazy that senior people can often allow themselves to get into a situation whereby it's only when a draft communication has already been produced that they start debating what it needs to say. This not only wastes your time, it's hardly a productive use of theirs, as the arguments about the purpose, content and style of the communication can all get muddled together, and leave people talking at crossed purposes in what is often already a sensitive and complex debate. How much better to separate out the debates, and take care of each of them at a time that makes the most logical sense from a production perspective.

The purpose and content debate

If you use the outcome-focused briefing process (summarised in Appendix A) you can generate a written brief which gives the communication a clear purpose (i.e. the outcome it's setting out to produce) and proposes the content that is causally linked back to that outcome.

If you can put in place a process which has any reader group signing off the brief before you start drafting the communication, that debate will not need to arise again later. Furthermore, having the debate up front should enable it to happen more quickly, not only because it's been separated from any debates about style, but also because the outcome should be nice and concrete for them, and the proposed content clearly demonstrating how it will produce that outcome.

The style debate

Given the numerous permutations that the mind's mouth, ear and eye can create, I'm not going to give you a pat solution to this problem, because no such solution exists. However, if you or any colleagues are experiencing a recurring problem with either drafting communications or getting them approved, you could benefit from talking through with the owner in question what he or she is doing when approving the text in question. Simply having that information in your mind as you sit down to write will make it that much easier for the words to flow. As a writer myself, I would want to find out of a communication owner:

1. Which mind's voice are you using?
2. Who do you perceive is using that voice (is it yourself, or do you see someone else using that voice – e.g. the CEO, Managing Director, etc – or even me?)
3. From which position is that person reading this text (Communicator, Audience or Detached Observer?)

This is quite a bit of information to gather and it may not always be the same with different communications, or even within the same one. But you don't have to get it all at once. I always begin by getting people to understand the three positions and three voices. Once they're comfortable with that, it's then quite easy to introduce the other elements. The important thing is to open up the dialogue, because then at least you'll be able to track when and how difficulties arise in the future. But many people have a problem with opening the dialogue in the first place. They tell me that they feel a bit awkward – even foolish – about asking their Managing Director, or CEO, what voices are going on in their heads. But I've found that the more senior a person is in an organisation, the more interested they often seem to be in understanding how they (and other people) function. I've never asked anyone about their mind's voices and been sent away with a metaphorical flea in my physical ear. In fact, they're usually grateful for the insight. After all, you may well be doing them a huge favour: saving them from having to do numerous re-approvals, while saving yourself the necessity of multiple redrafts.

The important point to recognise here is that the voice you use when writing or editing will tend to drive how you say what you say. And this in turn will affect at least the tonality of the voice that the reader hears. To make it as easy as possible to open up a dialogue with people about their mind's voices, I've summarised the concept in Appendix G. I produced this summary for my clients to use with their bosses, and they've found it extremely useful for breaking the ice.

And it's not only in the approval process that you can benefit from a conscious awareness of your mind's voice. It can spawn benefits in a number of other ways.

The Eileen test

When I was a corporate writer, one of the Marketing Directors would sometimes ask me to produce communications for the Marketing Division, or for the business as a whole. And I always used to give my text the Eileen test. Eileen worked in one of the marketing teams and was one of those ace people with an exceptionally fast mind, a razor sharp wit, and a forceful personality. She had the ability to sway the opinion of many people in the Marketing Division and was always quick to attack corporate bullshit. But equally, if she felt that something made sense she would be just as quick to get behind it.

It was only after I had left the company to set up on my own that I realised how I'd been using Eileen's voice whenever I was editing these internal marketing communications. I would tend to write the text in the voice of the Director who'd asked for it. But I'd then use Eileen's voice to edit it. I would imagine her standing by one of the coffee machines, reading the communication aloud to a group of others, and using her most sarcastic voice. And the test was this: would Eileen keep up with the sarcastic voice, or could I make it change? Usually there would be a telling phrase or two in the text, to which the sarcastic tone was building (and usually resulting immediately afterwards with the communication being thrown aside with a plaintive cry of 'Well honestly!'). If I couldn't stop this happening in my mind's eye, I knew the communication was in trouble. But if I could put together an argument that had Eileen dropping the sarcasm and saying, 'You know, this actually makes sense,' then I knew I was onto a pretty sure thing. And, if this sounds fanciful, I can only say that I was never proved wrong when those communications hit people's desks or screens. And it's a technique I've shared with numerous clients who've also found that it works for them. So who's your Eileen?

I'm not suggesting you do a wholesale re-draft after you've gone to all the trouble of identifying the owner's voice, position and so on. This is an editing technique which can simply help you to spot the chinks in your communication's armour. Indeed, once you've got your first draft down, you can then swap between the two voices – the one to do the checking, and the other to do the redrafting.

Challenges with speed-readers

Having said all this about the impact of the mind's voice, it's worth remembering that some people may speed-read the text they're approving. Speed reading is a visual process rather than an auditory one, so such people are likely not to be using any voice at all (I've also found this to be true of some people who have dyslexia). In these circumstances, the mind's voice can't cause any problems, but you may find that people who speed read get pedantic about the sequencing of particular groups of words. This happened to me with an important corporate communication project. The marketing director kept insisting that 'for the sake of consistency' a particular phrase was repeated in the same way throughout the communication – even though the different contexts in which it appeared meant that it wouldn't always make the best sense. For two and a half days we batted this communication back and forth. During all that time he was unable to see why I was so adamant about how the thing should be worded, and I was equally amazed that someone as intelligent as him should be asking me to write gibberish. Eventually, at lunchtime on the third day, I remembered he'd been taught to speed-read, and confronted him with the following idea:

'I think the problem, Jerry, is that you're spending too much time looking at the words.'

'How do you mean? We've got to get this right. Of course I'm spending time looking at the words.'

'Looking at them, yes. That's the problem. You're not listening to them – to what they're saying.'

I suggested that he try reading it again, but this time doing so by sounding out the words in his head, as he had originally been taught to do at school. And when he heard the words in his mind, rather than just seeing them on the page, he suddenly got it, and realised why I'd insisted on writing the piece as I had. Perverse though it may seem, then, it appears that speed-reading can sometimes slow down the approval process. Of course this won't always be the case, but it's another little nugget that's worth bearing in mind.

Customising standard text

The mind's voice is also useful for coaching people who have to customise standard letters. Customer service centres often have standard letters or paragraphs which staff can tailor to meet individual customer situations.

Often, when these staff drop in a sentence or two of their own, it's only too clear that this has been done. The lexicon and syntax of the inserted wording just doesn't match that of the standard text. It's almost possible to imagine you can see the sticky tape where the standard text ends and the customised text has been stuck in.

The problem usually arises because individual members of staff are taking over the communicator role, without taking over the communicator's voice. For example, readers might be using imaginary corporate or customer voices when reading through standard text. And when they begin inserting their own words, each person starts using his or her own voice. They might also be reading the standard text from the audience position and then, when they start inserting their own words, shift into the communicator position.

If you can make readers aware of the voices and positions they are using when reading the standard text, and then encourage them to hold those voices and positions when they add in their own text, you'll almost certainly find the lexicon and syntax flowing much more seamlessly.

I once worked with an Internet Banking team, who spent all day responding by e-mail to customer queries. And they were suffering from exactly this problem: a huge mismatch between the style and fluency of the standard text, and the tailored text they were inserting themselves. Not surprisingly, we discovered that many of them were reading the standard text in one voice, (usually, an imaginary 'corporate' voice) and then switching to their own individual voices when inserting their personalised text. By getting them to use the same voice throughout, they were able to smooth over the join so that it was no longer noticeable. Perhaps even more remarkable was the fact that they were able to start coming up with a second library of tailored inserts, which they would share with each other. And before long, no one could identify any longer who had originated the customised copy. It all just fitted together seamlessly.

Some people have told me they think this is a bit too sophisticated an idea to share with their customer service staff – some of whom have enough trouble just putting together a coherent sentence. But conscious awareness of the mind's voice can help such people improve their writing skills. Of the Internet Banking advisers I worked with, some were excellent writers while others struggled with basic grammar and syntax. With those whose written English was weak, I advised them to re-read their text before sending it, using their manager's voice rather than their own. (The manager was a very good writer.) When they did this, they started making observations such as: 'Oh my god, she'd never say that'. By using their manager's voice they were instantly able to identify and correct errors in their own grammar, syntax and punctuation they'd previously been unable to spot. I've replicated this with other groups, with the same results. By simply using the mind's voice of a good writer, then, it seems that almost anyone can become their own grammar teacher – instantly – without any need for textbooks. Children can often do this too.

The urban myth about capital letters

That many people are ignorant of the complexities of the mind's voice has perhaps never been more publicly demonstrated than by those people – somewhere in Microsoftland – who once managed to get the following unnecessary idea included in Microsoft Outlook's email tips:

'If you write in capitals, people will think you are SHOUTING.'

Really? Which people? And says who? Of course, having planted this idea in people's minds, it's possible that many will take on this belief, and indeed hear someone shouting when they read text written in capitals in an email. But quite possibly, it's only because the misguided souls at Microsoft have told them that they should. After all, that you should hear someone shouting is no more necessary or inevitable than that you should hear them LAUGHING, or WHISPERING, or SINGING, or USING A GERMAN ACCENT.

Unfortunately, though, the Microsoft technicians managed to get such ubiquitous prominence for their message that they had, in effect, hijacked the munificent flexibility of the mind's voice with their own limited belief. May I suggest that, if you've been suckered by this idea, you reclaim your right to use your mind's voice as you choose? And you might like to disabuse others of this thoroughly useless urban myth too. I'm not in any way suggesting that it's wrong to hear someone shouting when you read capital letters; simply that it's not inevitable. It's a matter of choice, not necessity.

The mind's voice as a self-editing aid

Another implication of the mind's voice concerns the way you use it when editing communications you own yourself. Whichever mind's voice you use when writing, you'll probably find that there's a natural flow to the way the words fall onto the page in front of you. Often, it can almost be as if you're taking dictation. Because of this, much of the meaning that you read into what you're writing can come from the inflexions and natural pauses that you hear in your mind's ear as you're doing so. But another reader, who's using a different voice, is unlikely to have the benefit of hearing that text in the same way you did when you were writing it.

It's therefore always a good idea to consciously choose a different mind's voice when you're editing your own text. This makes it easier to spot where your meaning may not be as clear as you might first have thought. The intention here is not to engage in a wholesale redraft, merely to check the punctuation and syntax to ensure that the sense is as you'd meant it. And just as with the Eileen test, you can then swap between the two voices to do your checking and redrafting.

Putting words together for someone else's physical voice

Finally, there can be times when communications are being passed on by word of mouth, such as happens during conferences or team briefings. It's worth bearing in mind that each person who's doing the briefing will usually be reading through the text before they deliver it. Interestingly, there are often people (and it seems usually to be the same people each time) who want to change the words – possibly changing the intended meaning in the process – because they don't feel comfortable expressing ideas in the way they're written in the team brief. Again you may be able to help them feel more comfortable about the words in front of them, by making them aware of how their minds' voices are creating their discomfort. But each of them is still going to have to stand up and use their own voice to say those words.

This problem may be something we just have to live with. Or is it? Maybe there's a way of writing communications for onward oral transmission that can address even this seemingly intractable problem. In fact, there is, and it's part of the solution to the sixth and final linguistic trigger, which we'll be coming on to next.

Chapter 19

To We or Not To We?
That Is the Question

'Up and down, up and down. I shall lead them up and down.'
Robin Goodfellow

In this chapter we will uncover:

➤ the different types of meaning that 'we' can have in business communications

➤ why people can sometimes drop out of the audience when those meanings change, and sometimes not

---

You could say I've saved the best 'til last. Or if not the best, then certainly the most intriguing. Arguably the final Detached Observer Trigger has the potential to create more problems than all the other triggers put together: 'We' is a whole lot more trouble than 'you' and 'I'.

Just imagine that Mother Nature, in her infinite diversity, had produced a creature with the qualities of both a chameleon and a mynah bird. Not only would it be able to all but disappear from view, it would also be able to mimic other creatures, fooling you into looking for something else entirely. Such an animal would be elusive to say the least, and tracking it down would be far too time consuming and frustrating for most people to bother with. It would be a fascinating creature, no doubt, but ultimately more trouble than it's worth. Probably best left to the television naturalists. But supposing we needed this animal in order to run our businesses? Supposing we had no choice but to track it down and tame it. This, in a nutshell, is the challenge presented by the word 'We'.

The English language has the most extensive vocabulary on earth – by far. The Oxford English Dictionary gives definitions and derivations for over 640,000 words, of which about 200,000 are in common usage today. Of these 200,000, 'We' is the 36th most frequently used*. Clearly it is crucial

*Source: *The Adventure of English* by Melvyn Bragg

to our ability to communicate; it has no realistic alternative; we simply can't get by without 'we'. But when you begin to understand the merry havoc it can wreak on your communications, you'll probably wish we could.

Together with its partners in crime, 'us' and 'our', the word 'we' is the ultimate linguistic chameleon, able to subtly change its meaning at the drop of a hat. It can crop up throughout a communication, seemingly a picture of innocent cooperation. Then, as you catch sight of it again, its meaning can give you the slyest of winks, a cheery wave of its hand, and say, 'I'm outta here'. And you can be left staring at it in a state of bemusement, wondering 'Where did its meaning just go?'

Three chapters ago, we looked at how the pronoun 'you' is able to act as a detached observer trigger when it changes between its two meanings – the singular and the plural. How much more problematic, then, will be a pronoun that has not two, but seventeen potential meanings? And how much trickier to grapple with if it can chop and change between some of those meanings with impunity, and then blow the audience away when it slips into other guises? Worse still, what if you were to decide upon a specific meaning for 'we', and stick rigorously to that meaning throughout a communication, only to find that this seemingly bewitched pronoun had hijacked itself, and taken on another meaning entirely? And what if it also possessed a mynah-bird-ability to mimic characteristics of every one of the other linguistic triggers?

Make no mistake; this pronoun is trouble. With a capital 'W'. Especially with internal communications.

With marketing, recruitment, customer or shareholder communications, it's reasonably easy to set up a clear relationship between the communicator and audience. In effect, it works out as follows: 'We' (the business) are talking to 'you' (the customer/recruit/investor) about 'this' (the proposition). With internal communications, though, it's much easier to get things muddled, because the relationship can often be like this: 'We' (the business) are talking to 'you' (the business) about 'us' (the business). It means that people receiving internal communications are more likely to become confused about who 'we' are supposed to be.

The following example, from a Board of Directors to their company's employees, illustrates this trigger in action. You may find it useful to imagine yourself as an employee of this business and, as you read, notice if and when you feel yourself becoming a detached observer:

Our markets, and the legislative environment in which we have to operate, mean it's important for us to communicate well. For some time, we have been concerned about the quality of our business's communications, so we recently brought in an external consultant to help us. Together, we have been conducting a review of our communications, and have decided that we really need to improve our standards. If you have any ideas about how we may do so, please let us know.

This is a short example (which is analysed in Appendix C) and, conceivably, you could go through it and tidy it up in a trice. But many internal communications are much longer, and become increasingly entangled as they go. Clearly we need to understand what this pronoun is up to.

How the trigger works

'We' has several characteristics that cause it to act as a detached observer trigger, the most significant of which is its ability to change its meaning:

- Sometimes a communication can come from a single individual, who will usually (but not necessarily always) use the word 'we' when he or she wants to talk about him or herself and the audience together.

   'It's been such a long time since we've seen each other; we really should get together.'
   We = me (the communicator) + you (the audience)

- Some business communications come not from individuals, but from groups. Even though it's usually one individual within the group that's doing the writing, the whole group is taking responsibility for what's being said. In such circumstances, the author will often use the word 'we' to identify that communicator group.

   'We've just completed our market research, and these are our conclusions.'
   We = us (the communicators)

- What happens, then, when a communication coming from a group wants to talk about themselves and the audience together? Again, they have to use the word 'we'.

   'Our customers need to know they can trust us, and we cannot afford to take that trust for granted.'
   We = us (the communicators) + you (the audience)

Therefore the word 'we' has the potential to include the audience sometimes, and exclude them at other times. When the communicator or audience is more than one person, and 'we' means the communicator(s) and audience together, the communicator and audience positions lose their distinct identities and become fused together. It's no longer a case of 'I' (the author) am talking to 'you' (the reader/listener/viewer). Instead, 'I' am talking among 'us' (the communicator and audience together).

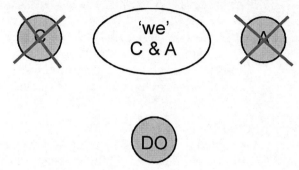

From this moment on, readers (or listeners or viewers) will need to continue feeling that they are part of 'us' in order to feel 'this is talking to me'. And if the meaning of 'we' then contracts, to mean only the communicator group, it will have excluded the audience who, without a distinct position of their own to return to, will have nowhere else to go but the detached observer position.

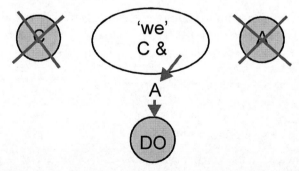

Importantly, after that point even using the word 'you' is unlikely to work any more, because it may then seem to apply only to people who are still part of 'we'. (Whether or not it does so usually depends on the individual reader's mind's voice which, as the author, you can only partially influence.)

In summary then, 'we' ('us' and 'our') will act as detached observer triggers if they ever mean 'the communicator and audience together' and then contract to exclude the audience.

Expanding 'we'

What happens, though, when things work the other way round? Surely if 'we' starts off excluding the audience and then expands to include it, there shouldn't be a problem, should there? Unfortunately it's not that simple. Although communicators may intend their meaning of 'we' to expand, they will usually fail to take the audience with them. The trouble is that, like 'you', 'we' can work retrospectively when it changes its meaning. Here's the opening line of a memo from a finance manager to all budget holders:

As of the next financial New Year, we will be introducing a new financial management system...

Before going any further, who's introducing the system? To whom does that opening 'we' refer? It's the finance team, is it not? So what are the implications of this new system? Here's how the memo continued:

...which means there will be new procedures for us all to follow. It's important that we all understand and follow these new procedures, as the mistakes we have been making with the old system have been costing us dearly.

If a reader had, quite understandably taken the initial 'we' to mean 'the finance department', who needs to be following the new procedures? The author's intention was to expand the meaning of 'we' at this point, so that it included the audience. But it's impossible to guarantee that people will read it that way. They would know that they had not been involved in introducing the new system, so it would be perfectly reasonable – indeed, logical – to take it that the new procedures were for all those people who had introduced it. This is how the 'we' trigger can make it seem as if the communicator group are simply talking among themselves. In some circumstances, the opening meaning of 'we' can be ambiguous. In this example, for instance, it's possible to take 'we' to mean 'the business'. And a reader could go back and re-think their original understanding of 'we'. The trouble is, you can't guarantee that everyone will do this. And often this option isn't even available. For example, the finance manager could have started his communication by saying:

We have been discussing the accounting procedures, and have decided that there need to be some changes. Therefore, as of the next financial New Year, we will be introducing a new financial management system.

There's no way that any reader outside the finance department could include themselves in that first meaning of 'we', given that they hadn't been involved in the discussions.

A clumsy solution

One way of ensuring that you don't confuse the meaning of 'we' is to state explicitly what you mean by it every time, e.g. *'As a business we need to be competitive, which means that, as a department we need to be as efficient as we can.'*

Such an approach can work in small doses, but it can rapidly become both cumbersome to write and excruciating to read. Many people, when going through four or five such sentences back to back, discover a capacity for whimpering they didn't know they possessed. Although this style of writing may not push people into the detached observer position, it's still likely to fail, because many readers will give up on it altogether. We therefore need a more elegant solution, one which can keep the meaning of 'we' consistent throughout any given communication, regardless of who's writing it, who's receiving it, or what it's about. This task may look simple enough but, as ever, there are numerous pitfalls waiting to ensnare the unwary.

The chameleon 'we'

'We', 'us' and 'our' are able to change their meanings so readily because they can be made up of numerous combinations of the following six parties:

1. the author (or the individual in whose name the author is writing)
2. a communicator group (which may or may not be being represented by a named individual)
3. the individual reader/listener/viewer
4. other members of the audience (when the communication is going to more than one person)
5. an identified 3rd party (which may be an individual or a group)
6. other people (who are outside any communicator, audience or 3rd party group).

These six parties can combine to provide 'we' with 17 potential meanings, which fall broadly into three categories:

1. 'We' includes the communicator and excludes the audience
2. 'We' includes both the communicator and the audience
3. 'We' excludes the communicator and includes the audience

And with the first two categories, when 'we' includes the communicator, there's another ingredient that can come into play – the different types of communicator from whom a business communication can arrive:

(a) **a single individual** – a communication comes from single individual when that person is writing on his or her own behalf, and no one else's
(b) **an individual representing a group** – a communication comes from an

individual representing a group when an individual is named as the communicator, but that individual is writing on behalf of a group of others, e.g. a note from the CEO on behalf of the Board, or a letter from a customer service representative on behalf of the company
(c) **a group** – a communication comes from a group when no individual is named as the communicator.

For our purposes, the only difference between a communication that comes from a group, and one from a group represented by an individual, is that when there's a named author involved, the option exists to use the 'I' pronoun on occasions, in place of 'we'. Otherwise, they're the same. And it allows us to categorise the 17 meanings of 'we' as follows:

	Communication coming from:	
'We'	Single individual	Group
• includes communicator and excludes audience	Category 1	Category 3
• includes communicator and audience	Category 2	Category 4
• excludes communicator and includes audience	Category 5	

If you want to avoid turning your audience into Detached Observers, you need to ensure that 'we' only ever uses one of these categories throughout a given communication. The moment it moves from one category to another, it's pretty much guaranteed to lose the audience. Appendix C lists all 17 meanings of 'we', and gives examples of what they look and sound like.

Sleight of meaning
That 'we' has so many meanings it can adopt is bad enough. But it's about to get worse. There are many magicians who perform tricks with curtains: e.g. they put a rabbit into a cage, pull down a curtain in front of it, and when they lift it up again the rabbit has changed into a brace of doves. 'We' can perform just such a trick linguistically. It simply uses the possessive pronoun 'our' as its curtain. With internal communications, the expression 'our company' could mean 'the company to which the author and individual audience member belong'. Equally, it could mean 'the company to which the author and communicator group belong'. 'Our' can therefore give the illusion that the meaning of 'we' has changed when it hasn't, or (and this is where it can really muck things up for you) that the meaning hasn't changed when it has. But how does it do this? Very sneakily indeed.

'Our' has all the 17 potential meanings of 'we', but each of those meanings can imply numerous different sorts of relationship. For the sake of simplicity, I'll suggest just three types: Directive, Associative and Dependent. For example:

Directive: that which belongs to us – e.g. this is our house

      those for whom we have responsibility – e.g. they are our children

Associative: that to which we belong – e.g. our golf club

      those with whom we associate – e.g. our friends

Dependent: those on whom we rely – e.g. our doctor

      those who are responsible to us – e.g. our MP

Some relationships can carry more than one quality at the same time: e.g. he is our MP. You could argue that, because we voted for him, 'we are responsible for him being our MP' (Directive) and, now that he's got that job, 'he is responsible to us' (Dependent).

These different types of relationship can create problems when you're writing, because it's so easy to slip unconsciously between two different meanings as you write or read back your own text. This, for example, is a phrase that appeared in a note from an IT manager:

It's vital to ensure that our systems are able to cope with growing business demands...

Out of context it may seem innocuous enough. But the expression 'our systems' can mean:

> 'the systems of the business to which we (the communicator group and audience) belong' (associative) or
> 'the systems for which we (the communicator group) are responsible' (directive)

This ability of 'our' to carry two meanings at once, one of which includes the audience, and the other of which doesn't, is where 'we' can do an almost imperceptible quick-change act:

We're[1] operating in an increasingly competitive market place and, to keep ahead of the competition, we[2] need to be able to give customers the service they expect 24/7.

It's vital to ensure that our systems are able to cope with growing business demand, and we[3] have been concerned for some time that much of the old hardware is getting close to its limits. We[4] have therefore been negotiating with an external supplier to upgrade the servers and some of the cabling over the next six months.

The first two meanings of 'we' are clearly meant to relate to the company (i.e. the communicator group and audience together). But meanings 3 and 4 are just as clearly referring only to the IT department; the audience is excluded (either that, or – with meaning 3 – it's having its attitude presupposed). If you read only as far as the word 'demand', the meanings of both 'we' and 'our' can be taken to be the same: including both communicator and audience. However, if you start reading from the beginning of the fourth line, 'It's vital …' through to the end, 'our' can also agree with meanings 4 & 5 of 'we'. 'We' has arrived at the word 'our' including the audience, and left it excluding the audience. This c an happen in almost any circumstance. And unless you know what you're looking for, and are extremely vigilant, you won't be able to see the join – because it's hidden behind the curtain of 'our'.

Taming the chameleon/mynah bird/trouble-maker-in-chief

You need to identify the meanings of 'we', 'us' and 'our' every time they appear, and establish whether they include the audience, exclude the audience or could be doing both. It's then a matter of using your skill and judgement to keep the meanings consistent throughout the communication. I've provided in Appendix C a summary of techniques you can use to do this, together with worked examples and other guidance notes. This trigger is complex, and can throw up all manner of unexpected challenges, some of which may be more relevant to you than others. I've therefore organised Appendix C into seven parts to make it easy to use:

Part 1: The seventeen meanings of 'we'

Many people, when they learn of this trigger, start to panic unnecessarily when they see the meaning of 'we' changing, even when its doing so won't have caused problems (i.e. it hasn't suddenly included or excluded the audience). I've therefore listed all 17 potential meanings of 'we', arranged in their appropriate categories, to help you allay anyone's concerns about whether or not a particular change in meaning is going to cause problems.

Part 2: Linguistic techniques for disarming the trigger

There are various linguistic techniques you'll need to bring into play to disarm this trigger in different circumstances. Some are too reliant on the way you use other techniques to make sense in their own right, but follow on naturally when you use any of the principal techniques. By an odd coincidence, there happen to be 17 principal techniques, all of which are illustrated in this part of the appendix.

Part 3: Using the 'sub-group' technique successfully

Of the 17 principal techniques, the 'sub-group' technique is one you're likely to need more often than most, and it's also somewhat delicate; used incorrectly, it can exaggerate rather than disarm the trigger. It therefore has its own section to show how you can and can't use it.

Part 4: The mynah bird 'we'

This section shows how 'we' can mimic the effects of the other linguistic triggers, and what to watch out for so you don't get suckered.

Part 5: Worked examples

To help you understand how the techniques work in situ, there's a whole bunch of worked examples you can study. Each one shows the trigger in action, and then gives three rewrites, illustrating how the techniques enable 'we' to include just the communicator, communicator and audience, or just the audience.

Part 6: 'The company', singular or plural?

This is a debate that can crop up from time to time. Some people feel very strongly on the subject. In this part of the appendix you'll find a cogent argument that's based not on subjective prejudices, but on the rules of what's grammatically permissible and an understanding of what the 'we' trigger can and can't do.

Part 7: Using 'we' to mean 'only the audience'

Team briefs and other cascade processes are notoriously unreliable in many businesses, partly because some managers lack the confidence to present to an audience, and partly because some managers go off message. Although it may seem strange, using 'we' to mean 'only the audience' can go a long way to removing these problems. This section explains why.

One way or another, Appendix C will enable you to keep the meaning of 'we' clean, tidy and under control in any circumstances. So, if the question is: 'To We or not to We?' I believe you've now got your answer.

Chapter 20

Going for Gold

'This very remarkable man, commends a most practical plan
You can do what you want, if you don't think you can't,
So don't think you can't, think you can.'

Charles Inge

In this chapter we will uncover:

➤ how best to use this book from now on, to help you exploit the potential of your communication goldmine.

Within these pages, we've looked at the potential value of your business's communication goldmine, and various obstructions that have kept much of that potential hidden or inaccessible in the past. In doing so we've also discussed, in principle, how it's possible to start bringing that value to the surface. So what now? You could just put this book down, say, 'Well that was nice,' and carry on as before. Or you might want to make some changes.

I'd therefore like to close this discussion with a look at how you might be able to make practical use of these ideas. Getting to grips with this stuff is rather like learning to drive a car. You may have been able to get the theory from a book, but you have to take it out on the road in order to really learn it. And as with learning to drive, you may feel at times that you'll never get it. Remember what it was like when you were trying to get the hang of changing gear? You may have been asking yourself, 'How can anyone think of all these things at once?' But over time, all those separate operations started to collapse together into a single one, which took up that much less 'thinking space' and freed you up to focus on other things. I would therefore advise against trying to put everything in this book into practice at once – particularly when it comes to the briefing process. I'd suggest instead going back to specific chapters and practising those insights one or two at a time, until they start to become at least semi-automatic, before moving on. People who've taken this approach have been surprised to discover within a few months just how much they're doing on autopilot.

However, what you do next depends, at least in part, on where you want to get to. I hope I've demonstrated how your role as a business communicator has the potential to add considerably more to your business's success than you, or the top tiers of management, might previously have realised. There's unquestionably a case for getting senior people to attach more importance to business communication: to recognise the influence it can wield, the value it can add and the commercial worth of those who are expert at it – if you want. The question is, do you want to do so? Many people, for example, get into full-time business communication roles because they find it interesting and have a talent for writing or design. But they don't necessarily have any high career ambitions. Indeed, in many businesses, the internal communication department can be a kind of career siding, in that it doesn't logically lead anywhere in particular. And that suits many people just fine – even if, from a purely hard-nosed business perspective, it's not in the best interests of the organisation.

So, what if you want to go further? What if you want to exploit more of your own potential and that of business communication in general. What if you wanted to get a new briefing process introduced, or a new approval process, or both? Doing so would inevitably affect the working practices of all the business's communication owners – even those at the very top – and any departments (e.g. legal, product development etc) who get involved in approving communications. And if you wanted to go the whole hog, getting a Strategic Communication Policy set up in your business, and revolutionising the very business planning process itself, you're looking at some big league stuff, involving HR, the finance division and the board of directors. And it's not the kind of thing your CEO and HR Director are likely to be up for just because you happen to have read this book.

I've therefore produced a series of appendices which you can use to start moving things forward. They are of two types: Quick Fix and Developmental. The Quick Fix appendices are reference documents that you can come back to time and again to help you in your day to day work. The developmental appendices are designed to help you make more radical changes, should you so wish, by enabling you to take these ideas to other parts of your business. They are as follows:

Quick Fix Appendices

A **Outcome-focused briefing** (a summary of all the briefing questions for you to refer to any time you sit down with a communication owner, or to produce a communication of your own)

B **Nice to know outcomes** (which explains how to intermingle the 'outcome' and 'content' questions when taking a brief for a 'nice to know' communication. It includes worked examples)

C **Taming the linguistic chameleon** (a full explanation of how the final trigger works, together with a summary of the linguistic techniques you can use to disarm it, and a number of worked examples)

D **The linguistic minefield simulator** (so you can practise disarming detached observer triggers before you have to do it in live situations)

E **Editing and heading principles** (which, given the purpose of business communication, go beyond those that work for recreational communications)

Developmental Appendices

F **Valuing the goldmine** (how to build a commercial case for introducing changes to the way your business communicates – which you can work on by yourself, or perhaps with people from finance)

G **Speeding up the approval process** (a summary of the problems caused by the mind's voice in the approval process, and a recommended way forward, which you can give to communication owners and approval group members to read)

The Quick Fix Appendices should enable you to change your own working practices so that you can add more value with greater ease. And if this book has got you all juiced up to go for it, the Developmental Appendices, together with the ideas we've already covered, are designed to help you start getting your business's centres of influence thinking along the same lines as yourself.

I hope you can use the ideas in this book to take your career to whatever level you want, because I'm passionate about what excellent communicating can do: its potential for bringing about extraordinary, positive change in your business. I'm passionate about it because I know that everyone can benefit from such changes; you, the communication owners, their audiences – everyone. You simply can't improve the way you communicate without improving the quality of business life for all the people whom your communications touch.

Developing your personal influence and career potential could in many ways be an extremely altruistic move – as the exponential benefits you can generate must always far outweigh any that you can get personally – even though those personal rewards could be considerable.

They may say all that glisters is not gold. But plenty of it is. And if you make these ideas work for you and your business, you'll more than earn your share of the riches that are lying in the communication goldmine as we speak, just waiting for you to start bringing them to the surface, now.

Good luck.

The practical value of the goldmine briefing process

Added Value for the business:

Lower communication costs

This process has the potential to reduce all ten of the communication costs. Naturally, identifying clear outcomes up front should help to stop the goalposts moving, and stop ill-thought through projects being started which would then have to be ditched later. This in turn can stop deadlines being pushed, making it easier to get better deals on any printing. It should also reduce the amount of time both you and communication owners need to spend on redrafts and re-approvals. And as unnecessary communications won't be happening, and those that are happening will be going only to people who need them, and will say only what's useful to those people, it will save on audience time too.

The last four costs result from communications failing. Identifying audiences accurately will reduce the possibility of the audience tripping out into the detached observer position and will inevitably reduce these costs, as will ensuring the communication is as user-friendly as possible. Valid outcomes, accurately defined audiences, causally linked content and user-friendly media will increase the likelihood of communication success, thereby reducing the need for repeat communications.

Less communication overload

A lot of the unnecessary back-covering costs occur because people don't know how to identify real audiences or intentional detached observers effectively. Helping communication owners to do so will therefore help to stop communications going to people who don't need them.

Reduced 'silo thinking'

Having a robust method for identifying Intentional Detached Observers will make it much less likely that the left hand no longer knows what the right hand is up to. And it will also mean that when people are included in a copies list, they know that it's worth their while to read what they've been sent, rather than dumping it unread in their waste basket.

Better staff morale

Many people feel disenfranchised when either left out of certain communication loops, or continually on the receiving communications that feel like they're talking to someone else. Ensuring that employees are getting everything they need, and always feel that what they're reading or listening to is talking to them will, over time, help them to feel more involved and more valued.

Better productivity

Reducing the communication overload will not only free up more of the audience's time, it will also reduce their stress levels. And by ensuring that everyone who needs to be informed is either included in an audience or an Intentional Detached Observer group, they're more likely to have the information they need to do their jobs right.

Added Value for the communication owners:
More time and confidence

Many communication owners lack confidence in their briefing skills. And they don't like the briefing process as a result, and therefore devote as little time to it as they can get away with. By making it easier for them to articulate what they want – in concrete terms, they can have more confidence in their decision-making, and may be inclined to devote more time to giving you a decent briefing. And by reducing the number of iterations, they need to go through, they'll save time as well.

Added value for yourself and your colleagues:
More time

Identifying outcomes clearly up front will stop some unnecessary communications from even being started, and having a clear brief will make it quicker and easier for you or your colleagues to produce the work, which should also need fewer amendments. All this should save you loads of time. And by ensuring that nothing unnecessary is being said, it may also save some of the audience's time as well.

Enhanced reputation

Your ability to help communication owners understand the concepts of the detached observer position, its triggers, its commercial and logistical implications, and how to deal with it all successfully, is likely not only to increase your personal reputation, but also your influence and your recognised commercial value.

More confidence and job fulfilment

Ultimately, this process will let you know you're getting it right. You'll be able to work quicker and smarter, safe in the knowledge that you are adding value, big time, to the communication owners and the business as a whole.

The practical value of the goldmine strategic approach

Added value for the business:
Business and project plan translation

● Distinguishing three different types of strategic communication plan will make it easier for everyone to know that they're talking about the same thing.

- With a project or business plan already couched in terms of audience behaviours, the communication strategy will be much simpler to put together and agree. And by making all business and project plans more concrete, everyone's thinking will be clearer and more precise.
- It may also make it easier to spot more opportunities in advance.
- This in turn will breed less confusion, more confidence, and quicker, better decision making as a result
- The business should be producing only the communications it needs, and doing so in the most cost-efficient manner, in terms of people's time (both producers and audience) and any print and distribution costs.

Communication ownership skills
- Ensuring that they have the necessary skills to do the job, with the necessary procedures to follow, management support, performance measures and reward and recognition set-up, will not only prompt and enable them to do the job effectively, but give them the confidence that they can and are doing so.
- And with the right level of communication expertise where it's needed, all planning and management activities will be more effective and less wasteful.

Perpetual, outcome-focused feedback
- Having an all-year-round feedback system, firmly focused on the SMARTIED principle, will enable the business to spot and seize more opportunities, and allow the business leaders to know instantly why something's not working, or not going to work, and what's needed to fix it.
- An effective feedback system should also engender a greater sense of ownership among staff, improving morale and productivity, and fewer sick days and lower staff turnover.

Value measurement
- By measuring the inputs and linking them to the unnecessary costs you'll be able to prove your value, while helping ensure that the incentive to improve communication performance is built into the business's management systems.

Added Value for you:
Enhanced reputation and influence
- Translating the business plan into communication planning language will demonstrate the pivotal nature of your role, in unambiguous terms to the business leaders.

- Measuring the inputs and linking them to falls in communication costs will enable you to prove your commercial value.
- Developing the understanding of communication owners will enable them to appreciate your skills, and the value you add.

Less stress, more time and more job fulfilment
- This whole strategic approach should enable you to be more proactive and less reactive.
- Your position in the business cannot help but be enhanced

The practical value of disarming the triggers

Added value for the business:
More income and lower costs
- Spotting and disarming these triggers will keep audiences switched on, and cut out many feelings of disenfranchisement that may currently exist. In turn, this is likely to lead to a more motivated workforce.
- With customer communications, it's likely to reduce the number of queries that come in from customers who say they don't understand their last letter, but have in fact been switched off by it – thus saving customer service time.
- Although these triggers don't often appear in any sales and marketing communications, removing any that do can increase response rates and help boost more sales.
- The business can audit its communications to identify how often these triggers occur, and review this regularly as one of its communication input measures.

Reducing communication overload
- When communications get through to the audience, they don't have to be repeated, which will reduce the volume and make it easier for people to devote more time to what they get. This in turn is likely to reduce communication failure still further.

Added value for communication owners:
More confidence
- Knowing how and why communications have failed in the past, and what's being done to solve the problems, can give them more confidence in the whole process – making it easier for them to take it 'seriously enough' – especially when combined with a robust briefing process.
- With internal communications, they'll also be able to feel more confident in front of their audiences, knowing that their written messages are getting through.

- Simply having the vocabulary with which to discuss their concerns about how something is phrased will help them to understand their own gut reactions in a way not available to them before.

More time

- Because you can explain people's gut reactions to them, they can have more confidence in your ability to do the job, and will be more likely to trust you, rather than wanting to tinker all the time.
- Understanding the mind's voice, and its impact on their gut reactions, can speed up approvals dramatically, releasing lots of time for both communication owners and approval group members.

Added value for you:
More confidence

Although these triggers result in subjective gut reactions, they are objectively provable. As such, you will be in a position to explain to communication owners how and why text needs to be written one way and not another – in terms they won't be able to argue with.

More time

Being able to remove subjective arguments from communication approvals will enable you to get your job done that much more quickly.

Enhanced reputation

Because these triggers have not been published until now, you will be able to introduce this new and hugely valuable idea to your business, and establish a reputation for yourself as a centre of unrivalled excellence. Truly you will be the expert when it comes to making sure business communications are well written – even compared to those who can spot split infinitives at a hundred paces.

More fulfilment

If you start reviewing your business's communications, you may be surprised at how many contain these triggers – and how much of an impact your newly acquired skills can have. Knowing the extent to which you're cleaning up your business's communication act may give you the biggest buzz of all.

Skim Read Version

Chapter 1
Being taken seriously ... enough

- You're worth a potential fortune to the people who pay you. (Page 11)

- Most senior managers will say they take communication, and communication professionals, seriously. Fewer are prepared to say they take them seriously enough (in part because they fear that communication could simply be a bottomless pit). (Page 12)

- You or your colleagues may therefore experience more stress and frustration than necessary, and have huge potential to be adding more value, getting more recognition and influence, and to have more confidence, job fulfilment and career potential. (Page 12)

- If the business is ever to exploit its communication goldmine, you may need more resource and authority, but there's often a vicious circle that stops you getting it. This may be something we need to tackle. (Page 13)

- Accountants can know they've got their sums right; Graphic Designers can know their design skills are 'special'. Neither of these comfort zones has been as readily available to account managers or copywriters – even those trained as journalists – until now. (Page 15)

Chapter 2
The end of the bottomless pit

- We can't realistically expect to improve our ability to fulfil the purpose of business communication without first establishing what that purpose is. (Page 18)

- If people claim 'Of course I'm a good communicator, I've been communicating all my life' they're talking about social communicating, not commercial communicating. (Page 19)

- Commercial communicating, whether to internal or external audiences, has a different purpose and rules from social or academic communicating.

• Splitting the commercial communication cake into 'need to know' and 'nice to know' is only one way of doing it; you can also distinguish between business communications and recreational communications. (Page 20)

• Recreational communications produce profit by simply getting people to engage in the process of being communicated with. Business communications don't. (Page 22)

• Business communication plays a pivotal role. On one side are people taking strategic decisions about the business results they want. On the other are the people whose behaviours turn those strategic decisions into business reality. (Page 23)

• Business communication has a functional purpose, behind which is an ultimate purpose (Page 24)
    - The functional purpose of business communication is:
      > Directly and/or indirectly
      > to prompt and/or enable people
      > to take and/or avoid actions
      > immediately and/or eventually.

    - The ultimate purpose of business communication is:
      > To help enable the business to fulfil its raison d'etre
      > as effectively as possible, and to develop its ability
      > to do so increasingly.

• Taking you seriously enough is not a bottomless pit; its dimensions are definable and even reducible (Page 24)
    - There can never be any such thing as 'a valuable 'for information only' business communication'. That concept is an oxymoron.

• Journalists are trained to produce recreational communication outcomes, not business ones (Page 25)

Chapter 3

Why you're worth a fortune

- All businesses have to communicate. Business leaders can't choose to not do it at all, only between how badly or how well it's going to be done. (Page 26)

- If money is the lifeblood of your business, then communication is its respiratory system: the more effectively you communicate, the less money has to be pumped through the system to produce the necessary results. (Page 27)

- Just because someone has good communication skills doesn't mean they have the necessary business communication ownership skills. (Page 28)

- Communication ownership skills include the ability to do the following: (Page 28)
  a) identify what needs communicating in the first place
  b) articulate that clearly to you or your colleagues
  c) objectively appraise your work
  d) provide only constructive feedback that's consistent with the original brief.

- Communication owners' skill shortfalls can create a whole raft of unnecessary challenges – any one of which is a clear sign that the business is not communicating effectively, and is sitting on a potential goldmine. (Page 29)
  You or your colleagues are:
  • having to produce communications for people who can't tell you what they want (although they'll know it's what they want when they see it)
  • having to do numerous re-drafts
  • not being given enough time to do the job properly
  • having people re-write the text (often quite badly) or just asking you to produce communications 'wot they've writed themselves'
  • having to spend ages getting communications approved, because so many people want to stick their oars in, and often correct each other's corrections
  • investing loads of time and effort into a project only to have it pulled at the last minute.

People around the business are:
- complaining that they aren't being kept informed
- complaining of communication overload.
- engaging in 'silo- thinking'
- unable to rely on cascade processes.

- These challenges are costing your business dearly, because communicating in business can have up to ten costs. (Page 30)
Necessary costs:
  1. the hard costs of producing them (print, distribution etc)
  2. the soft costs of people's time spent producing them
  3. the cost of the audience's time spent receiving them.
Wasteful production and distribution costs:
  4. ill-defined or moving goalposts
  5. ditching communications
  6. backside covering & ladder climbing.
Communication failure costs:
  7. re-communicating
  8. correcting mistakes
  9. missed opportunities
  10. lost audience good will.

The last seven are unnecessary, and it makes commercial sense to eliminate them.
But when money gets tight, the knee-jerk reaction of many businesses is to cut the communication budget (cost 1) thereby almost certainly increasing exponentially the communication failure costs.

- Reducing these costs can directly or indirectly spawn numerous upside benefits: (Page 36)
  a) increasing customer loyalty
  b) increasing income and stronger cash base
  c) better quality recruits
  d) a happier workforce and working environment
  e) greater staff productivity
  f) greater staff creativity
  g) less sick leave
  h) greater staff loyalty (meaning better skills retention)
  i) a more nimble business
  j) increased competitive edge
  k) more confident investors and a growing share price.

- **Appendix F will help you to start working out some of these costs so you can bring them to the attention of the key decision makers.**

Chapter 4

Briefing process ground rules

- **A robust, precise brief is the cornerstone of an effective communication. However:**
  - **communication owners are not taught to develop briefing skills, and**
  - **because the purpose of business communication is different from that of its recreational counterpart, so too does the briefing process need to be different. (Page 339)**

- **The 'Outcome Focused Briefing' Sequence (Page 40)**

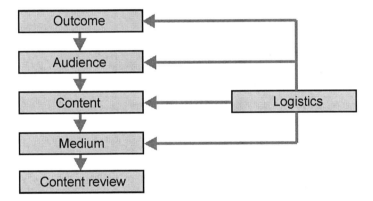

- **What a communication owner really wants is an outcome. But initially they may think they just want to say stuff. We therefore need to start by being clear about what a business communication outcome looks and sounds like. (Page 41)**

Chapter 5

Being clear about business communication outcomes

- When taking a brief, it's not enough to understand what a communication owner means; you need to understand what they mean in the same way that they do. (Page 42)

- You therefore need to be able to recognise how and why your 'meaning' may be different from theirs, and know how to close the gap. (Page 43)

- When coming up with reasons for communicating, people can put their attention on any of these different subjects. (Page 44):

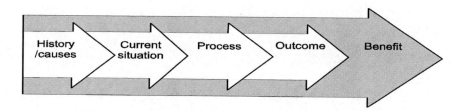

History /causes → Current situation → Process → Outcome → Benefit

- You can't make any process effective if you don't first know what outcome it has to produce.

- Objectives tend to focus people on the process of doing. Outcomes focus on the results of having done. (Page 46)
  - Many people think they're focusing on the outcome when in fact they're focusing on the process.
  - Therefore, never identify communication objectives, always identify communication outcomes.

- A communication process answer will tell you what the communicator is (or intends to be) doing in communicating. A communication outcome answer will tell you what the audience is doing as a result of having been communicated with. (Page 48)

- The key question to start any brief with is:
  - 'What do you want people to be doing (not doing/be able to do) as a result of having read (watched/listened to) this communication?' (Page 50)

- If you're producing a communication to generate feedback, the question is:
  - 'What do you want to be able to do as a result of having received their feedback?' (Page 51)

Chapter 6
How to light up the darkness

- Communication owners can sometimes respond to a question without giving you the answer you need. It's therefore crucial to your success that you can recognise the answers you're getting, and know what to ask next. (Page 52)

- People are motivated to move themselves or others away from discomfort and towards comfort. (Page 53)
  - If someone tells you only what they want to move the audience away from, you also need to find out what they want the audience to move towards instead, otherwise the audience may simply change one undesired behaviour for another that's equally undesired.

- Language can be concrete or abstract. (Page 55)
  - **Concrete language describes direct sensory experience which makes it easier to see in your mind's eye what someone means.**
  - **Abstract language describes intellectual concepts, which makes it difficult or impossible to see in your mind's eye what someone means.**
  - **To be clear in your own mind what a communication owner wants, you need to get them to make their language as concrete as possible.**
  - **You can use the questions What? Which? Who? When? Where? and How? to get someone to make individual abstract words more concrete.**
  - **You can use the following 'catch-all' questions to challenge entire abstract sentences:**
    - **'Can you give me an example of that?'**
    - **'How will you know?'**

- Language can be static or dynamic (Page 59)

- Abstract nouns tend to encourage static impersonal mental images. Changing them into dynamic verbs (i.e those with an 'ing' ending) tends to get people to make mental movies rather than static pictures. It also makes their images more concrete and personal.

- Language can be directive or permissive (Page 60000)
  - The word 'will' is directive, and narrows people's focus of attention. This is useful for stopping people dithering, and getting them to make a decision
  - The word 'could' is permissive, and opens up their focus of attention. This is useful for helping people find more options if they're stuck for ideas.

Chapter 7

How to spot and deal with the phantoms

- There are seven phantoms that a communication owner could come out with when asked for an outcome. They are as follows:

1. **A process answer (Page 62):**
   E.g.   *'We want to make sure people know about X'*
   Problem: The 'making sure' is being done by the communicator.
   Cause: It'll usually happen when the owner hasn't really heard the question.
   Response: *'What do you want them to do as a result of knowing?'*

2. **A benefit answer (Page 63)**
   E.g.   *'As a result of having read this press ad, they'll be buying our kitchens.'*
   Problem: 'Buying our kitchens' is the result of a whole series of communications, and could never be achieved with just one ad alone.
   Cause: It happens when the owner's thinking has jumped up to a higher 'logical level'.
   Response: *'How will this communication make/enable them to do that?'*

3. **A Subsequent outcome (Page 65)**
   E.g.   *'As a result of having received this invitation, I want them turning up for the team building day.'*

Problem: Although this is an outcome, it's not the most immediate one the owner needs

Reason: The owner's thinking has got ahead of itself.

Response: *'Is this the most immediate thing you need them to be doing?'*

4. No known outcome at all (Page 66)

    E.g.   *'I don't know what I want them to do,'* or *'I don't want them to do anything.'*

    Problem: There's no such thing as a valuable 'for information only' business communication.

    Reasons:
- You've asked the owner what they want the audience to 'do', when the communication is intended only to 'enable' actions.
- The owner has identified only the Current Situation they want to move Away From, and not the Outcome they want to move Towards.

    Response: *'If you don't want them to do anything, what do you want them to be able to do?'*
'What's the benefit of telling them?'
'What would happen if we just didn't tell them?'
(These questions often elicit the next phantom)

5. Intellectual or emotional responses (Page 68)

    E.g.   *'People will know X (believe Y/feel Z/understand A/be aware of B/buy into C/etc.)'* Or *'It's about employee engagement.'*

    Problem: Intellectual and emotional responses are not actions

    Reason: Again, owners are likely to have identified only the current situation they want to move away from, and no outcome to move towards.

    Response: *'What do you want them to (be able to) do as a result of knowing (feeling/believing/engaging in etc) this?'*
'What's the benefit of them knowing (feeling/believing/etc) this?'
'What would happen if they didn't know(feel/believe/etc) this?'

6. Deciding/Agreeing/Sanctioning (Page 69)

    E.g.   *'I want them to agree the new accounting procedures.'*

    Problem: Making decisions, while not merely an intellectual response, still falls short of an action.

Reason: The owners may want an action from their audience,
            but have pulled their own thinking up short. Or they
            either want:
            • to be allowed to do something themselves, or
            • the audience to push other people to act.
Response: *'So what are they going to be doing themselves, or
            getting other people to do, or allowing you to do, as a
            result of having agreed/decided?'*

7. Telling: (Page 70)
   E.g.   *'I want them to tell their staff about the store layout
               changes.'*
   Problem: The apparent audience for this communication are
               really just go-betweens. The ultimate audience are
               those whom these go-betweens will be telling – and
               their actions are still unidentified.
   Reason: The owner's thinking is again stuck in the process.
   Response: *'What do you want their staff to be doing as a result of
               having been told?'*

● You can use outcomes thinking for setting up and running
  meetings, with outcome-focused agendas, and for identifying
  training needs, setting up projects, and even having a valid reason
  for forwarding e-mails. (Page 71)

Chapter 8

Why audiences vanish and how to stop them

● It's common for people to read a communication and to start
  feeling it's talking to someone else. (Page 773)

● People can read communications from any one of three
  'positions': (Page 74)
   a) The <u>communicator</u> (i.e. the one who is saying the words on
      the page)
   b) The <u>audience</u> (the one to whom those words are being said)
   c) A <u>detached observer</u> (someone who is merely
      eavesdropping on a conversation between a communicator
      and a real or imagined audience).
   • When people adopt the detached observer position, they rarely

respond to what they're reading, so the communication fails and incurs some or all of the failure costs.

- There are nine 'triggers' which cause people to trip out of the audience and become detached observers, thus causing the communication to fail. (Page 77)
  - Two of these: <u>jargon</u> and <u>waffle</u>, have long been known about, are matters of subjective judgement, and cause people to switch off consciously.
  - The other seven have only recently been identified. They are objectively measurable and cause people to switch off unconsciously.
  - Six of these unconscious triggers are linguistic and are covered later.
  - Marcoms contain one of these triggers per 14 communications; with customer comms it's one in five, but with internal comms over 40% have at least one trigger, and there will be 11 triggers in every 10 communications.
  - Each trigger will lose between 50-100% of the audience, and most will lose 80%+.

- The triggers have gone unnoticed for so long because: (Page 79)
  - they work unconsciously
  - audiences rarely if ever tell authors when they know they've switched off
  - they often switch off without even realising it
  - the triggers don't affect academic or recreational communications, and the textbooks on how to write English have been compiled by academics or journalists.

- The first unconscious trigger is not linguistic, but is caused by the communication trying to talk to more than one audience. (Page 81)

- Once you have identified the outcome, you can identify your 'Total Potential Audience' with the following question: (Page 82)
  - 'Who do you want to be doing (able to do) the outcome?'
  - Your <u>Total Potential Audience</u> may be made up of a number of 'Real Audiences', because some members of the Total Potential Audience may be starting from a different 'current situation' from others.

- To avoid sending your readers (viewers/listeners) into the

detached observer position, you must produce a separate
communication for each Real Audience. (Page 83)

- Use the following question to start identifying your Real
Audiences. (Page 84)
  - Why aren't they doing it (the outcome) already?
  - If you've now identified distinct groups starting from different
current situations, you need to ask the following for each
group:
    - What are they doing instead?
    - Why would they want to stop doing what they're doing now,
and start doing what you want?

- To ensure the left hand knows what the right hand is doing, you
also have to identify any <u>Intentional Detached Observers</u> that the
communication may require. (Page 86)
  - Who else needs to know what the audience is being told?
  - What do you want them to be able to do as a result of knowing
it?

Chapter 9

How to identify content without leaps of faith

- It's easy for someone to say: 'Start at the beginning, work through
the middle 'til you get to the end, and then stop'. But some
communication owners can make it tricky to find the beginning.
(Page 88)
  - The outcome tells you where to end your story, and the
audience questions tell you about their current situation – thus
providing your starting point
  - We're not working in the recreational environment, which has
two crucial implications for us:
    - the people we're addressing usually haven't volunteered
themselves to be receiving the communication, and,
    - if it's an internal communication, we often can't afford to
have people self-select themselves out of the audience.
  - We need to identify all the reasons why they wouldn't do what
we want (or avoid what we want them to avoid etc) and knock
them over one by one:
    - they don't want to read the communication in the first place

- they don't want to do what you want
- the arguments put forward are incomplete
- they don't want to stop what they're currently doing
- they feel the communicator 'would say that wouldn't they'
- they don't know how to do it
- they couldn't do it even if they wanted to, because of other circumstances.

● Almost all communications need to prompt and enable actions. But whichever of the two is the primary purpose will determine how you need to identify the content. (Page 90)
  - There are up to five areas of content to identify:
    - content to prompt actions
    - content to enable actions
    - verifying the prompting and enabling content
    - presenting a balanced view
    - soliciting feedback

● Verifying the content before writing it will achieve the following: (Page 91):
  - check its validity
  - provide you with more necessary detail
  - speed up approval.

● 'Communication problems' are often nothing to do with communication at all. (Page 92)
  - Communicating often isn't enough to produce the outcomes that the owner wants.
  - Getting people to do/not do/be able to do things often means they need any or all aspects of the SMARTIED principle:
    Skills
    Money
    Authority
    Responsibility
    Time
    Information
    Equipment
    Desire

● The content to prompt actions can be of two types. (Page 93)
  - prompting the audience to move towards the outcome

- prompting them to move away from the current situation
- (the towards/away from dynamic is also true for the enabling content)
- When verifying the content, you'll be reducing any communication owner's leaps of faith, by checking, *'How will saying X cause outcome Y to happen?'*

- You often need to present a balanced view in order to close the credibility gap, and avoid people thinking 'Well they would say that wouldn't they'. (Page 97)

Chapter 10
Making the communication user-friendly

- Communication owners often start their briefing by telling you the medium they want to use. This is, yet again, back-to-front thinking. (Page 98)

- Any communication can have two moments of truth: (Page 101)
  - the moment it arrives with the audience
  - the moment they use it (which may or may not be a different time)
  - the way it needs to be used must drive how it's delivered, rather than the other way around.

- There are eight possible 'timeframes' within which a communication can be used: (Page 101)
  1. Just do it now (an immediate, one-off action) e.g. ring me now to arrange a meeting
  2. Do it now and continue doing it ad infinitum – e.g. obey the new security rules every time you enter or leave the premises
  3. Do it on an ongoing basis from now until a certain date – e.g. use the back entrance of the office until the building work is complete
  4. Just do it, as a one-off, by a certain date – e.g. reply to a seminar invitation
  5. Just do it on a certain date – e.g. turn up for an interview, or a blood donation session
  6. Do it from a certain date and continue doing it from then on – e.g. follow the new accounts procedures as of the beginning of the next financial year

7. Do it between one future date and another future date – e.g make alternative arrangements for feeding yourself in the middle of the day during the second week of December, while the official Christmas lunches are going on in the staff restaurant.
8. Do it at some indeterminable time(s) in the future – e.g. use this telephone directory; follow the fire exit signs etc.

- Some communication owners don't know how people may receive a communication, if it's to be delivered through a third party. (Page 104)
  - In these situations, you need to think 'Screwdrivers'. A screwdriver can be used in many ways other than that for which it was intended. But that doesn't stop it having to be designed to perform a clear function.

- Once you've identified the medium, you may need to review the content to ensure that the audience will know how the communication owner wants them to use it. (Page 109)

Chapter 11
Clarifying the very term: 'communication strategy'

- Even when communication strategies seem to be working well, there may still be ways in which they could be improved. (Page 110)

- Just as no one is likely to argue with the idea of being 'professional', so too are few people likely to disagree with the idea of having a communication strategy. But what is everyone agreeing to? (Page 111)

- The briefing process is limited by the fact that it may never occur to a communication owner to brief you in the first place – hence the need for a proactive communication strategy. (Page 112)
  - However, despite having the same label, communication strategies are rarely the same thing twice

- Senior managers can end up with a false sense of security when they get a 'communication strategy', as they've often had no idea what they've expected that strategy to look or sound like. (Page 113)

- But there is a way of thinking about strategies that can make it easy for everyone to know in advance what they need to look and sound like

- If we go back to the beginning, it's clear that a strategy is itself a communication which, like any other business communication, needs to take an audience from a current situation to an outcome. (Page 114)
  - In terms of current situations, communication strategies tend to be instigated as a result of:
    1. campaigns or other business projects
    2. poor staff survey results
    3. a new broom
    4. a new corporate structure
    5. a new round of business planning.

  These give rise the three types of strategic communication plan: (Page 115)
  - Project strategy (single issue, finite lifespan)
  - Perpetual strategy (multiple issue, indefinite lifespan)
  - Business plan strategy (somewhere between the other two).

Chapter 12
Making strategic communication plans outcome-focused

- Business plans are usually written in corporate speak, rather than the language of communication outcomes, but almost all business results come from the actions of the business's audiences. (Page 117)

- Before putting together a strategic communication plan, therefore, always translate the business plan (or any other plan that's driving the strategy) into 'communication outcome' terminology. (Page 118)
  - This can bring four benefits.
    1. Having the business plan expressed in communication outcome language would make it harder for people to get caught in process-focused thinking when planning communications.
    2. Any project plan or individual communication's outcome will

always be transparently traceable back to the business plan.
3. Each communication could be better and more quickly produced
4. Phrasing the business plan in terms of audience behaviours won't compromise the accountants' ability to do the sums. Indeed the sums are often done first on the basis of audience behaviours before being translated into corporate speak.

- Translation criteria: (Page x119)
  - Make it concrete
  - Make it personal
  - Focus on the end audience
  - Make it dynamic

- With truly strategic communication planning, it's not just the INFORMATION and DESIRE aspects of The SMARTIED principle that involve communication. (Page 122)
  - SKILLS development requires training and coaching
  - MONEY management involves financial reporting
  - AUTHORITY and RESPONSIBILITY are communicated through job descriptions, individual or departmental objectives, organisation charts, policies and procedures
  - These all need to be considered as part of the strategic communication plan.

Chapter 13
Building a strategic communication policy

- If a communication strategy has as its purpose: 'To enable the business to communicate as effectively as possible' that purpose will be focusing on the process, not the outcomes. (Page 124)
  - A more valuable purpose is: 'To enable the business to produce communication outcomes as effectively as possible.'

- Communication strategies should enable you to achieve any or all of the following benefits: (Page 126)
  1. enable you to plan in advance
  2. stop audiences from being swamped with ill-thought-through communications arriving from just about anywhere
  3. save money
  4. ensure that communications that need to happen actually do so

5. ensure that people don't get left out of the communication loop
6. ensure that communication is two-way.
  - But doing so relies on the skills of the communication owners

- Therefore, in addition to any strategic communication plans, your business also needs a strategic communication policy to ensure that people get ownership of communications only when they have adequate training, performance measures and management support. (Page 129)

- Communication ownership is not the same as writing, listening and talking; it involves all three, but is an arcane discipline in its own right. (Page 130)

- Communication owners need to be treated more like budget owners. (Page 132):
  - They get clear procedures to follow.
  - Their performance as a budget owner is monitored.
  - They receive the necessary training and coaching.
  - If they can't cut it, the budget gets taken away from them and/or their upward progression suffers as a result.

- Your business can take a hands-on or hands-off approach to communication ownership, depending on how much authority it wants to invest in communication professionals. (Page 134)

Chapter 14
Using communication as a tool for perpetual, measurable business development

- Thinking about 'two way communication' is process-focused. To be outcome-focused, we need to think in terms of two-way business development. (Page 136)

- The outcome of a strategic communication policy can be: Everyone on the business is communicating, at the best possible time, only whatever and with whomever they need to in order to:
  1. deliver the planned business outcomes and
  2. develop the business's ability to do so increasingly,
  And they're not communicating anything, nor with anyone they don't need to. (Page 137)

- Annual staff surveys are of only limited value because: (Page 137)
  - The business environment is changing too fast for annual surveys to be of much more than superficial value
  - When providing qualitative feedback, people tend to focus on what's most prominent now, rather than on what's most important year-on-year.
  - These surveys often follow the same agenda each year, regardless of whether it's relevant, which can mean throwing good information after bad.
  - They're unreliable, because they're not self-regulating. Respondents aren't encouraged to let the surveyors know if some of the survey's questions or statements are too vague or ambiguous for their answers to be useful.
  - Their purpose is usually process, rather than outcome-focused. The surveyors want to 'find out' X, 'assess' Y, or 'evaluate' Z. And they never identify what they want to be able to do as a result of having found out, assessed or evaluated.

- In addition to ironing out the problems of annual staff surveys, it makes sense to have an additional approach which has three key pieces (Page 141):
  1. Elicit feedback from every communication, even with a standard line such as:

     'If you've any questions, concerns or suggestions about what you're being told here, or any ideas about how I could improve the way I'm communicating it to you...'

     ...followed by details about the process for providing feedback.
  2. Have robust mechanisms in place to ensure that all feedback is:
     a) Received by the relevant person
     b) acknowledged
     c) acted upon and the reasons for any changes explained to those affected
  3. Measure the effect (as far as possible)

- You can only measure up to a point the impact of internal communication on stakeholder value, because other aspects of the SMARTIED principle may skew your results. (Page 143)

- You can measure the use of effective communication inputs: (Page 143)
  - written briefs

- business plans translated into communication outcome language
- communication plans which are causally linked back to the business plan
- adequate training and performance measures for communication owners
- adequate processes for eliciting, handling and responding to feedback
- the use of style guides and design templates
- the systematic removal of Detached Observer Triggers

    Some of the items in this list could also make communication owners' errors as easy and clinical to spot as those of budget owners.

- To make any staff survey outcome-focused – whether annual or ad-hoc, it must be eliciting answers that will tell the surveyors: (Page 144)
    - what else they have to do to get the outcome they're after from the communication/campaign/business plan/business vision in question, and/or
    - how they can reliably (or more reliably) get the outcomes they want in the future, should they have similar issues to tackle.

Outcome-focused survey questions
Core question for the communication owner:
  'What do you want to be able to do as a result of having assessed the feedback?'

Questions to put to the audience:
1. Not *'Do you now understand about Y?'*
   But *'Do you now want to do Y?'* and
   'Are you now able to do Y?'
2. If the answers to either question is 'no':
   'What has to happen for you to want to do Y?'
   'What has to happen for you to be able to do Y?'
3. You can then causally link the answers to questions 1 & 2, in order to remove any erroneous leaps of faith, and give the communication owner more detail, by asking:
   'How will changing X make you want to do Y?'
   'How will changing X make you able to do Y?'

Chapter 15

Understanding the linguistic minefield

- If people start out as detached observers (e.g. on the copy list of an email) there's no problem with them picking up on what's being said, but they won't act on the direct instructions. (Page 148)

- When people start out in the audience position and then get pushed out of it they not only switch off but also feel disenfranchised. (Page 149)
  - These triggers only affect audiences for business communications; they make no difference to academic or recreational audiences.
  - They are beyond traditional rules of grammar and syntax, so they aren't described in any standard English textbooks.
  - Knowing what they are, how they work and how to disarm them, may do wonders for your confidence, and will certainly improve your reputation and business value.

- People adopt the detached observer position when they feel: (Page 150):
  - the communication is talking to no one at all
  - it is talking to another audience
  - the communicator is talking to him- or herself
  - a group of people appear to be talking among themselves.

- There are six of linguistic triggers that can switch your audiences off. (Page 150)
  - Trigger 1 involves impersonal verbs & abstract nouns.
  - Triggers 2, 3 & 4 involve the pronoun 'you'. (See chapter 16)
  - Trigger 5 involves the pronoun 'I'. (See chapter 17)
  - Trigger 6 involves the pronoun 'we'. (See chapter 19)

- These triggers have gone unnoticed (at least consciously) for so long because: (Page 151):
  - not everyone gets switched off by every trigger
  - they only affect people who are 'subjectively' in the Audience position; communication owners and approval group members rarely are.

- Linguistic Trigger 1 can make people wonder if what they're reading is talking to anyone at all. (Page 153)

- You can disarm this trigger by using personal verbs.
- This solution may set off any one of the three 'You' triggers, but there are other ways of getting around the problems they cause.

Chapter 16

How to disarm the 'You' triggers

- **Linguistic Trigger 2**: Presupposing the audience's attitude or situation (Page 157)
  - This can make people feel that what they're reading is talking only to people who fit into one or both of the following categories:
    a) They have the necessary attitude or are in the necessary situation.
    b) They are prepared to be talked down to.
  - You can disarm this trigger by:
    - making the language flexible (Page 158)
    - making the language indirect (Page 159)
    - playing around with the attitudinal references (Page 160)
    - using one of the past tenses (Page 161)
    - using quotations or questions. (Page 162)

- **Linguistic Trigger 3**: Writing about the reader(s) (Page 162)
  - This can make people wonder if the person being spoken about is the person being spoken to.
  - You can disarm this trigger by replacing the third person noun with the second person pronoun 'you'.

- **Linguistic Trigger** 4: Quantifying the audience   (Page 163)
  - This changes the meaning of the word 'you' from singular to plural.
  - It not only makes people wonder if what they're reading is talking to them any more, it also makes them unsure about whether or not it ever has been talking to them.
  - There are four different linguistic structures which can set off this trigger, which require their own solutions:

    a & b) Flexible and inflexible quantifiers: e.g. 'some, many, most, all, each ... of you'. (Page 164)

Solutions:
- Make your language indirect (e.g. some people)
- Lose the quantifier (i.e. rather than 'some of you', simply say 'you)
- Make it flexible by using 'if'

c) Plurals   (Page 167)
Solutions:
- Lose the plural
- Use an oblique or flexible reference
- Make it flexible by using 'If'

d) Adverbs: e.g. 'separately', 'individually', or 'together' (Page 168)
Solution:
- Lose the adverb

Chapter 17
How to disarm the 'I' trigger

- Many people say they find Question and Answer formats condescending. (Page 170)

- Q & A formats suffer from the following difficulties.
  1. The heading can often presuppose the audience's attitude or situation. (Page 172)
  2. The answers often don't answer the questions. (Page 172)
  3. Some readers' questions often get left out. (Page 173)
  4. The reader's mind's voice can get muddled between the following: (Page 173)
  - their own
  - the author's
  - an imaginary voice.

- When the voice changes, the new voice can often be talking to someone else. (Page 174)

- The subliminal nature of the mind's voice means that most people can get pushed into the detached observer position without even realising it. (Page 175)
  - Therefore, even if some people say they like receiving information in a Q & A format, that opinion can't be trusted.

- Even when using the second person 'you' for Q& A questions, people can still end up putting words in their readers' mouths. (Page 177)

- You can solve the mind's voice problem by using statements and explanations instead. (Page 178)
  - This will also remove the possibility of the problematic heading, and the audience's expectations.

Chapter 18
Getting maximum value from the mind's voice

- Some people in approval groups want to correct each other's corrections and argue about 'the right way to write this'. (Page 180)

- When someone is approving your text, he or she can be doing so from any one of the three positions, and using any one of the three mind's voices. (Page 181)
  - When it's a group of people doing the approving, different individuals can adopt their own position and voice – hence different emotional responses to the same phraseology.

- The mind's voice is an emotional powerhouse. With many people, its impact can be huge. (Page 182)

- The voice with which you write will affect the vocabulary and syntax you use. It may also influence the angle you take on the content. Your choice of vocabulary and syntax is likely, in turn, to affect the mind's voice of the reader. (Page 183)

- To get communications approved quickly, it's best to find out from the owner which voice he or she is going to use, before you start writing – and to use that voice yourself when putting the draft together. In this way, your lexicon and syntax is likely to match theirs. (Page 184)
  - This may well enhance your confidence in your writing.
  - Appendix G will explain to communication owners what they're doing, and how to get around the problems.

- Any mind's voice can also be heard in different tones, e.g. authoritative, smiley, sarcastic, etc. (Page 185)
  - Approvers can also imagine that voice and tonality being used

by someone else and in different situations: e.g. their boss reading the text aloud in a sarcastic voice to his or her colleagues.
   - Some people write badly because they use the same voice to edit their text as they did to write it.

- Having written briefs, and getting them signed off before writing, will remove the purpose and content debate from the approval process. (Page 188)

- Giving any piece of text the 'Eileen Test' is a useful way of ensuring its quality. (Page 190)

- Speed reading is a visual process. Speed readers may therefore want to change text because they're not listening to what it's saying. (Page 191)

- Standard customer letters often feel like they've been written by two different people when staff insert their own customised text, because those staff are swapping from a 'corporate' voice to their own voice when they start writing. (Page 191)

- It's not inevitable that writing in capital letters causes people to think the author is SHOUTING. You can just as easily think they are WHISPERING, or LAUGHING, or SINGING, or USING A GERMAN ACCENT. Your mind's voice is yours to use as you wish. (Page 193)

- If you're writing a communication for yourself, it's useful to check your syntax and punctuation by using a different voice when you're editing. (Page 194)

Chapter 19
Tracking down the most elusive trigger of all

- The final trigger is a combination of chameleon and mynah bird, and can cause more problems than all the other linguistic triggers put together. (Page 195)

- 'We' is the 36th most frequently used word in English. (Page 195)

- 'We' can include or exclude the audience. (Page 196)
   - It will lose the audience if it changes from one to the other.

- 'We' has 17 potential meanings, made up of combinations of six parties: (Page 200):
  1. the author (or the individual in whose name the author is writing)
  2. a communicator group (which may or may not be being represented by a named individual)
  3. the individual reader/listener/viewer
  4. other members of the audience (when the communication is going to more than one person)
  5. an identified 3rd party (which may be an individual or a group)
  6. other people (who are outside any communicator, audience or 3rd party group).

- These 17 meanings fall into 3 main categories: (Page 200):
  a) includes the communicator and excludes the audience
  b) includes both the communicator and audience
  c) excludes the communicator and includes the audience.
  - When 'we' changes between meanings a & b or a & c, the audience feel excluded.

- 'Our' can take the following forms. (Page 202):
  Directive: that which belongs to us
  Associative: that to which we belong
  Dependent: those on whom we rely
  - It can carry more than one meaning at the same time, so the meaning of 'we' can change imperceptibly within 'our', from including the audience to excluding it, or vice versa.

- The solutions to this trigger are in Appendix C.

Appendix A
Outcome-focused Briefing Questions

This appendix brings together in one place all the questions you need to be asking if you want to put together an effective outcome-focused brief.

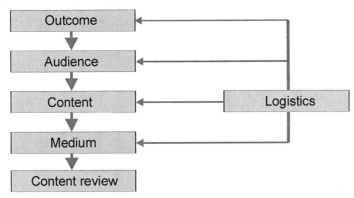

1. Always identify outcomes first, before the audience, content or medium.
2. The functional purpose of business communication is:
   > To prompt and/or enable people
   > to take and/or avoid actions
   > immediately and/or eventually.

Summary of the questions to identify the communication's outcome

1. *'What do you want people to be doing (avoiding or able to do) as a result of them having read/listened to/watched this communication?'*

If the answer is couched in terms of what the audience isn't doing, ask:

2. *'If you don't want them to be doing that, what do you want them to do instead?'*

If in response to the first question they say either, 'I don't know' or 'Nothing', ask:

3. *'If you don't want them to do anything, what's the benefit of telling them?'* Or

4. *'If you don't want them to do anything, what would happen if we just didn't tell them?'*

The responses to these questions are often that the audience will 'know, understand, feel or believe something' (or 'not know it') about the information being communicated, in which case, you can ask:

5. *'So what? What's the benefit of them knowing this?'* or
6. *'What do you want them to do as a result of knowing this?'* or
7. *'So what? What would happen if they didn't know this?'*

Keep repeating variants of these last three questions until you get a specific behaviour.

Summary of the questions to identify the audience
(and intentional detached observers)
1. *'Who do you want to be doing (able to do) this (the outcome)?'*
2. *'Why aren't they doing it already?'*

If you've now identified distinct groups starting from different Current Situations, you need to ask the following for each group:
3. *'What are they doing instead?'*
4. *'What's the single biggest reason why they would stop doing what they're doing now, and start doing what you want?'*

Then, to identify any Intentional Detached Observers:
5. *'Who else needs to know what the audience is being told?'*
6. *'What do you want them to be able to do as a result of knowing it?'*

The answer to this final question will give you the outcome for any mini-communications that you may need to send to the detached observers along with their copy of the main communication.

Summary of questions to identify the content
(Background question: *'What else needs to happen to get this outcome?'*
This may throw up some aspects of the SMARTIED principle)

Identifying content to move the audience towards the Outcome:
1. *'What can we say which will make them want to do what you want?'*
1a. *'And what else? And what else?'* etc.

Verifying this content – (ask these combinations of 2 & 3 for each item of content you've just identified)
2. *'What will we be saying in telling them this which will make them want to do what you want?'*
2a. *'And what else? And what else?'* etc.
3. *'How will telling them this make them want to do what you want?'*

Continue using combinations of these questions to drill down to the point that you're happy that your content is as concrete as possible.

Identifying content to move people away from the Current Situation:
4.   *'What can we say which will make them want to stop doing what they're doing now?'*
4a. *'And what else? And what else?'* etc

Verifying this content – (ask these for each item of content you've just identified)
5.   *'What will we be saying <u>in telling them this</u> which will make them want to stop doing what they're already doing?'*
5a. *'And what else? And what else?'* etc.
6.   *'How will telling them this <u>make</u> them want to stop doing what they're already doing?'*

Again, continue using combinations of these questions to drill down to the point that you're happy that your content is as concrete as possible.

Presenting a balanced view
7.   *'What could be the benefit to them of continuing as they are?'*
8.   *'What could it cost them to change?'*
9.   *'Why would they be better off changing?'*

(The benefits to individuals may come indirectly from benefits to the organisation)

Identifying content to enable the audience to deliver the outcome
1.   *'What do they need to know to be able to do what you want?'*
1a. *'And what else? And what else?'* etc.

Verifying this content – (ask these for each item of content you've just identified)
2.   *'What, specifically will we be saying <u>in telling them this</u> which will enable them to do what you want?'*
2a. *'And what else? And what else?'* etc.
3.   *'How will telling them this <u>enable</u> them to do what you want?'*

Prompting people to do achieve the outcome in the desired way:
4.   *'What's the benefit to them of doing it in this way?'*
5.   *'What could it cost them if they didn't do it in this way?'*

Summary of questions for identifying and verifying media
Usage
1. *'When is the audience likely to use the communication?'*
2. *'Where could they be at the time?'*
3. *'What actions do you expect them to take with it when using it?'*
4. *'What will remind them to use it when and how it should be used?'*
5. *'How are you going to get feedback from or through this communication?'*

Delivery
6. *'When are they likely to receive the communication?'*
7. *'Where could the audience be at the time they receive it?'*
8. *'What specific actions do you want them to take with it at that moment?'*
9. *'What will make or enable them use it as you want them to?'*

Supplementary questions
10. *'Does some or all of this communication need to be tailored to individual recipients?'*
11. *'Do you need a guarantee that everyone has received it?'*
12. *'Do you want to know who has chosen to receive it?'*
13. *'Is some or all of the information confidential?'*
14. *'If confidentiality is important, is the content of a personal nature, or can it be shared with a discrete group?'*

Logistics
15. *'How many people are you intending to communicate with?'*
16. *'How much can you afford to spend?'*
17. *'How far away is your delivery deadline?'*

Communications to Indirectly Prompt Actions

'Not every end is a goal. The end of a melody is not a goal. But if it did not reach its end it would also not reach its goal.'

Friedrich Nietzsche

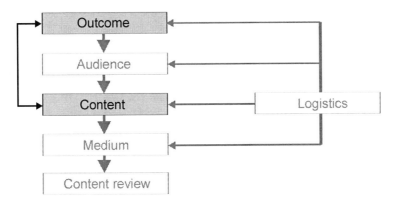

This appendix pulls together the ideas from the chapters on identifying outcomes and content, to show how you can combine the questioning techniques in order to make 'nice to know' communications as valuable as possible. If you are involved in producing such communications, you may already be thinking along these lines, but there may also be some useful nuggets of information here that you might not have noticed before.

All business communications could be said to generate two types of potential response: one hard and one soft. The hard responses are the actions which the audience will take (or be able to take) immediately and/or eventually as a direct result of having received the communication. The soft responses are the emotions engendered in the audience by the communication. These soft responses help to create what one might call the background ambience of the organisation. These are an inevitable outcome of any and all communications – whether formal or informal. Many businesses run ambient communications (such as in-house magazines) often with the sole intention of engendering soft responses. But closer inspection reveals that, with business communications, soft responses can never be an end in themselves.

When giving briefs for communications, people frequently start off by talking about the content they want to pass on. With a functional communication (one that's going to directly prompt/enable actions) they rarely have much difficulty identifying an outcome, when asked (albeit they might go through one or two phantoms first). But with social communications, they usually say that they don't expect the audience to do anything as a result of having been communicated with, that it's 'for information only'. Indeed, they often see no need for such a communication to produce any hard response.

But there are two problems with this. Firstly, there's the direct commercial impact. Remember, when an audience is receiving a business communication, they are consuming the business's money and, with internal communications, the business's time. This means that simply getting an audience to receive the communication does not contribute to the profit of the communicator. In fact, it costs profit. It's only when a business communication prompts or enables the audience to act that it generates profit. So although the communicator may want these communications to be enjoyable, their purpose has to be something beyond mere entertainment if they are to have any commercial justification.

The second problem is that, although it may not be openly talked about, everyone is aware (albeit unconsciously) that communicating costs money. If they read an in-house magazine and feel that it's wasted their time, they may feel, even subliminally, that they are working for an organisation that doesn't know how to prioritise its expenditure effectively (i.e. 'The business could have paid me the money it's wasted on this magazine). And with internal comms, because many people are under time pressure at work, they may resent the useless waste of their time as well. I've not yet come across an organisation that wanted to engender soft responses like this. But unless we take a fresh look at how we think through the briefing of social communications, such tacit outcomes are likely to continue.

Despite initial appearances to the contrary, social communications can indeed engender hard outcomes. But to ensure they do so, we need to take a longer term view.

When asked, people often give the emotional response they're going for with their ambient communications as something like 'a sense of belonging' or '…community' or '…loyalty'. And further probing reveals that the reason for engendering such responses is that they are believed to give rise to a whole range of behaviours. In other words, such a social communication is expected to engender audience actions as an *indirect* outcome of their having received it.

Before pursuing this idea any further, I feel it might be worth just thinking about this idea of 'Belonging'. I have come across numerous people who see this as the ultimate soft response, as they feel that it will provide exactly that ambience they are trying to engender. And while this may well be true, I think it's also worth recognising that it's not necessarily going to be everyone's priority. Many people are, indeed, very 'corporate minded' in their outlook at work; many are dedicated team players. But, equally, there are those who are more concerned with their own advancement. In the competitive cut and thrust of business, I think it's reasonable to suggest that not everyone is hugely interested in having a sense of belonging – in their own fulfilment, yes, but not necessarily belonging. But just because there are some people who have less desire or need for it than others doesn't mean that encouraging a sense of belonging isn't worth doing. It can bring numerous benefits, both financial and emotional. For example, a sense of belonging might result in people:

- answering a ringing phone on someone else's desk, rather than just leaving it
- contacting an unknown colleague for help, rather than mistrusting them, or thinking that they must be a bit of a wally simply because they are known to work in a department that people know 'stories' about
- washing up the mugs in the staff kitchen
- staying loyal to their employer, rather than moving to another company.

Naturally, all of these outcomes (and the many others that may come from people having a sense of belonging) are worth going for. But how can you get them? Clearly, getting these 'indirect outcomes' is more involved than getting direct outcomes. After all, you can't write an article about, say, a member of the customer service team winning an Open University degree, and expect everyone in the IT department to start washing up their mugs on the strength of it. That's not how it works.

Because of this, briefs for such communications can again involve owners in making major, perhaps erroneous, leaps of faith about the content that's likely to bring about the outcomes they desire. So what to do? In some instances, the answer may be for the owners to say nothing – because it's possible that nothing they say is going to make any difference.

Staff surveys abound these days, and when it comes to creating a sense of fulfilment, three factors have shown themselves to be more important than any number of social communications:

1. **The employee's interpersonal relationship with his or her immediate manager and colleagues** (something about which ambient communications can do pretty much diddly-squat).
2. **Being listened to as well as spoken to**. This means not just canvassing opinion, but actually doing something demonstrably useful with it – and not just once a year, but on an ongoing basis. For this reason, a business can make major strides in creating a sense of fulfilment and belonging among its staff by encouraging feedback on each and every communication – a subject we discussed in chapter 14.
3. **Honesty**. Many a business falls into the trap of feeling that it has to be a 'good news only' organisation, in the mistaken belief that this will motivate its staff more effectively. But such an approach is doomed to failure because, in the real world, things do go wrong. And when they do, a 'good news only' organisation can either clam up completely, or try to make out that this bad news is really good news. Either way, it loses credibility.

    Having thus undermined the credibility of its communications, such a business's genuine good news will have lost much of its motivating power, because its source will no longer be trusted. And the audience is likely to respond by thinking, 'Well they would say that wouldn't they'. A more effective approach is to offer a balanced perspective in all your business's communications, which is something we covered when we looked at identifying content in the chapter 9.

None of this means that ambient communications are unnecessary, but simply that they can't be expected to do the job on their own. If these three other factors aren't taken care of, ambient communications have about as much ability to warm employees' hearts as the Emperor's New Thermal Underwear. But when ambient communications are taking place against this supportive background, they can contribute to people's sense of belonging and fulfilment. And provided the people responsible for your organisation's internal communications are good enough writers, there are two options for building that emotional ambience:

1. Write a small percentage of ambient communications for pure 'feel good factor'.
2. Identify a valid business reason for writing the majority of ambient communications.

If you and your fellow communication professionals are skilled enough, a company magazine or newspaper can get away with writing the odd article just for fun. As with other communications, people get to know what to expect and, if done with finesse, the occasional fun article can encourage people to at least pick the thing up and read it each time it arrives – which is itself an important step.

For the majority of ambient articles, though, there can often be a valid business reason for writing them. Let's look again at the list of 'Nice to know' subjects we touched on briefly in the chapter 2:

1. Notification of a company party
2. One of the sales teams winning a major new contract
3. A member of staff graduating with a degree from the Open University
4. One of the company's new office buildings winning an architectural award
5. A pay rise

With the company party communication, even though the subject matter is undoubtedly intended to encourage a feel-good factor, it could be said to be a functional communication, as it has a very clear outcome in mind:

'As a result of having read the communication, people are turning up at the right venue at the right time on the right date, in the right attire, and ready to party.'

But with the other communications, the audience's reaction is perhaps less easy to spot – if indeed it exists at all. What, after all, would someone want the audience to do as a result of having been told about the architectural award? Maybe not all 'nice to know' communications are necessarily quite the same.

Interestingly, when the primary purpose of a communication appears to be indirect outcomes, a direct outcome may also become evident when you start identifying the content. (Or perhaps it would be more accurate to say that the content often starts coming out as you're identifying the outcome).

In these situations, communication owners usually start out saying that they don't expect the audience to do anything as a result of having been communicated with – but they want to tell their story anyway. There are two ways of dealing with this.

1. Use an alternative set of questions for identifying both the content and the outcome.
2. Use the briefing questions we've already discussed, but play around with the sequencing.

The alternative of questions are:

1. What has happened/is happening?
2. When did it/will it happen?

3. Where did it/will it happen?
4. Who was/will be/can be involved?
5. How can they get involved? or Why are you bothering to tell the audience this?

With this set of questions, of course, the outcome (which is the audience's involvement or re-action) is only going to become apparent at the end. Although you could ask the 'Why are you bothering...' question up front, you're often going to find it easier to get a useful answer from the owner once they've answered the other questions first. And it may be that there isn't a valid reason, so the communication may not need to happen. And while you may have spent twenty or thirty minutes of briefing time arriving at that conclusion, at least you won't waste any more time beyond that, writing something that doesn't need to exist.

The second method, which works just as well (often in conjunction with the first method) is to go for the outcome in the same way that you would for a functional communication. To illustrate how this method works, the following transcripts, which are taken from the opening parts of real briefing sessions, will give you an idea of how the outcome and content questions can work together. These transcripts also include the occasional 'specifier' question, to help clarify the thinking that's going on behind some of abstract language in the clients' answers.

Example 1
An article about a member of staff acquiring an Open University degree

What do you want people to do as a result of having read this article?
We don't want them to do anything?
So what's the benefit of telling them?
They'll know that one of their colleagues had just achieved something rather special. It was a lot of hard work for her, and I think her achievement ought to be publicly acknowledged.
Because?
Because... Well because people like to read about the success of others.
Perhaps, but when they've got 101 other things to be getting on with...
Yes, but it might encourage them to try to achieve something similar themselves, and it never hurts to have a better educated workforce.
Okay, so how will telling them about Jenny's achievement make them want to start learning again themselves?
Well Jenny got time off as study leave, time off for her exams, and £50 a year towards her textbooks. That's actually standard company policy, but it's not very

well known and some people might not realise that they could get it too. I'm sure lots of people would like to learn more, but feel they haven't got the time or the money.

So this article, as well as giving Jenny a well deserved pat on the back, can encourage some people to restart their learning, as well as letting everyone know that they're working in an culture that really encourages its people to grow and develop?

That's right.

Here a seemingly non-existent outcome has become something both specific and developmental. Interestingly, it doesn't have to encourage everyone to take the specific action as soon as they receive the communication. Instead, it acts in some ways a little like a telephone directory. It lets people know that the appropriate help to achieve what they want is at hand when they need it, if they ever should. And even if someone never uses its help from one year end to the next, they still find it comforting to know it's there. It's unlikely that anyone will ever say that it's been a waste of time and money issuing them with a phone directory, just because they happen not to have had a need for it.

Similarly, even the most cynical employee might find it more difficult to argue that such an employer doesn't genuinely believe in developing its people. Such a communication can therefore do much to build the credibility of corporate messages – but again, only if the business policies demonstrably support them.

Example 2
An article about a new company building winning an architectural award

What do you want people to do as a result of having read this article?
We don't want them to do anything?
So what would happen if we just didn't tell them?
They wouldn't know that we've won this prestigious award.
So what? What's the benefit of people knowing about this award?
Well our Facilities Management department are very proud of this award.
And?
And... it's good for people to know that we're winning things. Shows they work for a quality company that cares about doing things well.
And why is it important for people to know that?
So that they'll feel good about working here, because when people feel good about where they work, they're more enthusiastic and more loyal.
Right. Now you're a telecoms business, not a building firm. So how does winning

a building award show that you're a quality telecoms company, in such a way as to make people feel enthusiastic and loyal to it? If I were working for you, why should I suddenly get a rush of enthusiasm for my job, just because a bunch of architects I've never heard of have won an award for a building at the other end of the country that I'm never going to work in?

Okay. The main reason it won was because it's so energy efficient, so it's much more environmentally friendly, and that's part of our corporate policy – to become increasingly green. So this shows that it's not all talk, but that we actually mean it. And it should encourage people to 'think green'.

So apart from giving staff the ability to brag about their company in the pub, or defend it if other people attack it, you also want this article to prompt staff to be behaving in an environmentally friendly way at work?

Yeah, and taking our environmental message seriously. There's an important credibility issue here. I think that there's a tendency to disregard some of the company's messages as just so much hot air – or greenhouse gas. So this article should go some way to showing that our environmental stance is not just all talk.

In this instance, there is a valid outcome that can be won from this communication, but it's a close call. This example illustrates that many 'nice to know' communications are little more than vanity publishing exercises: people can often want to communicate something for their own sake (in this case: the FM department) rather than that of the audience. For this article, only the environmental angle made it worth pursuing in the end.

Example 3
Notification of a pay rise

What do you want people to do as a result of having read this article?

We don't want them to do anything?

So what would happen if we just didn't tell them?

But you can't not tell people they've had a pay rise. Why would you want to not tell them? People would wonder what was happening if they got a pay rise and you didn't tell them about it.

And what do you think would happen?

Well they'd start wondering what else they weren't being told.

Okay, so what's the benefit of telling them?

They'll be happy. Everyone likes to hear they're getting more money don't they.

Uh huh. And what else?

Well they can make plans for what they're going to do with it, and they can be motivated to stay here and work hard for us over the next year.

Right, and what will we be saying, in telling them about this pay rise, which will make them want to work hard over the next year?

You know, that's a very good question. Tell you what; we can link their pay rise to the business results they've helped us get, so that they can see how their efforts have been rewarded. And we could remind them of the results we're going for this year, so they know they've got a personal financial interest in getting those results.

So as a result of having received this communication, staff are working with equal or greater enthusiasm and loyalty?

Sounds good to me.

This is an example of a communication whose main purpose is to produce an 'Away-from' outcome (steering people away from ringing up the payroll department to query their pay cheques). But it also gives an opportunity to prompt indirect actions. And here, the communication alone can't achieve this – the money is the key motivator. Nevertheless, it can provide that important link in people's minds between their future work and future reward.

In each of these examples, the communication has been worth doing – and each for a subtly different reason. What's interesting is that, certainly with examples one and two, they were initially going to be produced only for the benefit of the people who were being talked about, rather than that of the audience or the business.

This is often the way a lot of ambient communications end up getting produced, without adding any real business value, and Corporate Communication Departments can frequently end up being little more than vanity publishing houses. In all these examples, though, the communications were worth doing because the subject matter fitted in with the business's policies (not just with its values). As such, they weren't simply trying to say something 'because they could'.

Appendix C

Taming the Linguistic Chameleon

Part 1: The seventeen meanings of 'we'
Part 2: Linguistic techniques for disarming the trigger
Part 3: Using the 'sub-group' technique successfully
Part 4: The mynah bird 'we'
Part 5: 'The company', singular or plural?
Part 6: Using 'we' in team briefs and cascades
Part 7: Worked examples

Part 1 – The seventeen meanings of 'we'

'We' can sometimes change its meaning with impunity, and sometimes not. And when people get to know about this trigger, many of them can get concerned if they perceive that the meaning has changed, even when its doing so won't have caused problems. (Remember, its ability to change meanings will only produce a Detached Observer Trigger if the change moves it between any of these categories)

	Communication coming from:	
'We'	Single individual	Group
• includes communicator and excludes audience	Category 1	Category 3
• includes communicator and audience	Category 2	Category 4
• excludes communicator and includes audience	Category 5	

You'll find examples here of all seventeen meanings of 'we', organised according to these categories. It should help you to allay anyone's concerns about whether or not a particular change in meaning is going to cause problems.

The communication is coming from a single individual
Category 1: 'We' includes the communicator & excludes the audience:
1. An individual communicator and a 3rd party (individual or group), e.g. a note to a delegate from the conference co-ordinator, talking about a joint decision taken with the catering manager.

   'I've talked to the catering manager about your special dietary requirements, and we've come up with the following menu.'

Category 2: 'We' includes both the communicator & audience:

2a. An individual communicator & individual audience member, e.g. a one to one email.

> *'Thank you for coming to see me. Here's a summary of what we agreed.'*

2b. An individual communicator & individual audience member + other audience members, e.g. a note from a department manager to his or her staff.

> *'Sally is leaving us today, and I'm sure we would all like to wish her well.'*

2c. An individual communicator & individual audience member + a 3rd party (individual or group), e.g. a note from a manager to one of his staff about a joint project with a 3rd party.

> *'I have raised your concerns about wheelchair access with the building manager and he suggests that the best way to solve it would be for the three of us to sit down together and talk it through.'*

2d. An individual communicator & individual audience member + others outside the audience, e.g. a mailshot letter from a member of a sales team, about a subject that affects people in general.

> *'We all need to have enough money to retire on.'*

2e. An individual communicator & individual audience member + other audience members + a 3rd party (individual or group), e.g. a note from a manager to all his staff about a project they're working on with a 3rd party.

> *'The finance team have taken a look at our proposal, and they want to arrange a meeting where we can all agree on a common way forward.'*

2f. An individual communicator & individual audience member + others both inside and outside the audience, e.g. a note from a department manager to his or her team about a subject that affects everyone in the business.

> *'Keeping customers happy is vital for all of us at XYZ company.'*

The communication is coming from a group
Category 3: 'We' includes the communicator & excludes the audience:

3a. A communicator group, e.g. a note from 'the board'.

> *'We are happy to announce an increase in profits for the third successive year.'*

3b. A communicator group & a 3rd party (individual or group), e.g. The IT department writing about a decision they've taken with a software supplier.

'We have been working on this problem with ABC software, and together we believe we've come up with a solution.'

Category 4: 'We' includes both the communicator & audience:

4a. A communicator group & individual audience member, e.g. a welcome note from a team leader to a new team member.

'I'm thrilled that you've joined the team. Your skills will be a great asset to us and I'm confident that, together, we can do great things for this business.

4b. A communicator group & individual audience member + a 3rd party (individual or group), e.g. a note from a manager to one of his staff about a joint project with a 3rd party.

'Janet, Mike and I have raised your concerns with the venue manager, and he suggests that the best way to solve it would be for all of us to sit down together and talk it through.'

4c. A communicator group & individual audience member + others inside the audience, e.g. the board talking to all employees about a subject that affects everyone in the company.

'As a business, we need to maintain our shareholders' confidence.'

4d. A communicator group & individual audience member + others outside the audience, e.g. an annual update from the company pension department.

'Here is your latest pension statement, showing the contributions you've made this year and the current value of your pension. As you can see, our funds have performed well over the past 12 months.'

4e. A communicator group & individual audience member + other audience members + a 3rd party (individual or group)' e.g. a note from the HR remuneration team to sales managers about new tax rules.

'Following the meeting we had with you last month, we took your ideas to the accounts team for a view on the legal position. They've come back with a series of questions and would like us all to meet up to thrash this out.'

4f. A communicator group & individual audience member + others both inside and outside the audience, e.g. Market Research writing to everyone in Marketing about customer survey results.

'As a business we need to be up to speed with what our customers want.'

The communication is a Team Brief or live cascade
Category 5: 'We' excludes the communicator and includes the audience

5a. The individual audience member & other audience members, e.g. a note from HR being communicated through a Team Brief.

'Human Resources have announced that the latest EU Health & Safety regulations will be introduced next year, so there will be new guidelines that we'll have to follow.'

5b. The audience group & others outside it*, e.g. a staff bonus being communicated through a team brief.

'These bonuses reflect our increased profit.'

*In these circumstances, the meaning of 'We' will often include everyone in the business, which with an internal communication does of course include the communicator group. However, they are being included only as members of the audience and, if referred to in their own right, would be talked about in the third person: 'they'.

Part 2 – Principles and techniques for disarming the trigger

Principles

1. To disarm this trigger, you must keep 'we' constant throughout any given communication. In other words, each instance of 'we', 'us' and 'our' must:
   - include the communicator and exclude the audience from beginning to end, or
   - include both the communicator and audience from beginning to end, or
   - exclude the communicator and include the audience from beginning to end.

2. It's usually simplest to go through a communication, noting what 'we' means each time (always bearing in mind that it can sometimes be ambiguous). Then you should know which meaning is dominant. If, for

example, there are twelve instances of 'we', nine of which exclude the audience, two of which include it, and one of which is ambiguous, you'll know that it will probably be simpler to change the meaning of the two inclusive instances, rather than the nine exclusive ones.

About the techniques

The complex nature of this trigger means that there are numerous techniques you'll need to use – in different circumstances – to keep the meaning of 'we' clear. You might expect that all these techniques would make clearer whom you're referring to in any given sentence or phrase. In the main this is true. But the paradoxical nature of this trigger means that some techniques will clarify the meaning of 'we' by obscuring, rather than clarifying whom you're talking about.

Either way, all the techniques involve playing around with either pronouns or verbs. The following list is not exhaustive, as to make it so would require us to descend to a prohibitive level of detail. But it does cover almost every situation you're likely to find. And any additional tweaks will almost always follow naturally from using these.

Unfortunately, it's impossible to name a technique, and distinguish it from the others, without using some technical terms, e.g. replacing 'we' with adjectives or articles. I've therefore provided a simple example or two for each technique, so you can see what the technical description means in practice. Although this will explain the technical terms, it won't give you the full context, which is often necessary to understand what the technique is doing in situ. I've therefore provided numerous worked examples which illustrate the 'we' trigger in action, and how the various techniques are disarming it.

For ease of reference, the techniques are grouped together according whether they will enable you to use 'we' to:

- **include the communicator and exclude the audience**
- **include both the communicator and audience**
- **exclude the communicator and include the audience.**

Techniques for excluding the audience from 'we'

The **pronoun** techniques will enable you to clarify 'we' by either:
- changing it for another pronoun
- replacing 'we' with something else entirely
- adding extra pronouns, or

- losing 'we' altogether.

The **verb** techniques will enable you to clarify 'we' by either:

- changing the action that 'we' are doing, or
- bypassing the question of who's doing the action.

Pronoun techniques

Using 'you'
Simply using the second person 'you' in preference to 'we' can often keep your meaning clear, e.g. *'so that we can get ourselves up to speed'* can become *'so that you can get yourself up to speed'* (Example 3A)

Using 'everyone', 'these', 'those', 'its'
You can often help avoid confusion and keep things clear by replacing personal pronouns ('we', 'us' & 'our') with general ones (e.g. 'everyone', 'these', 'those' & 'its'), e.g. *'our colleagues in sales'* can become *'those working in sales'* (Example 3A)

Substituting adjectives or articles for 'We'
You can often depersonalise the text to help avoid confusion and keep things clear by replacing personal pronouns (such as 'your' and 'ours') with adjectives or articles, e.g. *'our PC packages'* can become *'the outdated PC packages'* (Example 4A), or, *'our competitors'* can become *'the competition'* (Example 3A)

Emphasising the audience's separateness from the communicator group
To ensure that the audience are in no doubt about the meaning of 'we', you can explicitly separate them from the communicator group, by including the pronoun 'you' in the same sentence as 'we'. e.g. *'We all want this conference to be a success'* can become *'We want this conference to be a success for you.'* (Example 1A)

Losing unnecessary joint references to communicator & audience
It's often possible to lose joint references and focus solely on one party or the other, e.g. *'Further to our conversation'* can become *'Thank you for contacting us.'* (Example 8A)

Drop the pronoun
Sometimes, you can simply remove a pronoun to keep the meaning of 'we' clear., e.g. *'to provide our customers with the best value for money products'* can become *'to provide customers with the best value for money products'* (Example 3A)

Verb techniques
Changing the verb
Sometimes you can't change the meaning of 'we' without also having to change the action that 'we' are, need to be, or have been, engaging in, e.g. *'we'd only have to start following these rules later'* can become *'we'd only have to introduce these rules later.'* (Example 6A)

Using impersonal verbs
You can use impersonal verbs (sparingly) to remove a potentially confusing meaning of 'we', e.g. *'what we need to focus on'* can become *'what needs focusing on.'* (Example 3A)

Using infinitive verbs
Infinitive verbs (e.g. to walk, to breathe etc) involve no specific person, and are another useful way bypassing the question of who's involved in, or responsible for the actions, e.g. *'give me a ring so we can discuss this'* can become *'give me a ring to discuss this.'* (Example 8A)

Techniques for including both communicator and audience in 'we'

Pronoun techniques enable you to clarify 'we' by either:
- changing it for another pronoun
- replacing 'we' with something else entirely.

Verb techniques enable you to clarify 'we' by either:
- changing the action that 'we' are doing, or
- bypassing the question of who's doing the action.

Pronoun techniques
Using 'I'
If a communication is coming from an individual representing a group, it's sometimes possible to use the word 'I' rather than 'we' in order to keep the responsibilities clear, e.g. *'we are pleased to announce'* can become *'I am pleased to announce'* (Example 7B)

Naming names
Rather than relying on pronouns to do all the work, you may sometimes need to be specific about the individual groups you are describing. However, by naming names, you will be objectifying the group in question. Therefore, if the communicator were to name the group he or she was representing, it would appear that he or she was separate from it, rather than part of it. To avoid this, the communicator group itself cannot be named. Instead, you can

name either a sub-group, a super-group, or an extra-group, as follows:

i) **Sub-group:** an individual or collection of individuals who make up only part of the communicator group. Unless you're referring to an individual, a sub-group will always need to be plural, e.g. *'we have completed our research'* can become *'Mike and Jenny have completed their research.'* (Example 3B)

ii) **Super-group:** a group which includes, but also extends beyond the communicator group. As such, it may or may not include some or all of the audience. Whether it does or not, the communicator will always need to talk objectively about it, so a super-group must always be treated as singular, e.g. *'We have always striven to ensure our remuneration packages are competitive'* can become *'The company has always striven to ensure its remuneration packages are competitive.'* (Example 5B)

iii) **Extra-group:** a group which is completely separate from the communicator group, but who are the real people who are taking the action, or making the request. Because this group is separate from the communicator(s) it can be plural, e.g. *'we (Fleet Admin) need you to complete and return the enclosed form'* can become *'the Reward & Recognition Team need you to complete and return the enclosed form.'* (Example 5B)

Verb techniques
Changing the verb
Sometimes you can't change the meaning of 'we' without also having to change the action that 'we' are, need to be, or have been, engaging in, e.g. *'we'd only have to introduce these rules later'* can become *'we'd only have to start following these rules later.'* (Example 6B)

Using impersonal verbs/ellipsis
You can use impersonal verbs (sparingly) to remove a potentially confusing meaning of 'we', e.g. *'We should have the timetable completed shortly and we'll let you know...'* can become *'They should have the timetable completed shortly and will let you know...'* (Example 4B)

Techniques for excluding the communicator from 'we'

Pronoun techniques enable you to clarify 'we' by either:
- changing it for another pronoun
- making multiple pronoun changes

Verb techniques enable you to clarify 'we' by:
- changing the action that 'we' are doing.

Pronoun techniques
Using 'they'
When 'we' means only the audience, you will need to objectify the communicator group, so 'we' will become 'they', e.g. *'We have been working with the training department to put together a timetable of training so that we can all make the transition to the new software as easily as possible. We should have the timetable completed shortly.'* can become, *'IT have been working with the training department to put together a timetable of training so that we can all make the transition to the new software as easily as possible. They should have the timetable completed shortly.'* (Example 4C)

Naming names
You may sometimes need to replace 'We' with a proper noun to keep your meaning clear, e.g. *'As part of our ongoing commitment to provide customers with the best value for money products...'* can become *'As part of the company's commitment to provide customers with the best value for money products...'* (Example 3C)

Using 'everyone', 'these', 'those', 'its'
You can often help avoid confusion and keep things clear by replacing personal pronouns ('we', 'us' & 'our') with general ones (e.g. 'everyone', 'these', 'those' & 'its'), e.g. *'our new procedures'* can become *'these new procedures.'* (Example 2C)

Talking as rather than to the audience
If you're re-writing a cascade or team brief, so that 'we' means only the audience, you may sometimes need to flip several pronouns, e.g. *'We will let you know the details'* can become *'They will let us know the details'* (Example 4C)

Verb techniques
Changing the verb
Sometimes you can't change the meaning of 'we' without also having to change the action that 'we' are, need to be, or have been, engaging in, e.g. *'we'd only have to introduce these rules later'* can become *'we'd only have to start following these rules later.'* (Example 6C)

Part 3 – Using the sub-group technique successfully

This is an extremely useful technique, which will come into play only if you want 'we' to mean the communicator and audience together. If you're going to talk about a sub-group of the communicator, there are three points to bear in mind.

1 'Our' can simultaneously include and exclude the audience.
2 'We' will take on its most recently implied meaning.
3 Even though you may intend 'we' to include the audience, you can't always guarantee that the audience will read it that way.

This means that, just because you name a sub-group, it doesn't necessarily mean that the audience will include themselves within 'we'. After all, the communicator is still representing a group, and the context will often suggest that 'we' could be just that group.

Here's how such a problem can arise:

As of the next financial new year, we will be introducing a new financial management system, which means that there will be new procedures for us all to follow.

If you want 'we' to include both communicator and audience, its first meaning will have to change. But will doing so necessarily guarantee that the audience will read 'us all' to include them?

As of the next financial new year, Accounts Payable will be introducing a new financial management system, which means that there will be new procedures for us all to follow.

Even though the sub-group has been identified, it's still a finance bod talking, and it's certainly possible to infer that he or she is talking about procedures that apply only to the finance team (the communicators are talking among themselves).

But in this example, the sub-group was the first instance of 'we' in the communication. What happens if you've already used 'we' to mean the communicator and audience? Here too there can be problems. Here's part of a note from an IT Director to all the company's PC operators:

To ensure that our[1] systems are able to meet the demands of our[2] growing business, we[3] have been investigating new PC applications, and will be upgrading some of our[4] PC packages over the next six months.

In this example, the context suggests that 'our growing business' must surely mean the business to which both communicator and audience belong. And this then works retrospectively to make 'our systems' mean 'the business's systems'. The meaning of 'we' has therefore been established. But can it survive when a sub-group is introduced to take care of meaning 3?

To ensure that our systems are able to meet the demands of our growing business, <u>software support</u> have been investigating new PC applications, and will be upgrading some of our PC packages over the next six months.

There are three things going on here:.

1. Just as with the previous example, the audience can feel that the author is speaking on behalf of a group.
2. 'We' can take on its most recently implied meaning.,
3. By referring to 'software support' the author has drawn the audience's attention into the group he represents

Therefore although it's not inevitable, it's certainly possible for 'our PC packages' to be read as 'the PC packages used in IT'. The ambiguity (if you'll pardon the logic) is all too clear.

How to avoid the ambiguity

I think it's best to explain this with examples rather than theory. Each of the nine worked examples in part 7 of this appendix contains a version in which 'we' means both audience and communicator, and six of them use the sub-group technique. As you read them, the following three principles should become apparent:

1. It's best to assume a worst-case scenario every time. Different people will bring different attitudes to any given communication, and almost everyone is under time-pressure, so it's fair to assume that at least some members of an audience will disappear at the slightest provocation.
2. Just because you intend 'we' to include both communicator and audience, it doesn't mean you have to use 'we' in place of 'you'. In fact, unless you explicitly need to talk about the communicator and audience together, your pronoun of preference in most circumstances should be 'you'.

   Let's say, for example, that there were some new procedures being introduced. You could say, *'there are new procedures for <u>us all</u> to follow'* or *'there are new procedures for you to follow.'*

Even though the procedures will apply to the communicator group as well as the audience, it's not necessary, for reasons of comprehension, to use 'us all'. The meaning is perfectly clear when you use 'you'. As mentioned in Chapter 19, some people want to use the 'us all' version because they believe that it's more inclusive. In fact, in many circumstances it will achieve the opposite, and trigger each individual reader, or listener, to feel excluded.

3. When 'you' isn't appropriate, it's usually possible to talk objectively about a group that includes both communicator and audience (e.g. 'the company').

It may seem that, in some situations, you won't be able to use 'we' to mean the communicator and audience. And on a few occasions this can indeed be true (in which case, you'll have to use 'we' to mean just the communicator. The alternative is to try getting by with loads of impersonal verbs – which of course will switch people off as well.) But in most instances, 'we' can be used effectively to include both the audience and communicator together, as the examples in Part 7 will illustrate.

Part 4 – The mynah bird 'we'

Even when you know what you need to do with this trigger, it can sometimes be disorientating, because it appears to be mimicking certain characteristics of the other linguistic triggers.

Linguistic trigger 1: Using too many impersonal verbs and abstract nouns

Initially, you might think I'm potty for even suggesting that 'we' could mimic this trigger. By its very nature, impersonal verbs don't involve pronouns, so the moment you use 'we', it can't happen – can it? Up to a point you'd be right. However, the first linguistic trigger works by giving the impression that the communicator is talking to no one, but simply engaging in a soliloquy. Misusing the word 'we' can sometimes create an almost identical impression; the difference is that sometimes, rather than it being an individual talking to him or herself, it feels like it's the communicator group that's being addressed.

As we discussed in Chapter 19, the following example can create just such an impression:

As of the next financial New Year, we[1] will be introducing a new financial management system, which means there will be new procedures for us all[2] to follow. It's important that we all[3] understand and follow these new procedures, as the mistakes we[4] have been making with the old system have been costing us[5] dearly.

Some readers could easily take the first meaning of 'we' to be 'the Accounts Payable team' (the communicator group), which was, in fact, the author's intended meaning. From then on, though, the communicator intended his meaning to expand, and include the audience. But it would be quite possible for readers to stick with their first meaning throughout. In such circumstances, throughout the rest of the communication the author would appear to be addressing only the other members of the communicator group.

Often, then, expanding the meaning of 'we' to include the audience won't work. But there may sometimes be circumstances in which it can. Here's a note from the Head of a Facilities Management department to all the employees who work in the same building as him.

At the beginning of this year, we[1] were set the task of refurbishing all our[2] office buildings. Since then, John and Mark have been working with ABC company to plan these refurbishments. Together they have agreed a timetable for the work, which will commence on 15th of next month with an upgrade of the reception here in this building. This work should take two weeks, during which time, we will all[3] need to use the building's rear entrance.

In this example, the first meaning of 'we' is Facilities Management. The second instance: 'our' is a little ambiguous (for reasons we shall be looking at shortly). The author's intended meaning was to include the audience, but it's not a disaster if the audience reads 'our buildings' to mean: 'the buildings for which we, Facilities Management, are responsible'. However, although it's *possible* to read the final 'we' as referring only to the FM team, it's much more likely to include the audience. You could argue that this is because of the subject matter itself. But is this necessarily true? Does it any more obviously include the audience than did the previous example about financial procedures? The key difference is that the FM manager has cleverly *objectified* the specific members of the communicator group who are doing the work: 'John and Mark', and the third party 'ABC company'. By referring to this group as 'they', he's allowed himself to become, like the rest of the people who work in the building, someone who will have to go along with what 'they' have planned. This is one of the numerous techniques for dealing with 'we' that are explained and demonstrated in Part 2 of this appendix.

Linguistic trigger 2: Presupposing the audience's attitude or situation

When 'we' is used to mean 'you and I', it can put you in just as much danger of presupposing the audience's attitude or situation:

We all want to keep costs down

This is an extremely common mistake, which almost always seems to come from a well intentioned but misunderstood attempt to use 'we' to create a sense of inclusiveness. In fact, it achieves the opposite. And unlike other aspects of the 'we' trigger, this one can kick in right from the off; it doesn't have to wait for 'we' to change its meaning.

Linguistic trigger 3: Writing about 'the' reader

This piece of mimicry happens in two quite different ways. The first, and more obvious, comes from writing about the business while treating it as plural. This is a subject we deal with in section 5 of this appendix. The second way in which 'we' mimics this trigger is rather subtle. Just as authors may sometimes write about the reader, so too can they write about the group they're representing. The net result is that, bizarre though it may seem, the communicator group ends up in the detached observer position, and the audience is left wondering who, if anyone, the author now represents. Do that person's words need to be listened to any more? It seems not. This usually happens when an author trying not to change the meaning of 'we'. The following example was written by a Market Research Manager to his colleagues in the Marketing Division:

As part of our ongoing commitment to provide our customers with the best value for money products, Market Research have been conducting their latest round of research into what our competitors are up to. As our society is changing at an ever quickening pace, we all have a duty to our colleagues in sales and customer service to be aware of how our market stands currently, and what we all need to focus on in order to keep our company ahead of the game. Market Research will therefore be conducting a number of lunchtime presentations, on the 16th, 17th and 18th so that we can all get ourselves up to speed.

Whoa, just a second Mr Author, aren't you *part* of the Market Research Team? This is a classic example of how 'we' can behave in a very similar way to the linguistic minefield, as writers instinctively sidestep one trigger, only to tread on another. What makes 'we' all the more challenging is that it's just the one trigger; it just has numerous ways of being set off. Why, after all, would the Market Research Manager have disassociated himself from the his department? Why not simply include himself: 'my team and I' for example? Could it be that he's instinctively shying away from setting off this trigger in another way? Almost certainly.

Suppose he were to decide that he wanted 'we' to include both the communicator group and audience. Arguably, there are only two instances of 'we' that would need to change (although the first instance of 'our' on line two may also be a bit dodgy).

As part of our ongoing commitment to provide our customers with the best value for money products, we've been conducting our latest round of research into what our competitors are up to. As our society is changing at an ever quickening pace, we all have a duty to our colleagues in sales and customer service to be aware of how our market stands currently, and what we all need to focus on in order to keep our company ahead of the game. We'll therefore be conducting a number of lunchtime presentations, on the 16th, 17th and 18th so that we can all get ourselves up to speed.

This is how it could (and all too frequently does) go wrong:

As part of our ongoing commitment to provide our customers with the best value for money products, my team and I have been conducting the latest round of research into what our competitors are up to. As our society is changing at an ever quickening pace, we all have a duty to our colleagues in sales and customer service to be aware of how our market stands currently, and what we all need to focus on in order to keep our company ahead of the game. My team and I will therefore be conducting a number of lunchtime presentations, on the 16th, 17th and 18th so that we can all get ourselves up to speed.

Here 'we' combines three of its characteristics to create a web of confusion. Firstly, if you look only at the uses of 'we', 'us' and 'our', it's evident that the author has intended them to mean 'the communicator group and audience' every time. But 'we' has a knack of assuming its most recently implied meaning: in this example, 'my team and I'. So who are 'our competitors' now? Are they the market research teams in other companies – or independent market research operations. Couple this to the ability of 'our' to be ambiguous about whether or not it includes the audience, and the question arises about who is being referred to in the phrases 'We all have a duty', and 'so we can all get ourselves up to speed'.. Is 'we' now mimicking the first linguistic trigger? Are the communicator group now simply talking among themselves? It all depends on how someone reads it. But there's no question that it could just as easily be read this way as any other.

Therefore, although the author has stayed true to his intention of keeping only those meanings of 'we' that included the audience, this rapscallion of a pronoun has managed to perform a deft little 'jink' and got past him anyway.

Linguistic trigger 4: Splitting the audience's identity

Naturally, 'we' can't do this, given that it can only ever be plural, never singular. However, the very fact that 'we' can change its meaning enables it to replicate the fifth trigger's ability to work retrospectively, so that people question not only if the text they're reading is talking to them any more, but whether it ever has been. This is what happened when an HR team announced a new staff benefit scheme.

We all want to have more money to play with, and over the past few months we have been in discussions with a number of local businesses to negotiate a number of special deals.

Here, the audience may initially feel included in the first meaning of 'we' (although it is presupposing their attitude). But the second use of 'we' changes all that, making it look as if maybe its only members of the HR team who want more money to play with. And, as 'we' spins another web of confusion, this group may now be just talking among themselves. Or an aspect of the next trigger may be kicking in.

Linguistic trigger 5: Misusing the communicator position

There are two ways in which 'we' can mimic this trigger. Firstly, because 'we' can mean 'you and I', it can feel like it's combining linguistic triggers 2 & 5 so that it's not just presupposing their attitude, but actually putting words into their mouths as well.

Furthermore (and perhaps unsurprisingly, given its capacity for mayhem) 'we' can also play with the tonality of the mind's voice as a cat does with a ball of wool, with some remarkable repercussions. One of my clients was once analysing the one of the examples we've already discussed, and said she'd found a meaning of 'we' which included only the audience; the communicator was gone. But when I read it myself, I couldn't understand how she'd managed this. Try it for yourself:

As of the next financial New Year, we will be introducing a new financial management system, which means that there will be new procedures for us all to follow. It's important that we all understand and follow the new procedures, as the mistakes we have been making with the old system have been costing us dearly.

If you're like me (and the clients with whom I have subsequently shared this example) you may struggle to see how 'we' can mean only the audience. But imagine one of those bossy, maternal nurses from the 1960s, who would say to their patients, 'And how are we today?' With such a tone, the word 'we' actually means 'you'. Try reading the last sentence of the example with that tone of voice and notice what happens. Whether or not you 'get' this will depend a lot on your mind's voice. But even if you don't, most people tell me they realise just how condescending it can sound when read in that way. Certainly whenever I read it now, I can almost see the admonishing finger wagging in my face.

Part 5 – The company – singular or plural?

One of the perennial debates that goes on in many businesses concerns the vexed question of whether to refer to itself (or themselves) in the singular or the plural. Should you say, 'XYZ company is committed to quality' or 'XYZ company are committed to quality'? Some people feel strongly on the matter, and insist that there be a hard and fast ruling on this. Whether they can have such a ruling largely depends on how hard and fast they want it to be. To make any ruling robust, we need to take two criteria into account:

1. What is possible grammatically
2. What will work best commercially

Let's start with the grammatical issues.

The words 'company' and 'organisation' are technically known as nouns of multitude, which means they can be either singular or plural (even though grammar checkers sometimes struggle with this). Naturally enough, this also applies to the proper name of your business, and means that you can quite properly say 'the company is' or 'the company are'. Both are grammatically correct.

From a commercial perspective, there can be valid reasons for referring to your business as singular in some circumstances, and plural in others. This is partly because there are different dynamics in play with internal and external communications, and partly because you've often got a choice about whether to talk *about* the business (i.e. objectively) or *as* the business (i.e. subjectively).

If you say 'XYZ company is', the pronoun which represents 'XYZ company' is 'it'. So, when you refer to your business as a singular entity, you can't talk subjectively 'as' the business, only objectively 'about' it. Importantly, you will also be making 'the business' impersonal. If you say 'XYZ company are', the pronouns which can represent 'the business' will be 'we' and 'they'. So when you refer to the business as a multiple entity you are, by implication, talking about the people who make up that business. But you may be doing so subjectively (we) or objectively (they). You therefore have three options.

Writing *about* the business:
1. objectively and impersonally: 'XYZ company is'/'it is'
2. objectively and personally: 'XYZ company are'/'they are'.

Writing *as* the business
3. subjectively and personally: 'XYZ company are'/'we are'.

If you're writing external communications, the 'communicator group' can be the entire business. For legal statements, making the business singular is certainly useful, because it indicates a single legal entity ('XYZ company is...') When it comes to marketing, customer and recruitment communications, though, you're usually going to be better off making your business plural. Doing so will mean that customers and recruits will be more likely to think of your business not as a single, cold, impersonal entity, but as a group of people with whom they can interact. And because such communications are talking directly to the audience, it makes sense to talk as the business (XYZ company are.../We are...'). If talking through a third party though (e.g. a journalist's column in a newspaper) it generally works better to talk about the business, if you want the words to appear to be those of someone who's taking an objective view (XYZ company are.../They are...').

Internal communications are different, not least because the communicator group cannot be the whole business. How you refer to 'the business' therefore becomes a question of whether you want 'we' to include or exclude the audience. If you want 'we' to mean only the communicator group, you have no choice but to talk objectively about the business, because to talk subjectively as the business would have to include the audience. And you'll have to make the business singular (it), because to use the plural (they) would imply that 'the business' was a group of people to which the audience didn't belong; you would, in effect, be mimicking the third linguistic trigger: writing about the readers.

So, with internal communications, if 'we' excludes the audience:
• the communicators = we
• the audience = you
• the business = it.

If you want 'we' to include the audience, things get a little more involved, for example:

We've been doing really well. We've gone from strength to strength over the last 12 months; our profits are up, and the company is well set for the coming year.

In this note from a CEO to all employees, 'we' clearly means the business, as does the expression 'the company is well set'. Within one sentence, then, 'the business' has been both singular and plural, without causing any problems of either comprehension, or detached observer triggers. When it comes to hard and fast rules, then, the only one that holds true in all circumstances for internal communications, is that the business must be singular when it's talked about objectively.

With legal issues, for example, it is not the business as a group of people, but as a single legal entity that is involved. If, let's say, the business had just been fined by its regulator, it would not be the individual employees, but the corporation that would have to stump up the cash. Therefore, if you want 'we' to include the audience, it is not only possible, but sometimes necessary to refer to the business as both singular and plural in the same communication.

This is all very well when the audience is the whole business, but what happens when it's not; if the audience is, say, just the Marketing department?

We've had a really good year. We're beating our competitors hands down, but we cannot afford to be complacent. Keeping ahead of the game means we need to continue providing the best possible support to our colleagues in Sales and Customer Service. Only in this way can we be sure to provide our customers with the products and service they want, and make sure the business continues to grow.

Although 'we' hasn't acted as a detached observer trigger in this example, it has started to create a little confusion about who's responsible for what. This is a ticklish problem, which takes us into a largely under-utilised application of 'we': how to use it in Team Briefs and live cascades.

Part 6 – Using 'we' in Team Briefs and live cascades

In a team brief or other live cascade scenario, using 'we' to mean just the audience can work particularly well. Live presentations enable individuals to identify themselves with a specific audience group. And expanding that group beyond the confines of the room they're in won't stop them from belonging to it.

With a communication that people are going to read (or listen to/watch privately) a subtly different dynamic takes place. You can start out using 'we' to mean 'the business' and then contract it to mean just the discrete audience sector. However, once you've done this, you're best off leaving 'we' with this second meaning, because you're only going to need to communicate with a discrete audience group, if that group is going to be doing something different from everyone else in the business. As such, if the meaning of 'we' were to keep chopping and changing between the discrete group and the business as a whole, the audience might become unclear about who was responsible for taking which action. If you contract 'we' to mean only the audience, therefore, 'the business' will then need to be objectified ('it'). If you expand 'we' to mean 'the business', the discrete audience sector will need to be addressed as 'you'.

Not so with a team brief which is presented live, and is made up of a number of communications. Indeed, it is precisely because it is made up of several communications that you're usually better off using 'we' to mean just the audience. Some of the Team Brief items could be coming from single individuals, some from groups and some from individuals representing groups. And each is likely to have been expressed in its own idiosyncratic way – with the meaning of 'we' chopping and changing all over the place in the original drafts. Redrafting Team Brief, so that 'we' means only the audience, will remove this problem at a stroke. And it'll have another huge spin-off benefit too.

Cascade processes are notorious for their inconsistency, with some people giving dull, lifeless verbatim readings of the words, while others go way off message. We've already discussed the power of the mind's voice, and the impact it can have on people's emotional responses to what they're reading. How much more powerful an impact is it likely to have if they not only have to read the words, but say them aloud to other people: if the words are not only being put into their mind's mouth, but their physical mouth as well? Might not Team Briefers unconsciously know that, if they use 'I' and 'we' to express other people's views, desires and decisions, the words are going to ring somewhat hollow? Might that not, at least in part, explain why some of the less confident presenters lack conviction in their briefings, while the more confident ones are effectively tearing up the script and giving the messages their own unique spin?

For the core brief (as opposed to the local news stuff) although the team briefer is saying the words, he or she is as much a member of the audience as everyone else in the team. He or she just happens to have the job of being the mouthpiece of not one, but several communicators. Therefore, it makes sense to allow that reality to be reflected in the way the words are written: objectifying the numerous communicators (as 'he', 'she' or 'they') and allowing the 'team' (briefer included) to think of themselves as 'we'.

Part 7 – Worked examples

Example 1
The conference department writing to all conference delegates

Our[1] 25th annual sales conference will be on 1st June. We[2] want this conference to be a success. To ensure it is, we[3] all need to prepare properly, so we've[4] put together some guidelines to help things run smoothly. If we[5] follow these guidelines, we[6] should all get the most out of the conference.

Meanings that include the audience: 1, 3, 5 & 6
Meanings that exclude the audience: 2 & 4

A. 'We' includes the communicator and excludes the audience

The company's 25th annual sales conference will be on 1st June. We want this conference to be a success for you. To ensure it is, everyone needs to prepare properly, so we've put together some guidelines to help things run smoothly. If you follow these guidelines, you should get the most out of the conference.

B. 'We' includes both communicator and audience

Our 25th annual sales conference will be on 1st June. The Board want it to be a success. To ensure that it is, we all need to prepare properly, so the Directors have approved some guidelines to help things run smoothly. If we all follow these guidelines, we should all get the most out of the conference.

C. 'We' excludes the communicator and includes the audience

Our 25th annual sales conference will be on 1st June. The conference team want this conference to be a success for us. To ensure that it is, we all need to prepare properly, so the conference team have put together some guidelines to help things run smoothly. If we follow these guidelines, we should all get the most out of the conference.

Example 2
A senior finance manager writing to all budget holders

As of the next financial new year, we[1] will be introducing a new financial management system, which means that there will be new procedures for us all[2] to follow. It's important that we[3] all understand and follow our[4] new procedures, as the mistakes people have been making with the old system are costing us[5] dearly.

Meanings that include the audience: 2, 3 & 5
Meanings that exclude the audience: 1 & 4

A. 'We' includes the communicator and excludes the audience

As of the next financial new year, we will be introducing a new financial management system, which means that there will be new procedures for <u>you</u> to follow. It's important that <u>you</u> understand and follow <u>these</u> new procedures, as the mistakes people have been making with the old system are costing <u>the company</u> dearly.

B. 'We' includes both the communicator and audience

As of the next financial new year, <u>Accounts Payable</u> will be introducing a new financial management system, which means that there will be new procedures for <u>you</u> to follow. It's important that we all understand and follow <u>these</u> new procedures, as the mistakes people have been making with the old system are costing <u>the company</u> dearly.

C. 'We' excludes the communicator and includes the audience

As of the next financial new year, <u>the finance department</u> will be introducing a new financial management system, which means that there will be new procedures for us all to follow. It's important that we all understand and follow <u>these</u> new procedures, as the mistakes people have been making with the old system are costing <u>the company</u> dearly.

Example 3

The Market Research Manager writing to the rest of the Marketing Division

As part of our[1] ongoing commitment to provide our[2] customers with the best value for money products, we've[3] been conducting our[4] latest round of research into what our[5] competitors are up to. As our[6] society is changing at an ever quickening pace, we[7] all have a duty to our[8] colleagues in sales and customer service to be aware of how our[9] market stands currently, and what we all[10] need to focus on in order to keep our[11] company ahead of the game. We'll[12] therefore be conducting a number of lunchtime presentations, so that we[13] can all get ourselves[14] up to speed.

Meanings that include the audience: 1, 2, 5, 6, 7, 8, 9, 10, 11, 13 & 14
Meanings that exclude the audience: 3, 4 & 12

A. 'We' includes the communicator and excludes the audience

As part of <u>the company's</u> ongoing commitment to provide customers with the best value for money products, we've been conducting our latest round *of research into what <u>the competition</u> are up to. As society is changing at an ever quickening pace, <u>everyone in Marketing</u> has a duty to <u>those working</u> in sales and customer service to be aware of how <u>the</u> market stands currently, and what <u>needs to be focused</u> on in order to keep <u>this</u> company ahead of the game. We'll therefore be conducting a number of lunchtime presentations, so that <u>you</u> can all get <u>yourself</u> up to speed.*

B. 'We' includes both the communicator and audience

As part of our ongoing commitment to provide our customers with the best value for money products, <u>Mike and Jenny</u> have been conducting <u>the</u> latest round of research into what <u>the competition</u> are up to. As our society is changing at an ever quickening pace, we all have a duty to our colleagues in sales and customer service to be aware of how our market stands currently, and what we all need to focus on in order to keep our company ahead of the game. <u>Mike and Jenny</u> will therefore be conducting a number of lunchtime presentations, so that <u>you</u> can get <u>yourself</u> up to speed.

C. 'We' excludes the communicator and includes the audience

As part of <u>the company's</u> ongoing commitment to provide customers with the best value for money products, <u>Market Research</u> have been conducting <u>their</u> latest round of research into what <u>the competition</u> are up to. As our society is changing at an ever quickening pace, we all have a duty to our colleagues in sales and customer service to be aware of how our market stands currently, and what we all need to focus on in order to keep our company ahead of the game. <u>Market Research</u> will therefore be conducting a number of lunchtime presentations, so that we can all get ourselves up to speed.

Example 4
The IT Director writing to all staff

To ensure that our[1] systems are able to meet the demands of our[2] growing business, we[3] have been investigating new PC applications, and will be upgrading some of our[4] PC packages over the next six months. However, it's important that we[5] are able to continue working efficiently while the upgrade is taking place, and we[6] have been working with the training department to put together a timetable of training so we[7] can all make the transition to new software as easily as possible. We[8] should have the timetable completed shortly, and we'll[9] let you know the details in due course.

Meanings that may or may not include the audience: 1
Meanings that include the audience: 2, 4, 5 & 7
Meanings that exclude the audience: 3, 6, 8 & 9

A. 'We' includes the communicator and excludes the audience

To ensure that our systems are able to meet the demands of <u>the</u> growing business, we have been investigating new PC applications, and will be upgrading some of <u>the outdated</u> PC packages over the next six months. However, it's important that <u>you</u> are able to continue working efficiently while the upgrade is taking place, and we have been working with the training department to put together a timetable of training so <u>you</u> can make the transition to new software as easily as possible. We should have the timetable completed shortly, and we'll let you know the details in due course.

B. We includes both the communicator and audience

To ensure that our systems are able to meet the demands of our growing business, <u>software support</u> have been investigating new PC applications, and will be upgrading some of <u>the company's outdated</u> PC packages over the next six months. However, it's important that you are able to continue working efficiently while the upgrade is taking place, and <u>software support</u> have been working with the training department to put together a timetable of training so you can make the transition to new software as easily as possible. <u>They</u> should have the timetable completed shortly, and <u>will</u> let <u>you</u> know the details in due course.

C. 'We' excludes the communicator and includes the audience

To ensure that our systems are able to meet the demands of our growing business, <u>IT</u> have been investigating new PC applications, and will be upgrading some of our PC packages over the next six months. However, it's important that we are able to continue working efficiently while the upgrade is taking place, and <u>IT</u> have been working with the training department to put together a timetable of training so we can all make the transition to new software as easily as possible. <u>They</u> should have the timetable completed shortly, and <u>will</u> let <u>us</u> know the details in due course.

Example 5
Fleet management writing to all company car drivers

Owing to the introduction of new corporate and personal tax rules on company cars, we[1] are having to review our[2] car policy. We[3] have always striven to ensure that our[4] remuneration packages are competitive, and will continue to do so despite these legislative changes. We[5] therefore need you to complete the attached form to ensure that none of us[6] is unduly penalised.

Meanings that may or may not include the audience: 2 & 4

Meanings that include the audience: 1, 3 & 5
Meanings that exclude the audience: 6

A. 'We' includes the communicator and excludes the audience

Owing to the introduction of new corporate and personal tax rules on company cars, we are having to review our car policy. We have always striven to ensure that our remuneration packages are competitive, and will continue to do so despite these legislative changes. We therefore need you to complete the attached form to ensure that <u>you aren't</u> unduly penalised.

B. 'We' includes both the communicator and audience

Owing to the introduction of new corporate and personal tax rules on company cars, <u>the company</u> is having to review <u>its</u> car policy. <u>The company has</u> always striven to ensure that <u>its</u> remuneration packages are competitive, and will continue to do so despite these legislative changes. <u>The Reward and Recognition Team</u> therefore need you to complete the attached form to ensure that <u>you aren't</u> unduly penalised.

C. 'We' excludes the communicator and includes the audience

Owing to the introduction of new corporate and personal tax rules on company cars, <u>HR</u> are having to review <u>the company's</u> car policy. <u>The company has</u> always striven to ensure that our remuneration packages are competitive, and will continue to do so despite these legislative changes. <u>HR</u> therefore need each of us to complete <u>one of these new</u> forms, to ensure that we aren't unduly penalised.

Example 6

The HR Director writing to all staff

Health and safety is always an issue for us[1], and we[2] are introducing new guidelines which include the latest Best Practice recommendations from the European Union. Many of these guidelines will become legal requirements within the next couple of years, so we'd[3] only have to start following them later anyway. The attached leaflet tells you what our[4] new guidelines are, and what changes they will require in our[5] working practices.

Meanings that may or may not include the audience: 4
Meanings that include the audience: 1, 3 & 5
Meanings that exclude the audience: 2

A. 'We' includes the communicator and excludes the audience

Health and safety is always an issue for <u>the business,</u> and we are introducing new guidelines which include the latest Best Practice *recommendations from the European Union. Many of these guidelines will become legal requirements within the next couple of years, so we'd only have to <u>introduce</u> them later anyway. The attached leaflet tells you what the new guidelines are, and what changes they will require in <u>your</u> working practices.*

B. 'We' includes both the communicator and audience

As a business, Health and Safety is always an issue for us, and <u>the Health & Safety Group</u> are introducing new guidelines which include the latest Best Practice recommendations from the European Union. Many of these guidelines will become legal requirements within the next couple of years, so we'd only have to start following them later anyway. The attached leaflet tells you what <u>these</u> new guidelines are, and what changes they will require in our working practices.

C. 'We' excludes the communicator and includes the audience

Health and safety is always an issue for <u>the business</u>, and <u>HR</u> are introducing new guidelines which include the latest Best Practice recommendations from the European Union. Many of these guidelines will become legal requirements within the next couple of years, so we'd only have to start following them later anyway. <u>This</u> leaflet tells you what <u>the</u> new guidelines are, and what changes they will require in our working practices.

Example 7
The CEO writing to all staff

Our[1] end of year results are about to be published, and we[2] are pleased to be able to tell you that both our[3] profits and market share have increased significantly over this time last year. We[4] feel this is a testament to our[5] business strategy, and the hard work we[6] have all put in over the past twelve months.

Meanings that may or may not include the audience: 5
Meanings that include the audience: 1 & 3
Meanings that exclude the audience: 2, 4 & 6

A. 'We' includes the communicator and excludes the audience

<u>The company's</u> end of year results are about to be published, and we are pleased to be able to tell you that both profits and market share have increased significantly over this time last year. We feel this is a testament to <u>the business's</u> strategy, and the hard work <u>everyone has</u> put in over the past 12 months.

B. 'We' includes both the communicator and audience

Our end of year results are about to be published, and I am pleased to be able to tell you that both our profits and market share have increased significantly over this time last year. I feel this is a testament to our business strategy, and the hard work we have all put in over the past 12 months.

C. 'We' excludes the communicator and includes the audience

Our end of year results are about to be published, and the Board are pleased to be able to announce that both our profits and market share have increased significantly over this time last year. They feel this is a testament to both the business's strategy, and the hard work we have all put in over the past 12 months.

Example 8

A Customer Service rep writing to a customer

Further to our[1] conversation, I can confirm that we[2] have increased your overdraft facility as we[3] agreed. Your new limit will be £800 and our[4] standard terms and conditions apply. If you have any further questions about this, please give me a ring so we[5] can discuss them.

Meanings that include the audience: 1, 3 & 5
Meanings that exclude the audience: 2 & 4

A. 'We' includes the communicator and excludes the audience

Thank you for contacting us. I can confirm that we have increased your overdraft facility as agreed. Your new limit will be £800 and our standard terms and conditions apply. If you have any further questions about this, please give me a ring to discuss them.

B. 'We' includes both the communicator and audience

Further to our conversation, I can confirm that the bank has increased your overdraft facility as we agreed. Your new limit will be £800 and the bank's standard terms and conditions apply. If you have any further questions about this, please give me a ring so we can discuss them.

Appendix D
The Linguistic Minefield Simulator

This appendix summarises the linguistic triggers and contains five sample communications which you can use to develop your skill in spotting and disarming these triggers. Each sample has two 'solutions' at the back of the appendix. If you want to practice spotting the triggers, the first solution simply highlights where they are. If you want to practice disarming them, the second solution shows re-written versions, with the triggers taken out.

Some of the solutions may seem pedantic at first, but you need to remember that different people are more sensitive to some triggers than others. Therefore, even though you might not be switched off by some of the triggers, the potential danger remains – unnecessarily. The linguistic triggers are what they are, regardless of how you feel about them personally.

In the body of the book, I presented each trigger discretely to make it easy to understand. In the real world, though (from which the following examples come) they can combine to form multiple triggers. There are several such triggers in the examples.

The six linguistic triggers

Linguistic Trigger 1: Using too many impersonal verbs & abstract nouns
- You can disarm this trigger by using personal verbs

Linguistic Trigger 2: Presupposing the audience's attitude or situation
- You can disarm this trigger by:
    - making the language flexible (Page 158)
    - making the language indirect (Page 159)
    - playing around with the attitudinal references (Page 160)
    - using one of the past tenses (Page 161)
    - using quotations or questions (Page 162)

Linguistic Trigger 3: Writing about the reader(s)

- You can disarm this trigger by replacing the third person noun with the second person pronoun 'you'.

Linguistic Trigger 4: Quantifying the audience

- There are four different linguistic structures which can set off this trigger, which require their own solutions:

(a & b) Flexible and inflexible quantifiers: e.g. 'some, many, most, all, each ... of you'. (Page 164)

Solutions

- Make your language indirect (e.g. some people).
- Lose the quantifier (i.e. rather than 'some of you', simply say 'you').
- Make it flexible by using 'if'.

(c) Plurals (Page 167)

Solutions

- Lose the plural.
- Use an oblique or flexible reference.

(d) Adverbs: e.g. 'separately', 'individually' or 'together' (Page 168)

Solution

- Lose the adverb.

Linguistic Trigger 5: Putting words in people's mouths

- You can disarm this trigger by using the second person (You) instead of the first person (I), and by using statements and explanations instead of questions and answers.

Linguistic Trigger 6: 'We'

- You can disarm this trigger by making the meaning of 'we' consistent throughout the communication, i.e. it either:
  - always includes the communicator and excludes the audience, or
  - always includes both communicator and audience or
  - always excludes the communicator and includes the audience.
- The linguistic techniques for doing this start on page 195.

Example 1
An HR Director writing to all staff

We *once again have a need to develop more managers to cope with our business growth. We will therefore be expanding the Management Development Programme (MDP) we instigated last year.*
Who is eligible?
The MDP is available in all countries except Cyprus. Employees who applied for the MDP last time and are still interested do not need to complete a new form. However, they do need to notify their manager of their continued interest. The manager should then advise their Director.
How do I apply?
Details of the MDP process and how to apply will be communicated at the country level as the process varies from country to country.
Where can I find more information?
If you have questions not answered here or in your country specific communication, you should speak with your manager or local HR contact.
We are committed to developing the organisation so that we can achieve growth now and in the future and fulfil the potential we all know this company has. And what all of you can take pride in is the continued improvement of our business results.

Example 2
The Managing Director of XYZ company writing to all staff

The Board and I recently reviewed the results of the latest staff survey. We were very impressed with what you told us and the openness of your comments. The good news is the results tell us that most of you like working for the company.
As for the most pressing issue we need to address, you told us the decision making process is not working very well. Clearly this is a major concern for us and we have set up a project team to look into how we can improve the situation.
Finally, our end-of-year results have been benchmarked against other companies operating in our industry and I am pleased to announce that we compare favourably with our competitors.

Example 3
A plc's Chief Executive writing to all staff

I know you are all very busy and I appreciate you taking the time to read through these messages.

I am receiving very valuable feedback from many of you on the issues we need to fix to better serve our customers and out-perform our competitors. My fellow Directors and I are taking many of your suggestions on board and following through with the appropriate people. Please continue to provide your ideas on how we can improve our business.

Example 4
A briefing pack for Line Managers

Welcome to the Customer Relationship Briefing pack. This pack contains overviews, product descriptions, fact sheets and diagrams to assist Line Managers and staff in their understanding of the new Customer Relationship Programme (CRP).

The successful implementation of the CRP relies on each Line Manager understanding the concepts and changes involved and passing this information on to their teams. For those readers who have attended a CRP briefing session, your feedback has been positive overall, even though finding time to attend was difficult. Because you've been to these sessions, you can go straight to Page 7. For those readers who have not attended a CRP briefing session, please go to Page 2.

Example 5
An HR manager writing to company car drivers

From next year, new rules will be introduced regarding business trips. The current system has been reviewed, including accounting practices and reward and recognition structure. The decisions taken will result in better cost management, procedure simplification and reductions in paperwork.

Employees who, for business reasons, are required to drive more than 2,000 miles a month will no longer be required to complete weekly returns. These can now be done monthly through the existing Intranet form.

Employees who make ad-hoc business trips will be required to visit the Travelmaster web page on the Intranet to identify the cheapest travel option. As many of you know, Travelmaster enables the employee to enter details of their journey, together with the make and model of their car, and provides a comparison of different travel options. Employees will be required to forward their options page to HR for approval before booking tickets.

First class travel on trains and business class on planes will be restricted to Grades G3 and above.

Example 1 – Solution i: Exposing the triggers

An HR Director writing to all staff about a Management Development Programme

We[1] once again have a need to develop more managers to cope with our[2] business growth. We[3] will therefore be expanding the Management Development Programme (MDP) we[4] instigated last year.
Who is eligible?
The MDP is available in all countries except Cyprus. Employees[A] who applied for the MDP last time and are still interested do not need to complete a new form. However, they[B] do need to notify their[C] manager of their[D] continued interest. The manager should then advise their Director.
How do I apply?[E]
Details of the MDP process and how to apply will be communicated at the country level as the process varies from country to country.
Where can I find more information?[F]
If you have questions not answered here or in your country specific communication, you should speak with your manager or local HR contact.
We[5] are committed to developing the organisation so that we[6] can achieve growth now and in the future and fulfil the potential we[7] all know[G] this company has. And what all of you[H] can take pride in is the continued improvement of our[8] business results.

The triggers
- A, B, C & D – *Linguistic Trigger (LT) 3*: Writing about the readers
- E & F – *LT 5*: Putting words in people's mouths
- G – *LT 2*: Presupposing the audience's attitude or situation
- H – *LT 4*: Splitting the audience's identity
- *LT 6*: We:
  - Meanings of 'we' that may or may not include the audience: 1, 3 & 4
  - Meanings of 'we' that include the audience: 2, 6, 7 & 8
  - Meanings of 'we' that exclude the audience: 5

Solution ii: Disarming the triggers

We once again have a need to develop more managers to cope with our business growth. We will therefore be expanding the Management Development Programme (MDP) we instigated last year.
Who is eligible?

The MDP is available in all countries except Cyprus. <u>If you</u> applied for the MDP last time, and are still interested, <u>you</u> do not need to complete a new form. However, <u>you</u> do need to notify <u>your</u> manager to confirm <u>your</u> continued interest. <u>Your</u> manager should then advise his or her Director.

How to apply

Details of the MDP process and how to apply will be communicated at the country level as the process varies from country to country.

Where to find more information

If you have questions not answered here or in your country specific communication, you should speak with your manager or local HR contact.

The Board are committed to developing the business so that it can achieve growth now and in the future, and <u>give you the opportunities to fulfil your potential</u>. And <u>you</u> can take pride in the continued improvement of <u>the business's</u> results.

Example 2 – Solution i: Exposing the triggers

The Managing Director of XYZ company writing to all staff

The Board and I recently reviewed the results of the latest staff survey. We[1] were very impressed with what you told[A] us[2] and the openness of your comments[B]. The good news is the results tell us[3] that most of you[C] like working for the company.

As for the most pressing issue we[4] need to address, you told[D] us[5] the decision making process is not working very well. Clearly this is a major concern for us[6] and we[7] have set up a project team to look into how we[8] can improve the situation.

Finally, our[9] end-of-year results have been benchmarked against other companies operating in our[10] industry and I am pleased to announce that we[11] compare favourably with our[12] competitors.

The triggers

- A & B – *LT2*: Presupposing the audience's attitude or situation
- C – *LT 4*: Splitting the audience's identity
- D – *LT2*: Presupposing the audience's attitude or situation
- *LT 6*: We:
  - Meanings of 'we' that may or may not include the audience: 4, 6 & 8
  - Meanings of 'we' that include the audience: 9, 10, 11 & 12
  - Meanings of 'we' that exclude the audience: 2, 3, 5 & 7

Solution ii: Disarming the triggers

The Board and I recently reviewed the results of the latest staff survey. We were very impressed with <u>the information we got</u> and the openness of <u>the comments</u>. The good news is the results tell us that <u>most people</u> like working for the company.

As for the most pressing issue we need to address, <u>we learned that</u> the decision making process is not working very well. Clearly this is a major concern for us and we have set up a project team to look into how we can improve the situation.

Finally, <u>the company's</u> end-of-year results have been benchmarked against other companies operating in <u>the</u> industry, and I am pleased to announce that <u>XYZ company</u> compares favourably with <u>the competition</u>.

Example 3 – Solution i: Exposing the triggers

A plc's Chief Executive writing to all staff

I know[A] you are all[B] very busy and I appreciate you taking the time[C] to read through these messages[D].

I am receiving very valuable feedback from many of you[E] on the issues we[1] need to fix to better serve our[2] customers and out-perform our[3] competitors. My fellow Directors and I are taking many of your suggestions[F] on board and we[4] are following through with the appropriate people. Please continue to provide us[5] with your ideas[G] on how we[6] can improve our[7] business.

The triggers
- A – *LT2*: Presupposing the audience's attitude or situation
- B – *LT 4*: Splitting the audience's identity
- C & D: *LT2*: Presupposing the audience's attitude or situation (I may be reading this message, but you can't know I've read any others, nor that I'll do so in the future)
- E – *LT 4*: Splitting the audience's identity
- F & G- *LT2*: Presupposing the audience's attitude or situation (Both these presuppose that I've already offered at least one suggestion/idea)
- *LT 6*: We:
  - Meanings of 'we' that may or may not include the audience: 1 & 6
  - Meanings of 'we' that include the audience: 2, 3 & 7
  - Meanings of 'we' that exclude the audience: 4 & 5

Solution ii: Disarming the triggers

As always, it seems everyone is very busy, so I appreciate you taking the time to read this.

I am receiving very valuable feedback from many people on the issues we need to fix to better serve our customers and out-perform our competitors. I am taking many of these suggestions on board and ensuring they are followed through by the appropriate people. If you have any new ideas on how we can improve our business, please let me know.

Example 4 – Solution i: Exposing the triggers

A briefing pack for Line Managers

Welcome to the Customer Relationship Briefing pack. This pack contains overviews, product descriptions, fact sheets and diagrams to assist Line Managers[A] and staff in their understanding of the new Customer Relationship Programme (CRP).

The successful implementation of the CRP relies on each Line Manager[B] understanding the concepts and changes involved and passing this information on to their teams[C]. For those readers[D] who have attended a CRP briefing session, your feedback has been positive overall[E], even though finding time to attend was difficult[F]. Because you've been to these sessions, you can go straight to Page 7. For those readers[G] who have not attended a CRP briefing session, please go to Page 2.

The triggers
- A, B & C – *LT3*: Writing about the reader
- D – *LT 4*: Splitting the audience's identity
- E – *LTs 2 & 4*: Presupposing the audience's attitude or situation/ splitting the audience's identity
- F – *LT2*: Presupposing the audience's attitude or situation
- G – *LT 4*: Splitting the audience's identity

Solution ii: Disarming the triggers

Welcome to the Customer Relationship Briefing pack. This pack contains overviews, product descriptions, fact sheets and diagrams to assist you and your staff in understanding the new Customer Relationship Programme (CRP).

The successful implementation of the CRP relies on you understanding the concepts and changes involved and passing this information on to your *team. We have run a series of CRP briefing session, <u>to which the feedback has been positive overall</u>, even though <u>some people had to struggle to make the time to attend</u>. If you have attended one of these sessions, please go straight to Page 7. <u>If you</u> have not attended a CRP briefing session, please go to Page 2.*

Example 5 – Solution i: Exposing the triggers

An HR manager writing to company car drivers

<u>*From next year, new rules will be introduced regarding business trips. The current system has been reviewed, including accounting practices and reward and recognition structure. The decisions taken will result in better cost management, procedure simplification and reductions in paperwork.*</u>[A]

Employees[B] *who, for business reasons, are required to drive more than 2,000 miles a month will no longer be required to complete weekly returns. They*[C] *can now do these monthly through the existing Intranet form.*

Employees[D] *who make ad-hoc business trips will be required to visit the Travelmaster web page on the Intranet to identify the cheapest travel option. As <u>many of you</u>*[E] *know, Travelmaster enables the employee*[F] *to enter details of <u>their</u>*[G] *journey, together with the make and model of <u>their car</u>*[H]*, and provides a comparison of different travel options. <u>Employees</u>*[I] *will be required to forward their options page to HR for approval before booking tickets.*

First class travel on trains and business class on planes will be restricted to <u>those of you</u>[J] *in Grades G3 and above.*

The triggers
- A – *LT1*: Impersonal verbs
- B, C & D – *LT 3*: Writing about the readers
- E – *LT4*: Splitting the audience's identity
- F & G – *LT3*: Writing about the readers
- H – *LTs 2 & 3*: Presupposing the audience's attitude or situation/writing about the readers
- I – *LT3*: Presupposing the audience's attitude or situation
- J – *LT4*: Splitting the audience's identity

Solution ii: Disarming the triggers

From next year, <u>the company will be introducing</u> new rules for business trips. <u>We have ben working with the Finance Team to review</u> the current system, including the accounting practices and the reward and recognition structure. The decisions <u>we've</u> taken will result in better cost management, simpler procedures and <u>less paperwork for you</u>.

<u>If you need</u> to drive more than 2,000 <u>business</u> miles a month, you will no longer need to complete weekly returns. You can now <u>do these</u> monthly through the existing Intranet form.

<u>If you</u> make ad-hoc business trips, <u>you</u> will need to visit the Travelmaster web page on the Intranet to identify the cheapest travel option. <u>In case you don't know</u>, Travelmaster enables <u>you</u> to enter details of <u>your</u> journey, together with the make and model of <u>your</u> car (<u>if you have one</u>*) and provides a comparison of different travel options. <u>You</u> will need to forward <u>the</u> options page to HR for approval before booking tickets.

First class travel on trains and business class on planes will be restricted to Grades G3 and above.

*This caveat would be redundant if the audience could be identified with enough precision up front (e.g. if company car drivers were being targeted directly).

Appendix E
Editing and Titles

'While we're talking, envious time is fleeing.'
Quintus Horatius Flaccus

Because business communication outcomes go beyond those of recreational communications, the disciplines necessary to edit these comms effectively need to do likewise. Similarly, with recreational communications, the audience has effectively volunteered themselves to receive whatever's being said. This is rarely the case with business communications, so the audience's motivation to even begin reading is quite different – which affects the way you need to write headings. What I'm about to share with you may be similar to what you do yourself, or there may be some additional subtleties you might want to take on board. Either way, like many people, you might not have consciously articulated quite how you go about editing the communications you work on. And this can make it tricky to pass on that expertise to your colleagues, or to convince other people that you're right. So you may find the next few pages useful whatever your background.

A useful attitude

When I first became a corporate copywriter, I felt somewhat nervous. My employer was a financial services company, so we didn't manufacture anything but pieces of paper with words and numbers on, together with the occasional picture or diagram. And this meant that there were hundreds of people around the business who were producing these marketing, internal, customer, recruitment, shareholder, distributor and press communications. But I was the company's first dedicated copywriter, which meant that all the other writers had additional skills or technical knowledge – other ways of adding value to the business; all I could do was write. And I was concerned that I might be considered no better a writer than anyone else, and turfed out.

As it happened, I was there for over five years, after three of which I was asked to start setting the standards by which other people in the business would do their writing. And paradoxically, I discovered that it had been my very lack of confidence in my ability that seemed to have turned me into an effective business writer. While most other people in the company appeared to be fascinated with the intricacies of pension plans and investment bonds, I could think of no reason why any normal person would voluntarily wish to read about them. And without realising it, I had developed an attitude which, while it may sound a trifle extreme or even melodramatic, is nonetheless useful – however much confidence you have. My thinking went something like this:

'If I write something that I expect other people to read, I'm effectively asking those people to give up that portion of their lives for me. And whether that amount is 30 seconds or 30 minutes, I'm going to have to give them a damned good reason for doing so.'

This attitude came into play whether I was writing headings or editing my own or anyone else's text. And as I studied in detail what I was doing in my mind as I was editing, I realised that several questions were in residence. A couple would pop up only on specific occasions, but two others were there in the background all the time – challenging every sentence to justify its existence. And when I finally got myself to write them down, I found that they were really the same question expressed in two different ways:

'So what?'

'Why are you bothering to tell me this?'

I later discovered that these questions are also taught in marketing circles as WIIFM:

'What's In It For Me?'

If the sentence I was reading could answer these questions, it was probably worth having in the communication. If not, it may not have been worthy of inclusion. But the more I looked into it, the more I started to realise that it would be unwise to make snap decisions about ditching any waffle. Waffle, it appears, is not just waffle. When I discussed with authors around the business why they had written what they'd written, I discovered that there were different varieties of waffle.

We know now that some text can appear to be waffling because an author has:

- used a load of abstract language
- not put together an effective brief and has no clear outcome or audience in mind
- stumbled over one of the linguistic detached observer triggers.

We've already discussed how to deal with these sources of waffle, but there are still four other types you can encounter. And each of these four might need to be treated in different ways:

1. introductory text
2. technically superfluous text
3. incomplete text
4. disordered text.

We'll spend a few moments looking at each of these types of waffle, and then discuss how you can wipe them out.

Introductory text

Some writers need to get themselves revved up before their writing starts doing its job properly. They can often take two or three sentences just to get into their stride, as it were. And they sometimes forget (or simply don't think) to go back to those opening phrases and delete them. So those words just hang around there, like an abandoned supermarket trolley on a public footpath, inconveniencing people who want to get by – and putting off a lot of people from continuing at all.

Often, you can simply discard these sentences. Indeed, many editors would tell you to do just that. But I would advise a little caution before doing so, because the apparent uselessness of these opening sentences may not be the result of a writer who's just trying to get going. It may be any one of the other types of waffle.

Technically superfluous text

This can happen a lot when someone is producing a communication on a subject about which he or she knows lots of stuff, and hasn't first put together an outcome-focused brief. Without such briefs, some authors will frequently struggle to discriminate between what's possible to say and what's useful to say. In such circumstances, they often include a lot of extraneous information simply 'because they can'. This information can pop up pretty well anywhere in the communication – even at the beginning. The problem for you, if you don't have the technical knowledge of the author, is that you may find it difficult to tell if the text you're reading is this type of waffle, or the next type.

Incomplete text

This one's a bit sneaky, because many people think that text only waffles when writers use more words than necessary. But in fact, it can just as easily do so when they've used too few.

Some people often leap in a few steps beyond the point that the audience is starting at – assuming a level of knowledge that these readers simply don't have. In such circumstances the text can appear to be waffling, but this is not because the information isn't relevant to them. Instead, it's because the author hasn't taken the preliminary step of explaining to them why it is so (WIIFM). And this can happen not only at the beginning of a communication, but at any point throughout it.

Disordered text

Sometimes the explanations as to why a given piece of text is relevant to the reader never arrive, and sometimes such explanations do crop up – but not until later on in the text. The problem here is that the audience may already have given up on the communication before discovering why they shouldn't have done so.

Wiping out waffle

Given what it's possible for you to know about the words you're trying to edit, it makes sense to work back in reverse order through these four types of waffle.

Disordered text

This is the only one which may be decipherable without having to go back to the author. You'll know that the text is disordered if the author explains why a piece of information that appeared earlier in the communication was useful for you to know. And it's often pretty straightforward to lift that explanation, tweak it a bit, and insert it before the info to which it refers. But with the other types of waffle, you'll have to go back to the author in order to find out which of them it is.

To tease out this information, I've found it useful to revert to the following briefing questions:

'What would happen if we didn't say this?'

and

'So what? What would happen if they didn't know that?'

Incomplete text

If the text is incomplete, the author will be able to explain how they believe it will help produce the communication's desired outcome. Their explanation will suggest that the text in question is designed to either prompt people to act, or enable them to do so. And from there you should be able to divine 'what's in it for the audience' and insert that information before the text in question. (With internal communications, sometimes the benefit is only indirectly for the audience, because the direct benefit is for the business. It may therefore be useful to discover what benefit the audience would get from that benefit to the business.)

Technically superfluous and introductory text

Although these two types of waffle occur for subtly different reasons, identifying and dealing with them is the same procedure. With either of them, the author won't have any explanation as to how the questionable text will help bring about the desired outcome, so you need to simply take it out, and knit the remaining text together.

These methods for identifying and dealing with waffle seem simple enough, but they do need you to discover the author's desired outcome and audience. And if these haven't been identified up front, it may be that the whole communication is facing the wrong way, or doesn't even need to exist. Simple though these approaches are, then, they can often lead to a wholesale re-think on the part of the author, and may help give you the leverage you need to get them to start putting together effective briefs up front.

Completing the story

The 'so what' question is a handy one for finding your way back to the beginning of the story. But how about the end? Even when it comes to giving people instructions about how to act on the communication, authors sometimes make assumptions about the audience's attitude or situation, and say things like:

'Please complete and return the form to confirm that you are eligible for a full bonus.'

Because we're now into 'enabling mode' rather than 'prompting mode' some people seem to drop their guard. At this point, all the 'so what's?' should have been taken care of, but that only means it's time to think about the 'what ifs?' What if the audience's situation is different from the one scenario being described? For example, what does someone do if they think they might be eligible for a partial bonus? Or what if they're just not sure?

It's often when people fail to include the other scenarios that audiences get on the phone and start eating up call centre time (or the author's time etc). The 'what if' question can therefore save a huge amount of time. And to increase response rates that little bit further, the question 'what next?' is a useful one to introduce into your thinking towards the end of a communication.

It seems that audiences are more likely to respond if they understand what will happen after they've completed their side of the bargain. Giving them clear instructions about what to do is vital. But if they can then see beyond their own actions, and understand how the process unfolds, it seems to increase their confidence and comfort in the process itself. For example, someone could end their 'story' with the instruction:

'Please complete and return the form to us in the envelope provided, or visit our website at www.helpful-ish.com and fill in the form there.'

Alternatively, they could go that extra step to complete the story for their audience, by telling them what will happen next:

'Once we've got your reply, we'll deal with it within 48 hours, and the bonus will arrive in your bank account (or a cheque on your doormat) within a further three days.'

These final little touches won't necessarily make or break a communication's effectiveness, but they can certainly help increase and expedite audience responses. Before being able to do that, though, we've got to get them to read the communication in the first place.

Titles and headings

The 'What's In It For Me?' attitude is a critical one to have in mind when writing titles or headings. Any business communication is having to compete with a whole raft of others for its audience's attention. And if your communication's title doesn't answer the WIIFM question, many members of your audience may never even bother to read the text.

When writing titles for some communications, many people seem to feel they have to emulate advertising or tabloid newspaper headlines in order to grab the audience's attention. Although this can sometimes work, I've found that it can just as readily backfire, with authors often sacrificing effectiveness for creativity. When it comes to writing a title for a business communication, or the headings that appear within it, the creative headline is not always guaranteed to work; it's very much a case of horses for courses. And there are four simple guidelines you can follow which have shown themselves time and again to be effective in getting people to want to read on. These guidelines by no means constitute the only way to write effective titles and headings – but they're certainly reliable:

1. Imagine the title or heading as the second half of a sentence, the first half of which never appears in writing, but which says: 'You're really going to want to read this because it's going to tell you...'
2. Make sure that it answers the 'what's in it for me?' question.
3. Make the language you use concrete, personal and as dynamic as possible.
4. Include one of Kipling's six honest serving men: 'What, Why, When, How, Where or Who' (or 'Which', if you prefer).

If you follow these simple rules, you'll almost always be able to grab people's attention and get them to want to read on – whatever else is competing for their time. And this includes emails. Interestingly, it seems that even many professional copywriters seem to switch off when it comes to writing the 'Subject' for their emails. Why this should be I've no idea, but these rules work just as readily on emails as they do on any other medium. Indeed, given the number of emails competing for people's attention, it's at least as important to write an effective title for these communications as it is for any other.

Getting it read and keeping it tight

- Because business communication outcomes go beyond those of recreational communications, so too may the editing disciplines. (Page 294)
  - Recreational audiences also volunteer themselves to receive communications, unlike those for most business communications, so titles and headings need to reflect this.

- To find waffle, you can ask: (Page 295)
  - *'So what?'* Or
  - *'Why are you bothering to tell me this?'*

- These questions may turn up any one of seven types of waffle:
  1. Abstract language (See chapter 6)
  2. Irrelevant communicating resulting from no brief, or from an ineffective brief with no clear:
     - outcome (See chapter 5)
     - audience (See chapter 8)
     - verified content (See chapter 9)
  3. The linguistic Detached Observer Triggers (See chapter 15)
  4. Introductory text (Page 296)
  5. Technically superfluous text (Page 296)
  6. Incomplete text (Page 296)
  7. Disordered text (Page 297)

- Each has its own technique for wiping it out. (Page 297)

- You can make sure you've completed the story for the audience by using the 'What if?' and 'What next?' questions. (Page 298)

- There are numerous ways of writing effective titles and headings for business communications.
  1. Imagine the title or heading as the second half of a sentence, the first half of which never appears in writing, but which says: 'You're really going to want to read this because it's going to tell you...'
  2. Make sure that it answers the 'What's in it for me?' question.
  3. Make the language you use concrete, personal and as dynamic as possible.
  4. Include a verb, and one of Kipling's six honest serving men: What, Where, When, How, Why or Who (or Which, if you prefer).
  5. Use these techniques even for the 'Subject' of your emails

Appendix F
Valuing the goldmine

For your business to exploit the potential of its communication goldmine it may well need to make some changes to the way it does things at present. Possibly some quite profound changes. It could mean introducing new briefing and approval procedures, which would affect the working practices of communication owners – even those at the very top of the business – and any departments (e.g. legal) who get involved in approving communications.

It could also mean some fundamental changes to HR policy, in terms of how people get to be communication owners, the management support they receive, the measures by which their performance is evaluated, and the rewards they receive. This is big league stuff, and not the kind of thing your CEO and HR Director will necessarily be up for just because you've read this book. You'll probably need a commercial case for making such changes. The question is, how robust a case will you need? Some business leaders simply need to understand the general principles, and maybe have some rough ballpark figures to back them up. Others want a detailed business case with watertight calculations. Either way, you'll probably need something to grab their attention in the first place and the following calculations are designed to help you do just that.

If you're only going to need rough ballpark figures, what follows may be enough. But if it's going to take more detailed calculations to get the top bods to move, you'll probably need to get the business's finance team involved. With this second scenario, you should be able to use these ballpark figures to build a case for them doing so. One way or another, what you need to do with these figures is to get the senior management to believe it's at least worth looking into further – whether that means giving the green light straight away, or getting the accountants to do some further number crunching.

How to avoid double-counting

I mentioned in chapter 3 that I've separated everything out to make clearer what's going on. This means we sometimes look at the same cost more than once – so here's how to avoid counting it twice. The costs fall broadly into three categories:

- **money** – direct financial expenditure
- **time** – paying people to do unproductive work
- **emotion** – upsets that reduce people's willingness to do what the business needs.

It's the wasted time costs you need to be wary of. The calculations for costs

2 (production time) & 3 (audience time) will give you totals to start from. The subsequent calculations, for costs 4 – 7 will show you how much of those totals is being wasted, while cost 8 will look at the time wasted clearing up afterwards. Cost 9 is where this wasted time comes home to roost. Importantly, though, it can have two distinct impacts depending on who's having their time wasted. Wasting sales people's time, for example, leaves them with fewer hours in which to generate income. Wasting background staff time (e.g. IT, HR, Finance etc) can mean the business is employing more people than necessary to get those jobs done – so there's potential to save on headcount.

When you're identifying the wasted time elements of costs 6-8 (which involve wasted audience time) you'll need to do each calculation twice, once for income-generators, and once for non-income-generators.

(Importantly, many people in non-income-generating roles can affect sales indirectly. IT people, for example, may be developing systems which will make sales people more efficient and thus release more sales time. Or if there were a greater amount of productive customer service staff time available, the phone calls could be answered more quickly – helping with customer good will. And, of course, Board Directors probably aren't spending much time, if any, making sales to customers. But releasing more of their time could give them the space to be better leaders. Although these are important subtleties to be aware of if you're going to present your figures to senior management, calculating this 'middle ground' figure is probably best left to the accountants – if the business wants it.)

Calculating Cost 1 – the hard costs of producing & distributing communications

In this you can include any print budgets the business has (if no formal budgets exist, the business may well have preferred supplier, from whom you can find out how much it's spending each year). You can also include the cost of paper and toner cartridges the business is buying to feed its printers and copiers, and the servicing bills for those machines. If the business holds conferences or annual business meetings, there's probably a budget set aside for them too. You could go further and include the telephone bill if you want, and any other incidental hard communication costs you can think of (although the hard cost of running an intranet is probably something to leave out, as it's probably a fixed cost and wouldn't be any cheaper if the business were more communication-efficient).

Calculating Cost 2 – people's time spent commissioning, producing and vetting communications

You may want to do separate calculations for different types of communication if averages are too difficult to work out.

Owners' briefing time

1. What's the average salary of the business's communication owners?
2. Divide this by 1,000 to arrive at a rough figure for how much their time costs the business per hour.

    (Dividing a person's salary by 1,000 to arrive at a rough hourly cost is a widely accepted practice. It's done on the basis that an average person will work for about 2,000 hours a year, but costs roughly twice their salary to employ, once you take into account National Insurance, the cost of running the workplace and other benefits such as company cars, pensions etc.)

Owners' hourly cost

3. How much time do you and others spend taking briefs from these people in an average month?
4. Multiply by 12 to get an annual figure
5. Multiply this by their hourly cost.

    Owners' time: £   a year

Approvers' time

6. On average, how many people in the business get involved in approving communications (whether on their own or as members of an approval group)?
7. Multiply this figure by the average number of hours they will spend vetting and editing these communications in a month (including reiterations of course).
8. Multiply this figure by the average cost per hour to the business of employing these people (roughly their annual salary divided by 1,000).
9. Multiply this figure by 12 to give you the annual cost.

    Approvers' time: £   a year

Comms professionals' time

10. If you belong to an in-house team, double your own salary and that of your colleagues. (This doubling is to take account of the other costs involved in employing you, such as national insurance, office space etc.) If you work as a freelance or belong to an agency, you should add your fees to Cost 1 if they're not already included.
11. Add all three costs together to get a total for Cost 2

    Cost 2: £   a year

Calculating cost 3 – audience time

Here you will need to do different calculations for income-producers and non-income-producers, because the commercial impact of consuming their time can be quite different. And you may want to do them for different departments if the averages across the whole business are too complex to work out.

Income producers

What percentage of their total work time do income producers spend receiving internal communications?

_____%

Non-income producers

1. How many non-income-producing employees does the business have?
2. Multiply this figure by the amount of time each of them spends reading, listening to or watching internal communications, in an average week (including emails and meetings)
3. Multiply this number by 50 to arrive at a rough annual figure (I've put 50 rather than 52 because people have holidays etc, when they're not receiving communications. They do have more to catch up on when they get back, but tend to skim many of these, especially those that are already out of date.)
4. Multiply this figure by the average hourly cost of employing them (their average annual salary divided by 1,000)

**Annual cost of paying non-income producers
to receive communications £ _____**

These two figures (the income-producers' percentage, and the cash figure for non-income-producers) will form the basis for some of the following unnecessary costs...

Wasteful production and distribution costs

Calculating cost 4 – ill-defined or moving goalposts

This is a tricky one to work out in terms of the real financial impact. After all, how many drafts or redrafts is reasonable? This is a wholly subjective view, but I would say that as a general rule of thumb, if you're having to present more than three drafts to the person who's commissioned you, that communication hasn't been produced as efficiently as it could have been. (I say this on the basis of producing a first draft as a sighting shot, a second draft to get it 95% of the way there, and a third draft to prune and polish). If this seems reasonable to you, then perhaps you could consider what percentage of your time (or that of your colleagues) is taken up with producing more than three drafts of communications, and getting them approved. This could represent a percentage of *Cost 2 (production time)* that's being spent unnecessarily. And are there times when printers hike the price because of the consequent rush jobs? Any such price differentials would be an unnecessary part of *Cost 1 (hard budgetary cost)*.

Percentage of **cost 1** that's wasted:

Percentage of **cost 2** that's wasted:

Calculating cost 5 – ditched communications

If you think back over the past year, maybe you can identify projects in which you or your colleagues have been involved, which got canned before the communication went out, and work out how much time and hard cash was wasted in this way. Then you can compare those figures with the totals for *Costs 1 & 2*. What sort of percentages do they amount to? And how much money does that equate to?

Percentage of **cost 1** that's wasted:

Percentage of **cost 2** that's wasted:

Calculating cost 6 – back covering and ladder climbing

You can base this on your own experience, or ring round a few people in different departments to find out what their figures are.

If you think about your own in-tray and in-box, what percentage of the communications you get are of no use to you? And what percentage of your time do you spend in, say, an average month, attending meetings that are of no value to you? And if it's reasonable to extrapolate those percentages across your entire department or business, how much of *Cost 3* would it account for? If such an extrapolation wouldn't be reasonable across the whole business, then what percentages would be, and what kind of cost does that equate to?

Percentage of **cost 3** that's wasted for income-producers:

Percentage of **cost 3** that's wasted for non-income-producers:

When it comes to pre-printed communications, what percentage of those are a waste of time?

Percentage of **cost 1** that's wasted:

Communication failure costs

Calculating cost 7 – re-doing communications

What percentage of communications (internal and external) need to be sent out twice, or even a third time? What percentage of *Costs 1, 2 & 3* would that account for?

Percentage of **cost 1** that's wasted:
Percentage of **cost 2** that's wasted:
Percentage of **cost 3** that's wasted for income-producers:
Percentage of **cost 3** that's wasted for non-income-producers:
You're now ready to identify how much of *costs 1 & 2* are being wasted. Add together the wasted percentages of *cost 1* from your calculations for *costs 4-7*.

From cost 4_____%
From cost 5_____%
From cost 6_____%
From cost 7_____%
Total wasted percentage of cost 1_____%
Multiply *cost 1* by that total percentage _____ x £ _____

Annual wasted communication budget £ _____
Add together the wasted percentages of *cost 2* from your calculations for *costs 4, 5 & 7*

From cost 4_____%
From cost 5_____%
From cost 7_____%
Total wasted percentage of cost 2_____%
Multiply *cost 2* by that total percentage _____ x £ _____

Annually wasted production time £ _____

Calculating cost 8 – correcting mistakes and misunderstandings

With failing customer communications, this means that sales and/or customer service staff will be having to spend time with customers, either face-to-face, on the phone or through correspondence, helping them to understand their last letter or bill. What percentage of sales and customer service staff time is taken up with this? (A senior customer service manager may well be able to give you a reasonably accurate figure for this.)

Failing internal communications will mean that staff are not following instructions properly, or are making ineffective decisions. In addition to the cost of their own and other people's time, it can often involve a hard cash cost if they're working with external suppliers. Again, if you do a straw poll of a few people in both income-producing and non-income-producing roles (including one or two senior managers) you should be able to get a credible ball-park figure.

Income producers
What percentage of their total working time are they spending correcting mistakes & misunderstandings?

Non-income producers
What percentage of their total working time are they spending correcting mistakes & misunderstandings?

On top of these, there may also be other costs involved in getting things wrong or putting them right: additional staff overtime, compensation to unhappy customers, legal fees, regulatory fines, increased insurance premiums and so on. The business will probably have records of these for at least the last financial year if you care to look for them.

Calculating cost 9 – missed opportunities
This is two types of cost: missed opportunities to generate income and to save expenditure.

Missed income opportunity
This calculation is in two parts
1. Add together the percentages for income-producers from your calculations for *costs 6 & 7*
2. Multiply this figure by the percentage you came up with for *cost 3*. This will give you the percentage of time that income-producers' waste going through communications.
3. Add to this the percentage of income-producers' time wasted correcting mistakes and misunderstandings (that you identified in *cost 8*).
4. Take that total percentage figure away from 100 to give you the percentage of productive income-producing time

In crude terms, last year's sales were produced with that remaining percentage of people's time.

Would it be reasonable to assume that, without the time wasting, that additional percentage of time would have been available for generating income at the same rate? If so…
5. How much money did the business generate last year through product/service sales?
6. Divide that number by your answer to point 4 above. This will give you a figure for income produced in every 1% of productive sales time.
7. Multiply by 100 to give you the potential income that could have been produced if none of the income-producers' time was being wasted
8. Take away last year's actual sales total (i.e. answer 5 above). What

you're left with is the value of sales lost due to wasted income-producers' time.

Crucially, this does not take into account sales lost due to people not having the right information available – which is again usually down to poor communication, or lost customer good will (i.e. part of *cost 10*).

Missed expenditure reduction

1. Take the percentages from your calculations for costs 6 & 7 – for non-income-producers, and add them together.
2. Multiply your non-income-producers' total for Cost 3 by that percentage. This will give you the cost of paying non-income-producers' to go through useless communications.

A. The annual cost of non-income-producers receiving useless comms £ _____

3. How many non-income-producing employees does the business have?
4. Multiply this figure by the average annual cost of employing them: the average annual salary multiplied by 2 (to take into account the cost of National Insurance, office space etc)

   The annual cost of employing non-income producers: £ _____
5. Multiply this figure by the percentage of non-income-producers' time wasted correcting mistakes and misunderstandings (that you identified in cost 8)

   x _____ %

B. The annual cost of paying non-income-producers to correct mistakes and misunderstandings   £_____

6. Add together totals A & B to identify the overall annual wasted cost you can attribute to ineffective communications:

   The business's annual wasted expenditure on non-income producers: £ _____

It's unreasonable to expect that the business could recoup all of this cost by raising its communication game, but it does illustrate that if people weren't wasting so much time, the business could get the same amount of work done with fewer people. Also, headcount is only one aspect of expenditure. If non-income producers are making ineffective decisions thanks to poor communications, there are likely to be other opportunities to save money gone begging as well.

Calculating cost 10 – lost audience good will.

This is tricky to put a figure on. It's common business practice to put a value on customer goodwill (or 'brand equity'). But it's more unusual for such value to be applied to the business's own staff, distributors, suppliers and shareholders, even though the same principles still apply. Indeed, customer goodwill is largely dependent on that of staff, distributors and suppliers. And the goodwill calculations are designed to show what the value is and not what it could be if all those things that detract from it were removed.

The previous calculations may therefore enable the business's finance bods to start identifying that 'value gap'.

A worked example

The following calculations are based on a company with 500 employees, 250 of whom are income producers. It has an annual turnover of £40,000,000

Cost 1 – hard costs
A total annual budget for all forms of internal communication has been set at: **£250,000**

Cost 2 – production time
Communication owners
Communication owners' average salary £70,000

	÷ 1000
Owners' hourly cost	£70
x 50 hours per month	£3,500
x 12 months	
Owners' time	**£42,000 a year**

Communication approvers

15 approvers	
x 5 hours a month	
Hours per month	75
@£70 an hour	£4,900 per month
x 12 months	
Approvers' time:	**£58,800 a year**

Comms professionals
2 in-house comms professionals
@ £30,000 a year each = £60,000
x 2

Comms professionals' time:	**£120,000 a year**

Total for Cost 2:	**£220,800**

Cost 3 – audience time
Income producers
Percentage of total work time spent receiving
    internal communications: 7%
Non-income producers
Number of non-income-producing employees: 250
    x 6 hours a week
Time per week   1,500 hours
    x 50 weeks
Annual time   75,000 hours
    x £30 an hour

Cost of non-income producers' time to receive communications:
£2,250,000

Cost 4 – ill-defined or moving goalposts
Percentage of *cost 1* that's wasted: 4%
Percentage of *cost 2* that's wasted: 10%

Cost 5 – ditched communications
Percentage of *cost 1* that's wasted: 1%
Percentage of *cost 2* that's wasted: 3%

Cost 6 – back covering and ladder climbing
Percentage of *cost 3* that's wasted for income-producers: 25%
Percentage of *cost 3* that's wasted for non-income-producers: 25%
Percentage of *cost 1* that's wasted: 20%

Cost 7 – re-doing communications
Percentage of *cost 1* that's wasted: 2%
Percentage of *cost 2* that's wasted: 2%
Percentage of *cost 3* that's wasted for income-producers: 6%
Percentage of *cost 3* that's wasted for non-income-producers: 6%

Wasted percentages of *cost 1* from your calculations for *costs 4-7*.
From cost 4_____4%
From cost 5_____1%
From cost 6_____20%
From cost 7_____2%
Total wasted percentage of *cost 1*   27%
Annual Budget (£250,000) x 27%
Annual wasted communication budget   £67,500

Wasted percentages of *cost 2* from your calculations for *costs 4, 5 & 7*

From *cost 4*_____	10%
From *cost 5*_____	3%
From *cost 7*_____	2%
Total wasted percentage of *cost 2*	**15%**

Annual cost of production time (£220,800) x 15%

Cost of annually wasted production time   £33,120

Cost 8 – correcting mistakes and misunderstandings

Percentage of **Income producers**' total working time
spent correcting mistakes and misunderstandings?   25%

Percentage of **Non-income producers**' total working time
spent correcting mistakes & misunderstandings?   30%

Cost 9 – missed opportunities

Missed income opportunity

Wasted income-producers' percentages of *cost 3* from *costs 6 & 7*

From *cost 6*	25%
From *cost 7*	+ 6%
Total % of cost 3 wasted	**31%**

Total working time consumed by *cost 3*	x 7%
% of total work time wasted receiving useless communications:	2.17%
Percentage of income-producers' time wasted in *cost 8*	+ 25%
Total wasted income-producers' time	27.17%

Last year's income: £40,000,000 was generated with

100% – 27.17% =	**72.83%** productive time.
Income produced per 1% of productive time:	**£549,224**
Potential income @ 100% productivity	**£54,922,400**
Actual income	**£40,000,000**
Lost income through ineffective communication:	**£14,922,400**

Missed expenditure reduction

Wasted non-income-producers' percentages of *cost 3* from *costs 6 & 7*

From *cost 6*	25%
From *cost 7*	+ 6%
Total % of cost 3 wasted	**31%**

Cost of paying non-income producers
to receive communications: **£2,250,000**

Annual cost of non-income-producers receiving useless comms:	**£697,500**
Number of non-income producers	**250**
Average salary	**x £30,000**
Annual cost of employing non-income producers:	**£7,500,000**
Percentage time wasted correcting mistakes and misunderstandings:	**x 30%**
Annual cost of paying non-income-producers to correct mistakes and misunderstandings	**£2,250,000**
The business's annual wasted expenditure on non-income producers:	**£2,947,500**

Appendix G
How to Save Time on Communication Approvals

Although almost everyone experiences a mind's voice when they're reading, many people feel uneasy about asking others which voice they're using when approving communications. If you're one of these people, the following pages are designed to make it much easier. Rather than broaching the subject directly, you can give any communication owner or approval group member the following few pages to read. Having them read about the principles of the three positions and mind's voices before asking them about their individual experiences should make the conversation that much easier.

A guide for communication owners and approval group members

If you feel that you occasionally have to spend more time than necessary vetting and/or approving communications, it may be because of a couple of unconscious mental processes that people quite naturally engage in when they're reading and writing. These processes often give rise to instinctive gut reactions that can make people feel uncomfortable with the words in front of them – even if those words are technically accurate and grammatically perfect.

Once you are aware of these processes, you can understand your own gut reactions, and make conscious choices which can dramatically reduce the need for rewrites, and thus save you time. (If you're part of an approval group, it naturally helps if everyone in the group understands these processes.)

Unconscious process 1: positioning

When reading anything – whether it's a business communication, a newspaper, a novel or even a recipe, you can do so from any one of three different perspectives or 'positions'. None of these is right or wrong, they're simply different possibilities.

1. The communicator position

People often adopt this position when, say, filling in a mailshot response coupon, which would be phrased something like this:

'I would like more information about your special offer...'

Because it's written in the first person ('I') this phraseology is designed to make you feel that it is you who's saying the words you're reading: in short, that you are the communicator. (Many people adopt this position when approving communications that are either going out in their own name, or from a group to which they belong.)

2. The audience position

In this position, you do not feel that you are saying the words, but that they are being said to you. Many people adopt this position when approving communications – putting themselves in the audience's shoes, as it were. But this approach is by no means universal.

3. The detached observer position

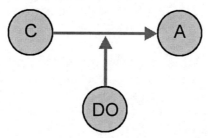

This is the position people unconsciously adopt when, for example, they are on a 'copies' list for an email. It's a fly-on-the-wall position, which, if you adopt it yourself, will make you feel as if you're eavesdropping on a conversation that's going on between a communicator and an audience: the words are not being said by you, nor to you, but by someone else and to another someone else (or even a group of others). Again, it's possible for many people to adopt this position when approving communications.

None of these three positions is right or wrong for approving communications. But it doesn't take a genius to see that the same communication may elicit different responses from you if you read it from different positions. Problems may arise, then, if you're using a different position from the one the author used when drafting it. And this problem can be exacerbated if the communication is being approved by an entire group, each member of which may be using any one of these three positions. On top of that, there's a second unconscious process waiting to stick its oar in.

Unconscious process 2: the mind's voice

Although the term 'the mind's eye' has found its way into common parlance, it's rare to hear anyone mention 'the mind's mouth', or 'the mind's ear'. Yet when most people read, they don't do so out loud. Instead, almost everyone uses their mind's mouth to say the words, and their mind's ear to hear them. This means that almost everyone is hearing a mind's voice when they're reading. But most people have a selection of three different types of voice they can use:

1. their own voice
2. the voice of the author (if they know who that person is, and what that person's voice sounds like)
3. an imaginary voice (any voice that isn't their own or that of the author).

Very few people have no mind's voice at all. Some readers can hear only their own voice, but most people (over 97%) have access to all three types. For most people, these voices can change – even when reading the same communication. Stop for a moment, and notice which mind's voice (if any) you've been using while reading this page. Even if you've got just the one voice for this communication, chances are you may well have access to others (as could happen if you were reading a novel, perhaps, in which different characters were conversing).

There's no right or wrong mind's voice. But different mind's voices can dramatically impact on how people respond emotionally to the words they're reading. (This is particularly so if someone feels they're having words put into their mind's mouth that they wouldn't naturally have put there themselves.) And when approving communications, if you're using a different mind's voice to the one used by the author (or other people in an approval group) it's likely to affect how comfortable (or uncomfortable) you feel about the text in front of you. It can cause you (or others) to want to change text which, when read with a different mind's voice, or from a different 'position' feels fine just as it is.

Saving time on communication approvals

To save yourself time on approvals when only you and the author are involved, you can agree up front which voice and position you'll both use. This will make it easier for the author to instinctively find the lexicon and syntax that will fit comfortably in your mind's mouth.

If you're part of an approval group, ideally the entire group together with the author need to agree upon a position and mind's voice to work with. Naturally this can be more challenging, given that not everyone can necessarily access three mind's voices. But at least it will give everyone a vocabulary with which to articulate why they feel the way they do about the words in front of them.

These simple insights have been proven to massively reduce the need for re-writes, and to save everyone loads of time.